365 Amazing Burger Recipes

(365 Amazing Burger Recipes - Volume 1)

Rita Morrow

Content

5

365 Awesome Burger Recipes

***

---

1. Ahi Fish Burgers With Chives Recipe

Serving: 4 | Prep: | Cook: 20mins | Ready in:

Ingredients

- 1 pound fresh tuna steaks, finely diced
- 1/3 cup breadcrumbs, or panko crumbs
- 2 eggs
- 1 carrot, grated
- 1/2 cup onion, diced
- 1 tbsp olive oil
- 1 tbsp mayonnaise
- 1/2 cup fresh chives, chopped
- garlic salt and freshly ground black pepper, to taste

Direction

- Combine the tuna, breadcrumbs, eggs, carrot, onion, mayonnaise, and chives in a large bowl. Season with garlic salt and black pepper, to taste, then make into patties.
- In a skillet, over medium heat, heat the oil then add the patties, do not crowd. Cook, uncovered, for 10 minutes per side, or until they become a golden brown. Serve.

---

2. All American Burgers Recipe

Serving: 4 | Prep: | Cook: 12mins | Ready in:

Ingredients

- Although we usually enjoy our burgers medium-rare, with extra ingredients added, tasters found that the burgers were too soft unless cooked through (basically, well-done).
- 1 1/2 pounds 85 percent lean ground chuck
- 1 cup shredded sharp cheddar cheese
- 8 strips cooked bacon , chopped fine
- 4 teaspoons yellow mustard
- 2 teaspoons worcestershire sauce
- 1/2 teaspoon table salt
- 1/2 teaspoon ground black pepper

Direction

- 1. Break beef into small pieces in medium bowl. Add cheese, bacon, mustard, Worcestershire sauce, salt, and pepper. Using fork, toss until evenly distributed. Divide mixture into 4 equal portions and lightly pack into 1-inch-thick patties.
- 2. When coals are ready and grate is hot, dip wad of paper towels in vegetable oil and use tongs to rub oil over grate. Grill burgers over very hot fire, without pressing down on them, until well seared on both sides and cooked through, 8 to 12 minutes. Transfer to plate, tent with foil, and let rest 5 minutes. Serve
- Note: We love burgers loaded with a lot of flavorful toppings, but a "Dagwood" style burger can be nearly impossible to eat. The toppings slide out from beneath the bun and end up covering everything but the burger itself. Is there way of putting the toppings inside the burger where they can't fall out? Here's what we discovered:
- Test Kitchen Discoveries
- Add the ingredients straight into the burger mix. Fine-chopped, cooked bacon, shredded cheese, mustard, and Worcestershire sauce can all be mixed directly into the ground beef.
- Use firm cheese like sharp cheddar so that the burger doesn't become mushy.
- To prevent the cheese-infused burger from being too greasy, use relatively lean 85 percent lean ground beef.

- Combine the ground beef and flavorings gently; otherwise the burgers may be tough.
- Because of the ingredients mixed into the meat, we found it best to cook the burgers to well-done. The cheese keeps them from being dry or tough.

3. Aloha Burger Steaks Recipe

Serving: 6 | Prep: | Cook: 25mins | Ready in:

Ingredients

- 1 1/2 lbs lean ground beef
- 1/4 cup finely chopped green pepper
- 1 egg
- 1 tsp seasoned salt
- 6 slices canned pineapple
- 1 (8 oz) can Hunt's tomato sauce
- 1 Tbls soy sauce
- 2 tsp brown sugar
- 2 tsp vinegar
- 1/2 tsp dry mustard

Direction

- Combine beef, green pepper, egg and salt; shape into 6 patties.
- Press pineapple slice firmly into each patty.
- In skillet, brown quickly, pineapple side up; turn, brown pineapple side down.
- Drain fat, turn patties pineapple side up.
- Combine remaining ingredients, pour over patties.
- Simmer covered 5 to 10 minutes.
- Serve over rice with extra sauce.

4. Alton Browns Burger Of The Gods Recipe

Serving: 4 | Prep: | Cook: 10mins | Ready in:

Ingredients

- 8 ounces chuck, trimmed, cut into 1 1/2-inch cubes
- 8 ounces sirloin, trimmed, cut into 1 1/2-inch cubes
- 1/2 teaspoon kosher salt
- toasted kaiser rolls

Direction

- In separate batches, pulse the chuck and the sirloin in a food processor 10 times.
- Combine the chuck, sirloin, and kosher salt in a large bowl.
- Form the meat into 4-ounce patties.
- Heat a cast iron skillet or griddle over medium-high heat for 2 to 3 minutes.
- Place the hamburger patties in the pan.
- For medium-rare burgers, cook the patties for 4 minutes on each side.
- For medium burgers, cook the patties for 5 minutes on each side. Flip the burgers only once during cooking. Do not mash.

5. Amazingly Good Turkey Burgers Recipe

Serving: 8 | Prep: | Cook: 15mins | Ready in:

Ingredients

- 2lb ground turkey
- 1/2 pack saltine crackers
- onion to taste (opt. - recipe is even easier without it!)
- 3/4 cup spaghetti sauce
- Grated parmesan cheese (in the can)
- Pam spray
- olive oil

Direction

- Thaw turkey, if needed.
- Roll crackers in a zip lock bag to crush.

- Chop onion, if using.
- Place turkey in large bowl. Add crackers, onion, and spaghetti sauce.
- Add as much Parmesan cheese as needed to form burgers; however, the softer they are, the more tender and juicy they fry up.
- Make 8-10 burgers, denting in the middle of each one.
- Spray large skillet then add olive oil; heat over medium heat.
- Fry burgers slowly.
- Serve with ketchup and spicy mustard on a wheat bun.

6. Andouille And Blue Cheese Beef Burgers With Spicy Mayo And Caramelized Onions Recipe

Serving: 6 | Prep: | Cook: 10mins | Ready in:

Ingredients

- Spicy mayonnaise:
- 3/4 cup mayonnaise
- 1 tablespoon fresh lemon juice
- 1 teaspoon Cajun or creole seasoning blend
- 1/4 teaspoon hot pepper sauce
- ****
- Burgers:
- 1/2 pound andouille sausage, cut into scant 1/4-inch cubes
- 3/4 cup pecans, toasted, chopped
- 1 teaspoon salt
- 1/4 teaspoon ground black pepper
- 1 1/2 pounds ground beef chuck or ground beef (20 percent fat)
- ****
- caramelized onions:
- 1 1/2 pounds onions, thinly sliced
- 2 tablespoons olive oil plus more for brushing grill rack
- 3 garlic cloves, minced
- 1 tablespoon golden brown sugar
- ****

- 6 large hamburger buns, split
- 8 ounces crumbled blue cheese
- ****
- Optional:
- 12 pickled okra pods, halved lengthwise*
- 3 cups watercress tops

Direction

- For mayonnaise:
- Mix all ingredients in small bowl. Cover and chill.
- Mayo Note: Can be made 2 days ahead. Keep chilled.
- ****
- For burgers:
- Toss first 4 ingredients in large bowl. Add beef; blend gently. Shape mixture into six 1/2-inch-thick patties. Transfer patties to small baking sheet.
- Burger Note: Can be made 1 day ahead. Cover and chill.
- ****
- For caramelized onions:
- Prepare barbecue (medium-high heat). Toss onions and next 3 ingredients in large skillet. Place skillet on grill; cook until onions are golden, stirring often, about 25 minutes. Remove from grill; season with salt and pepper.
- Onion Note: Can cook on stovetop in a heavy lightly-oiled sauté pan over medium-low heat for 25-30 minutes, or until caramelized. Season as directed above.
- ****
- Brush grill rack with olive oil. Grill buns, cut side down, until golden, about 2 minutes. Transfer buns to work surface.
- Grill burgers until brown on bottom, about 3 minutes. Turn over; sprinkle with cheese. Grill until burgers are cooked to desired doneness, about 3 minutes for medium.
- Place some onions, then burger, on each bun bottom. Top each with okra and watercress (optional). Spread mayonnaise on cut side of bun tops; place on burgers. Serve with remaining mayonnaise.

- ***Shopping tip: Look for pickled okra where the pickles and relishes are displayed.

7. Andouille Bayou Burgers With Red Pepper Mayo And Fiesta Corn Salsa Recipe

Serving: 6 | Prep: | Cook: 12mins | Ready in:

Ingredients

- BURGERS:
- 1/2 lb Andouille sausage
- 2 1/2 lb ground chuck (15% - 20% lean for burgers)
- 1/2 small red onion, minced
- 1 1/2 t salt
- 1 1/2 t fennel seeds, crushed
- Couple grinds black pepper
- Pinch cayenne pepper
- RED pepper MAYO
- 1 jar (3-4 oz) roasted red peppers, drained
- 1/2 c Kraft real mayo
- 1 T minced shallots
- FIESTA corn salsa
- 1 1/2 c cooked corn, drained
- 1 small red onion, diced
- 1 jalepeno, seeded and finely diced
- 1/2 pint grape tomatoes, quartered
- 1/2 c fresh cilantro, chopped
- 2 T capers, drained
- 1 T olive oil
- 1/2 t salt

Direction

- RED PEPPER MAYO (make first and set aside)
- Combine all ingredients in food processor or blender, process until smooth
- BURGERS
- In a large mixing bowl, combine all ingredients and gently shape into 6 patties, approx. 1 inch thick

- Lightly oil grill rack, and grill until desired degree of doneness (4-6 minutes each side for med rare, and so on)
- RESIST ALL URGES TO FLATTEN WITH SPATULA, as this makes for less juicy burgers
- Flip only once
- FIESTA CORN SALSA
- Place all ingredients in medium serving bowl, stir to combine well.

8. Andouille And Beef Burgers With Spicy Mayo And Carmelized Onions Recipe

Serving: 6 | Prep: | Cook: 35mins | Ready in:

Ingredients

- Spicy mayonnaise
- 3/4 cup mayonnaise
- 1 tablespoon fresh lemon juice
- 1 teaspoon Cajun or creole seasoning blend
- 1/4 teaspoon hot pepper sauce
- Burgers
- 1/2 pound andouille sausage, cut into scant 1/4-inch cubes
- 3/4 cup pecans, toasted, chopped
- 1 teaspoon salt
- 1/4 teaspoon ground black pepper
- 1 1/2 pounds ground beef chuck or ground beef (20 percent fat)
- caramelized onions
- 1 1/2 pounds onions, thinly sliced
- 2 tablespoons olive oil plus more for brushing grill rack
- 3 garlic cloves, minced
- 1 tablespoon golden brown sugar
- 6 large hamburger buns, split
- 8 ounces crumbled blue cheese
- 12 pickled okra pods, halved lengthwise*
- 3 cups watercress tops

Direction

- For mayonnaise: Mix all ingredients in small bowl. Cover and chill.
- Do ahead: Can be made 2 days ahead. Keep chilled.
- For burgers: Toss first 4 ingredients in large bowl. Add beef; blend gently. Shape mixture into six 1/2-inch-thick patties. Transfer patties to small baking sheet.
- Do ahead: Can be made 1 day ahead. Cover and chill.
- For onions: Prepare barbecue (medium-high heat). Toss onions and next 3 ingredients in large skillet. Place skillet on grill; cook until onions are golden, stirring often, about 25 minutes. Remove from grill; season with salt and pepper.
- Brush grill rack with olive oil. Grill buns, cut side down, until golden, about 2 minutes. Transfer buns to work surface. Grill burgers until brown on bottom, about 3 minutes. Turn over; sprinkle with cheese. Grill until burgers are cooked to desired doneness, about 3 minutes for medium. Place some onions, then burger, on each bun bottom. Top each with okra and watercress. Spread mayonnaise on cut side of bun tops; place on burgers. Serve with remaining mayonnaise.
- *Shopping tip: Look for pickled okra where the pickles and relishes are displayed.

9. Anniversary Burgers Recipe

Serving: 8 | Prep: | Cook: 15mins | Ready in:

Ingredients

- 2 eggs beaten
- 2 tablespoons milk
- 2 slices bread torn up
- 1 tablespoon dried minced onion
- 1-1/2 teaspoons salt
- 2 teaspoons prepared horseradish
- 1/4 teaspoon black pepper
- 1/4 teaspoon dried thyme
- 1/2 teaspoon dry mustard
- 2 pounds lean ground beef
- 1/2 cup unsalted butter
- 1/2 cup catsup

Direction

- Light a charcoal fire.
- Mix eggs with cream and milk.
- Add bread, onion, salt, horseradish, pepper, thyme and dry mustard.
- Stir well and let stand for 10 minutes.
- Stir well again until all is moistened and the bread is no longer in pieces.
- Add ground beef and mix well.
- Melt butter with catsup and keep warm.
- Measure out beef in 1/2 cup increments and form patties.
- Grill over hot coals on one side then turn and brush with butter catsup mixture.
- Grill other side and serve hot.

10. Asian Burgers With Wasabi Slaw Recipe

Serving: 4 | Prep: | Cook: 10mins | Ready in:

Ingredients

- wasabi Slaw:
- 1/3 cup mayo or enough to bind as desired, low mayo fat okay
- 1 1/2 tsp wasabi powder
- 3 cups pkg. coleslaw mix (cabbage and carrots)
- 1/2 cup red bell pepper strips
- 1/4 cup chopped green onion
- Burgers:
- 1 lb ground beef, as lean as possible
- 4 Tbs soy sauce (low salt is okay, too)
- 1 1/2 tsp minced garlic
- 4 large romaine or Boston lettuce leaves

Direction

- Mix coleslaw ingredients, blend well and chill.
- Combine beef, 1 Tbsp. soy sauce and garlic.
- Shape meat into 4 patties.
- Grill uncovered 11 to 13 minutes or done, basting with remaining soy sauce.
- Place burgers in lettuce leaves and top with the slaw.
- Yield 4 servings.

11. Asian Salmon Burgers With Pickled Cucumber On Pumpernickel Recipe

Serving: 4 | Prep: | Cook: 10mins |Ready in:

Ingredients

- 1 large cucumber (about 1 pound)
- 1 tablespoon cider vinegar
- 1 1/2 teaspoons sugar
- 1/4 teaspoon dried hot red pepper flakes
- 1 large egg white
- 1 tablespoon soy sauce
- 1/2 teaspoon grated peeled fresh gingerroot
- a 3/4-pound piece salmon fillet, skin discarded and fish cut into
- 1/4-inch pieces
- 1/2 cup fine fresh bread crumbs
- 2 scallions, chopped fine
- 1 teaspoon mustard seed
- 1 teaspoon vegetable oil
- 4 small green-leaf lettuce leaves
- 8 slices firm pumpernickel (about 10 ounces)

Direction

- With a Japanese rotary slicer (see note this page) cut cucumber into 1 long spiral. (Alternatively, with a sharp knife cut cucumber into very thin slices.) In a bowl toss cucumber with vinegar, sugar, red pepper flakes, and salt to taste.
- In another bowl whisk together egg white, soy sauce, and gingerroot until combined well and

stir in salmon, bread crumbs, scallions, mustard seeds, and salt to taste. In a food processor purée 1/3 cup salmon mixture and return to salmon mixture remaining in bowl. (Alternatively, chop 1/3 cup salmon mixture fine and mash to a paste with flat side of a knife.) Stir mixture to combine and form into four 3/4-inch-thick patties. Drain cucumber well.
- In a large non-stick skillet heat oil over moderately high heat until hot but not smoking and cook patties until golden, about 2 minutes on each side. Cook patties, covered, over moderate heat until just cooked through, about 5 minutes more. Arrange lettuce leaves on 4 pumpernickel slices and top with salmon burgers, pickled cucumber, and remaining 4 pumpernickel slices.

12. Asian Style Mushroom Burgers Recipe

Serving: 4 | Prep: | Cook: 20mins |Ready in:

Ingredients

- 1-1/2 pounds ground chuck
- 6 dried shitake mushrooms soaked in hot water 30 minutes finely chopped
- 3 cloves garlic finely chopped
- 1 scallion finely chopped
- 1/4 cup chopped cilantro
- 3 tablespoons soy sauce
- 1 tablespoon sesame oil
- 1 tablespoon chopped fresh ginger
- 1 teaspoon five spice powder
- 1/4 teaspoon salt
- 1/2 teaspoon freshly ground black pepper

Direction

- Combine all ingredients in mixing bowl and mix thoroughly with your hands.
- Form gently into 4 patties and grill over hot coals turning once halfway through cooking.

13. Asian Turkey Burger With Apple Slaw

Serving: 4 | Prep: | Cook: 20mins | Ready in:

Ingredients

- 3 green onions, finely chopped
- 2 tablespoons hoisin sauce
- 1 tablespoon minced fresh gingerroot
- 2 garlic cloves, minced
- 1/2 teaspoon salt
- 1/4 teaspoon pepper
- 1-1/4 pounds ground turkey
- 1 tablespoon olive oil
- SLAW:
- 3 tablespoons olive oil
- 1 tablespoon cider vinegar
- 1 teaspoon Dijon mustard
- 1/4 teaspoon salt
- 1/8 teaspoon pepper
- 2 medium apples, julienned
- 2 green onions, finely chopped
- ASSEMBLY:
- 4 hamburger buns, split and toasted
- 2 tablespoons hoisin sauce

Direction

- In a large bowl, mix green onions, hoisin sauce, ginger, garlic, salt and pepper. Add turkey; mix lightly but thoroughly. Shape into four 3/4-in.-thick patties.
- In a large cast-iron or other heavy skillet, heat oil over medium heat. Cook burgers until a thermometer reads 165°, 7-9 minutes on each side.
- Meanwhile, for slaw, in a large bowl, whisk oil, vinegar, mustard, salt and pepper. Add apples and green onions; toss to coat.
- To assemble, spread bun bottoms with hoisin sauce. Top with burgers and slaw; replace tops.

- Freeze option: Place patties on a plastic wrap-lined baking sheet; wrap and freeze until firm. Remove from pan and transfer to a freezer container; return to freezer. To use, cook frozen patties as directed, increasing time as necessary for a thermometer to read 165°.
- Nutrition Facts
- 1 burger with 1 cup apple slaw: 526 calories, 26g fat (5g saturated fat), 94mg cholesterol, 1024mg sodium, 41g carbohydrate (15g sugars, 4g fiber), 33g protein.

14. Asian Turkey Burgers Recipe

Serving: 6 | Prep: | Cook: 7mins | Ready in:

Ingredients

- Asian turkey Burgers
- 1 1/2 pounds lean ground turkey
- 1 small onion, very finely chopped
- 1 large egg, lightly beaten
- 1 cup panko (Japanese-style bread crumbs)
- 1/4 cup freshly chopped cilantro
- 2 tablespoons freshly chopped parsley
- 2 tablespoons sesame oil
- 1 tablespoon sesame seeds
- 2 teaspoons red chili paste
- 1 green onion, chopped
- 1 1/4 teaspoon coarse salt
- 1/4 teaspoon freshly ground black pepper

Direction

- Step 1
- Mix together the turkey, onion, egg, panko, parsley, cilantro, sesame oil, sesame seeds, chili paste, and green onion in a large bowl until well combined. Add the salt and pepper, or more to taste. (To test the flavor, cook a teaspoon or two of the mixture in the microwave or a small skillet.)
- Step 2
- Divide the mixture into 6 equal portions and shape them into patties, gently pressing the

center of each to create a slight indentation. This will prevent the patty from bulging in the center, so that you end up with a flat, evenly cooked burger. Refrigerate the patties until the grill is ready.

- Step 3
- Prepare a charcoal fire or a gas grill to medium-hot. Wipe the rack with canola oil and lay the burgers on it indentation-side up. Let them cook, without pressing down on them, until the bottoms are well seared, about 5 to 7 minutes. Flip the burgers and continue grilling until they are completely cooked through (the juices will run clear), another 5 to 7 minutes.

15. Asian Salmon Burgers With Pickled Cucumber On Pumpernickel Recipe

Serving: 4 | Prep: | Cook: 20mins | Ready in:

Ingredients

- 1 large cucumber (about 1 pound)
- * 1 tablespoon cider vinegar
- * 1 1/2 teaspoons sugar
- * 1/4 teaspoon dried hot red pepper flakes
- * 1 large egg white
- * 1 tablespoon soy sauce
- * 1/2 teaspoon grated peeled fresh gingerroot
- * a 3/4-pound piece salmon fillet, skin discarded and fish cut into 1/4-inch pieces
- * 1/2 cup fine fresh bread crumbs
- * 2 scallions, chopped fine
- * 1 teaspoon mustard seed
- * 1 teaspoon vegetable oil
- * 4 small green-leaf lettuce leaves
- * 8 slices firm pumpernickel (about 10 ounces)

Direction

- In a bowl toss cucumber with vinegar, sugar, red pepper flakes, and salt to taste. In another

owl whisk together egg white, soy sauce, and gingerroot until combined well and stir in salmon, bread crumbs, scallions, mustard seeds, and salt to taste.

- In a food processor purée 1/3 cup salmon mixture and return to salmon mixture remaining in bowl. (Alternatively, chop 1/3 cup salmon mixture fine and mash to a paste with flat side of a knife.)
- Stir mixture to combine and form into four 3/4-inch-thick patties.
- Drain cucumber well. In a large non-stick skillet heat oil over moderately high heat until hot but not smoking and cook patties until golden, about 2 minutes on each side.
- Cook patties, covered, over moderate heat until just cooked through, about 5 minutes more.
- Arrange lettuce leaves on 4 pumpernickel slices and top with salmon burgers, pickled cucumber, and remaining 4 pumpernickel slices.

16. BBQ Turkey Burgers Courtesy Of Kraft Foods Recipe

Serving: 4 | Prep: | Cook: 79mins | Ready in:

Ingredients

- 1 pkg. (16 oz.) frozen LOUIS RICH Pure ground turkey, thawed
- 1/4 tsp. onion powder
- 1/4 tsp. garlic salt
- 1/4 cup BULL'S-EYE Original barbecue sauce
- 4 KRAFT 2% milk Singles
- 4 hamburger buns, split
- 4 lettuce leaves
- 4 slices tomato

Direction

- PREHEAT lightly greased grill to medium heat. Mix turkey and seasonings; shape into 4 patties.

- GRILL patties 7 to 9 minutes on each side or until cooked through, brushing occasionally with the barbecue sauce.
- TOP burgers with 2% Milk Singles; continue grilling until 2% Milk Singles begin to melt. Fill buns with lettuce, tomato and burgers.

17. BBQ Burger Pocket Recipe

Serving: 4 | Prep: | Cook: 30mins | Ready in:

Ingredients

- 1 lb. ground beef
- 1-1/2 Tbsp. BBQ sauce
- 1-1/2 tsp. chili powder
- 1 tsp. cumin
- 1 tsp. garlic powdr
- 1 tsp. onion powder
- 1 or 2 tomato, 8 slices
- 2 cups romaine, shredded
- 2 Tbsp. ranch dressing
- 2 Tbsp. Dijon mustard
- 2 whole wheat pitas

Direction

- Preheat Char-grill.
- Combine beef with bbq sauce and seasonings.
- Divide into 4 portions.
- Slowly press the patty flat with palm of your hand, the patty should be 3/4 inch thick.
- Place on hot grill for 3-4 minutes each side for medium-well doneness.
- You should see clear juices coming through burger when meat is done.
- Place pita pockets on grill to warm bread, 30 seconds each side.
- Blend ranch dressing and mustard.
- Cut pitas in half, spread 1 Tbsp. of ranch/mustard mix evenly on bread, lay in a 1/2 cup shredded romaine, 2 slices of tomato and a burger.

18. BBQ Spoon Burgers Crock Pot Sloppy Joes Recipe

Serving: 6 | Prep: | Cook: 420mins | Ready in:

Ingredients

- 1 1/2 lb. ground beef
- 1/2 cup onion, chopped
- 1/2 cup green pepper, chopped
- 1 clove garlic, minced
- 1 Tbsp worcestershire sauce
- 1 tsp. dry mustard
- 1 tsp. salt
- 1/2 tsp. paprika
- 1/8 tsp. pepper
- 1 6 oz. can tomato paste
- 3/4 cup water
- 2 Tbsp vinegar
- 2 tsp. brown sugar

Direction

- Brown ground beef in skillet, drain fat. Combine all ingredients in crockpot; stirring well. Cook on low for 6-8 hours or on high for 3-4 hours. Serve over warm hamburger buns, noodles or rice.

19. BLT Turkey Burgers Recipe

Serving: 4 | Prep: | Cook: 12mins | Ready in:

Ingredients

- 4 slices bacon
- 4 lean ground turkey patties, about 1 lb.
- 1 tbsp dry chicken rub, such as McCormick's Grill mates
- 1/2 cup bottled chunky blue-cheese salad dressing
- 4 seeded sandwich rolls
- 1 tomato, sliced

- 4 pieces green-leaf lettuce
- 1 avocado, pitted, peeled, thinly sliced

Direction

- In 12-inch non-stick skillet, over medium-high heat, cook bacon until crisp, 5-6 minutes. Drain on paper towels. Reserve 1 tbsp. fat. Cool pan; wipe clean with paper towel.
- Sprinkle both sides of patties with rub. In skillet, heat reserved bacon fat over medium-high heat. Add turkey patties, in batches if necessary; cook, turning once, until no longer pink in centers, 5 minutes per side. Spread dressing over cut sides of rolls. Fill with turkey patties, tomato slices, lettuce, bacon and avocado slices.

20. BLUE MOON BURGERS Recipe

Serving: 4 | Prep: | Cook: 20mins | Ready in:

Ingredients

- 1 LB ground beef
- 4 LARGE toastED hamburger buns
- 4 OZ CRUMBLED blue cheese
- 4 OZ SOFTENED cream cheese
- 4 SLICES monterey jack cheese
- TOPPINGS
- MAYO
- SHAVED onions
- lettuce
- tomato

Direction

- COMBINE BLUE CHEESE AND CREAM CHEESE AND BEAT WELL
- SET ASIDE TO GIVE THE FLAVORS TIME TO MELD
- FORM THE GROUND BEEF INTO 4 PATTIES
- SALT AND PEPPER, IF DESIRED
- GRILL AS DESIRED

- WHEN BURGERS ARE DONE, ADD 1/4 OF THE BLUE CHEESE MIXTURE ON TOP OF EACH BURGER
- TOP WITH A SLICE OF JACK CHEESE
- SPREAD MAYO ON GRILLED BUNS
- WHEN JACK CHEESE IS GOOEY PLACE BURGERS ON BUNS
- ADD REMAINING TOPPINGS
- DON'T ADD KETCHUP. KETCHUP ABD BLUE CHEESE DO NOT GO TOGETHER

21. Bacon Double Cheese Stuffed Burgers Recipe

Serving: 6 | Prep: | Cook: 20mins | Ready in:

Ingredients

- 1/4 lb chopped, crisp cooked bacon
- 1/2 lg onion diced
- 1 cup cheddar cheese - shredded
- 1 1/2 pounds ground beef
- 1/2 tsp Spike (or seasoned salt)
- 2 Tbsp beer

Direction

- Combine bacon, onion, cheddar cheese and set aside.
- Combine beef, spike and beer, mix thoroughly, the shape into 6 thin patties.
- Put bacon/onion/cheese on 3 patties.
- Top with remaining patties and press edges to seal.
- Grill, broil or pan fry until well done, about 4 minutes per side.

22. Bacon Lettuce And Tomato Pork Burgers Recipe

Serving: 4 | Prep: | Cook: 20mins | Ready in:

Ingredients

- 1 pound ground pork
- 1 teaspoon freshly ground black pepper
- 1 clove garlic minced
- 1/4 teaspoon salt
- 8 slices Canadian bacon
- 4 lettuce leaves
- 4 tomato slices

Direction

- Mix together ground pork and seasonings then shape into 4 patties.
- Heat non-stick skillet over medium heat then place patties in skillet and cook 5 minutes.
- Turn and cook 5 more minutes then serve on toasted buns with bacon, lettuce and tomato.

23. Bacon Pan Burgers Recipe

Serving: 0 | Prep: | Cook: 25mins | Ready in:

Ingredients

- • feta cheese
- • italian seasoning/pepper
- • 1 egg
- • bread crumbs
- • 1 lb ground meat
- • olives
- • bacon
- • cheddar/Swiss/provolone cheese

Direction

- 1. Mix Feta, seasoning, egg, bread crumbs and ground beef in a mixing bowl.
- 2. Form into patties and fry over medium heat.
- 3. Top with olives, sliced cheese and bacon.
- 4. Serve on hamburger buns, or toasted sourdough bread.

24. Baked Beans With Sausage Patties Recipe

Serving: 4 | Prep: | Cook: 105mins | Ready in:

Ingredients

- 1 pound pork sausage
- 2 cups dried navy beans
- 1 teaspoon salt
- 1/2 teaspoon mustard
- 1/4 cup brown sugar
- 2 tablespoons molasses
- 2 tablespoons sausage or bacon drippings
- 2 cups water

Direction

- Wash beans then cover with water and soak overnight.
- Cook slowly for 1-1/2 hours and drain.
- Combine beans with drippings, water and seasonings then place in baking dish.
- Cover and bake at 250 for 8 hours then remove cover.
- Make 6 patties of pork sausage and brown lightly in skillet.
- Place on top of beans and bake an additional 30 minutes or until sausages are done.

25. Baked Beer Burgers For The Brawlers Recipe

Serving: 5 | Prep: | Cook: 10mins | Ready in:

Ingredients

- 2 lb of ground beef
- 1/2 package of dry onion soup mix (Lipton beefy Onion is arguably the best)
- 1 garlic clove, crushed
- A couple of shots of A1 Sauce
- A quarter as much Tabasco sauce as A1
- A handful of grated parmesan cheese
- 6 pack of beer with some body

- salt and pepper to taste

Direction

- Preheat your oven to 400 degrees. Combine the ground beef, A1 sauce, Tabasco sauce, garlic, dry onion soup mix, cheese, salt, pepper, and 1/4 cup of the beer. If you're going to use Coors Light here, you might as well piss in the bowl. You're better off adding a hearty beer like Samuel Adams, giving the whole burger a bit of distinction. Shape the beef into 5 patties.
- Bake them at 400 degrees until brown which should be about 10 minutes. Baste the burgers with the remaining open beer while you continue baking them for an additional 10-15 minutes, until they are well done. As I mentioned, you can also grill the burgers over medium heat.
- Serve them with the remaining 5 beers, alternating between taking a bite of the burger and a swig of the beer, punctuated with a resounding "Ahhhh."

26. Baked In Beef Burgers Recipe

Serving: 8 | Prep: | Cook: 30mins | Ready in:

Ingredients

- beef mix:
- 3/4 pound ground beef
- 3/4 cup minced onion
- 1/2 cup diced celery
- 2 tablespoon shortening
- 1 teaspoon salt
- 1/4 teaspoon pepper
- 1/3 cup tomato sauce
- flour mix:
- 2 cups flour
- 3 teaspoon baking powder
- 1 teaspoon salt
- 1/8 teaspoon marjoram
- 1/2 teaspoon sage

- 1/4 cup shortening
- Other:
- 1/2 cup tomato sauce
- water

Direction

- Preheat oven to 375 F.
- For beef mixture brown ground beef, onion, celery, in the shortening.
- Add salt, pepper, and tomato sauce. Cook until it is thickened. Cool.
- For flour mixture sift together flour, baking powder, salt, marjoram and sage. Cut in shortening until mixture resembles coarse meal.
- Combine the other tomato sauce with enough water to make 2/3 cup. Add to flour mixture, mixing only until all the flour is dampened. Knead gently on a floured board for a few seconds.
- Roll out to 12x9 inch rectangle. Spread with cooled beef mixture.
- Roll as for jelly roll, starting with 9inch side.
- Place on greased baking sheet.
- Bake for 30-35 mins.

27. Banana Blossom Burger Recipe

Serving: 0 | Prep: | Cook: 30mins | Ready in:

Ingredients

- INGREDIENTS: (Veggy Recipe)
- 1 piece medium banana blossom (puso ng saging)
- 1 egg
- 1 cup flour
- 2 cloves of garlic, minced
- 1 medium onion, minced
- ¼ teaspoon ground black pepper
- 1 teaspoon spoon salt
- A pinch of Ginisa Flavor Mix or Magic Sarap (optional)
- Oil for frying

Direction

- Remove outer covering of banana blossoms. Pull together and remove the tough part. Tough part looks like a match inside the banana blossom. When soft leaves could be felt, usually light in color and would easily break, slice thinly, cross-sectional. Immerse with water and drain to retain its light color.
- Put in a pot and bring to boil for about 10 minutes to remove the pungent taste of the banana blossom. Remove from fire and drain. Squeeze remaining water from the blossom.
- In a bowl, combine banana blossom, egg, flour, garlic, onion, black pepper and salt. Mix well.
- Heat oil in a frying pan. Make patties depending on your desired thickness and shape and dip it into frying pan. Cook until golden brown and drain excess oil.
- Another alternative Ingredient for Banana Blossom Burger
- (For those who want a taste of meat)
- Add flour and egg, and ¼ kilo of ground pork or beef. And add a pinch of Ginisa Flavor mix or Magic Sarap to taste but this is optional.
- Then Follow the same procedure as above.

28. Barbecue Spoon Burgers Recipe

Serving: 8 | Prep: | Cook: 23mins | Ready in:

Ingredients

- 1 1/2 lbs ground beef
- 1/2 c.onion,chopped
- 1/2 c. green pepper chopped
- 1 clove garlic minced
- 1tb worcestershire sauce
- 1 ts dry mustard
- 1 ts salt
- 1/2 ts paprika
- 1 6oz can tomatoe paste
- 3/4 c. water
- 2 tb vinegar

- 2 ts brown sugar

Direction

- Brown ground beef in skillet, drain fat
- Combine all ingredients in crockpot, stirring well
- Cook on low for 6-8 hrs. or on high 3-4 hours.
- Serve warm over hamburger buns.

29. Barley Beef Burgers

Serving: 2 | Prep: | Cook: 15mins | Ready in:

Ingredients

- 1/2 cup water
- 1/4 cup quick-cooking barley
- 1/2 small onion, halved
- 1 tablespoon barbecue sauce
- 1-1/2 teaspoons all-purpose flour
- 1/4 teaspoon salt
- 1/8 teaspoon pepper
- 1/2 pound lean ground beef
- 2 hamburger buns, split
- Optional toppings: lettuce leaves, tomato slices and onion slices

Direction

- In a small saucepan, bring water to a boil. Stir in barley. Reduce heat; simmer, covered, 8-10 minutes or until barley is tender. Remove from heat; let stand 5 minutes. Cool slightly.
- Place onion and barley in a food processor; process until finely chopped. Remove to a bowl; stir in barbecue sauce, flour, salt and pepper. Add beef; mix lightly but thoroughly. Shape into two 1/2-in. thick patties.
- Grill, covered, over medium heat 4-5 minutes on each side or until a thermometer reads 160°. Serve on buns with toppings as desired.
- Health Tip: Including barley adds 3 grams fiber and saves 5 grams fat compared to an all-beef burger the same size.

- Nutrition Facts
- 1 burger: 395 calories, 12g fat (4g saturated fat), 69mg cholesterol, 625mg sodium, 42g carbohydrate (5g sugars, 5g fiber), 29g protein. Diabetic Exchanges: 3 lean meat, 2-1/2 starch, 2 fat.

30. Bbq Chicken Burgers Recipe

Serving: 4 | Prep: | Cook: 15mins | Ready in:

Ingredients

- For the bbq sauce:
- 1/2 cup ketchup
- 1/4 cup molasses
- 2 tbsp very finely chopped (or grated) onion
- 2 tbsp worcestershire sauce
- 2 tbsp Dijon mustard
- 2 tbsp cider vinegar
- 1 tbsp brown sugar
- hot sauce, to taste
- For the burgers:
- 1 lb ground chicken
- 1/2 cup crumbled cornbread or 1/4 cup cornmeal
- 1 scallion, minced
- 1 tbsp minced fresh cilantro
- 1/2 tsp paprika
- 1/4 tsp garlic powder
- 1 tsp dry mustard
- 1/2 tsp kosher salt
- Pinch cayenne
- 2 tsp brown sugar
- 2/3 cup chopped pulled pork
- 5 tbsp bbq sauce (homemade or store-bought), divided
- 1/2 red onion, sliced into rings
- 4 slices extra sharp cheddar
- 4 burger buns
- olive oil
- For serving:
- Grilled red onion slices
- sharp cheddar cheese, sliced

- Additional bbq sauce
- hamburger buns

Direction

- To make the sauce:
- Combine all sauce ingredients in a small saucepan and heat over medium heat. Cook the sauce about 7 minutes or until thickened, stirring occasionally. The sauce should be reduced down to approximately 1 cup. Remove from heat and allow to cool. Refrigerate until ready to use. The sauce will keep, refrigerated, for about 1 week.
- To make the burgers:
- Prepare grill.
- In a large bowl, combine the chicken, cornbread, scallion, cilantro, paprika, garlic, mustard, salt, cayenne, brown sugar, pork, and 2 tablespoons of the bbq sauce. Lightly but thoroughly mix with your hands to incorporate all the ingredients. Add the remaining 3 tablespoons of bbq sauce to a small bowl.
- Form the mixture into 4 equal-sized patties. Brush the grates of the grill with olive oil. Place the burgers and onions on the grill, and cook the burgers 5-6 minutes, then flip. Turn the onions as well. Brush the cooked sides with half the reserved bbq sauce. After 3-4 minutes, flip the burgers again. Glazing the other side with the remaining bbq sauce. Place a slice of cheese on each patty, and lay the buns, cut side down, on the grill. Close the lid and allow the cheese to melt and the buns to toast.
- Remove all the food from the grill, assembling the burgers as desired. Serve with additional bbq sauce if desired.

31. Beef 'n' Pork Burgers Recipe

Serving: 8 | Prep: | Cook: 12mins | Ready in:

Ingredients

- 4 bacon strips, diced
- 1 large onion, finely chopped
- 1 garlic clove, minced
- 1-1/2 cups soft bread crumbs
- 1 egg, lightly beaten
- 1/2 cup water
- 1 tablespoon dried parsley flakes
- 2 to 3 teaspoons salt
- 1/4 teaspoon dried marjoram
- 1/4 teaspoon paprika
- 1/4 teaspoon pepper
- 1 pound ground beef
- 1 pound ground pork
- 8 hamburger buns, split and toasted
- mayonnaise or salad dressing, lettuce leaves and tomato slices
- want it a little spicy add jalapeno peppers

Direction

- In a small skillet, cook bacon, onion and garlic over medium heat until the bacon is crisp; drain and place in a small bowl. Stir in the bread crumbs, egg, water, parsley, salt, marjoram, paprika and pepper. Crumble beef and pork over the mixture and mix well. Shape into eight 3/4-in.-thick patties.
- Grill, uncovered, over medium-hot heat for 5-6 minutes on each side or until meat is no longer pink. Serve on buns with mayonnaise, lettuce and tomato.

32. Beef And Andouille Burgers With Asiago Cheese Recipe

Serving: 6 | Prep: | Cook: 20mins | Ready in:

Ingredients

- 4 oil packed sun dried tomatoes drained
- 1/2 cup mayonnaise
- 1 tablespoon whole grain Dijon mustard
- 8 ounces andouille sausage cut into 1" pieces
- 2-1/2 pounds ground beef

- 2 large shallots minced
- 2 teaspoons salt
- 2 teaspoons freshly ground black pepper
- 1 teaspoon fennel seeds crushed
- 6 large sesame seed hamburger buns
- 6 thick slices red onion
- olive oil
- 1 cup coarsely grated asiago cheese
- 7-1/2 ounce jar roasted red peppers drained

Direction

- Finely chop tomatoes in food processor then blend in mayonnaise and mustard then set aside.
- Finely chop sausage in food processor then transfer to a large bowl.
- Add beef, shallots, salt, pepper and crushed fennel seeds then stir with fork just until blended.
- Form mixture into six patties and prepare grill to medium heat.
- Grill buns 2 minutes then transfer to a platter.
- Brush onion slices with oil then sprinkle with salt and pepper and grill 7 minutes per side.
- Grill hamburgers 5 minutes per side then sprinkle cheese over top of burgers.
- Spread cut sides of hamburger buns with sun dried tomato mayonnaise.
- Top bottom halves of buns with hamburgers then red peppers and top with onion slices.
- Cover with top halves of buns and serve.

33. Beer And Maple Syrup Burgers Recipe

Serving: 4 | Prep: | Cook: 20mins | Ready in:

Ingredients

- 1 lb. lean ground beef, 90/10 or higher - I used grass fed, organic 93/7
- 1/4 cup beer - I used Stella Artois
- 1 Tbs. Worcestershire sauce
- 2 Tbs. pure maple syrup - not pancake syrup!

- scant 1/4 tsp. of black pepper
- 4 slices of sweet onion
- 8 slices maple bacon, cooked
- 4 slices cheddar cheese
- 4 buns, lightly toasted or grilled

Direction

- Mix ground beef, beer, Worcestershire sauce, maple syrup and pepper together in a large bowl until combined. It doesn't seem like it will go together at first, but it will. Keep mooshing. Form into four thin patties.
- Place patties on a pre-heated, burger ready grill. My grill is a charcoal grill. Grill for 3 to 4 minutes each side. When second side has 1 minute left, add onion, 2 pieces of bacon and cheese and grill until cheese has melted. Place burgers on buns and add any other of your favorite toppings and/or condiments.

34. Best BBQ Turkey Burgers Recipe

Serving: 14 | Prep: | Cook: 9mins | Ready in:

Ingredients

- 1.5 pounds ground turkey
- 1/2 cup chipolte bbq sauce
- 1 table spoon hickory liquid smoke
- 2 table spoons low sodium soy sauce
- 2 table spoons tried oregeno
- 1 1/2 cups bread crumbs
- 4 gloves fresh minced garlic
- 1 bunch green onion
- 1/2 cup old cheddar
- 1/2 cup fresh parmesan cheese
- 1 tea spoon fresh ground pepper
- 1 egg

Direction

- Mix all of the above together well.
- Roll into balls, all the same size

- Press out meat into 1 inch burgers
- Place in freezer 20-30 minutes to firm
- Grill on medium heat 8-10 minutes per side
- Remove from grill when done.
- Add condiments as desired.
- Along with a glass of wine. Cheers!

35. Best Chickpea Burgers With Tahini Sauce Recipe

Serving: 4 | Prep: | Cook: 58mins | Ready in:

Ingredients

- 1 19-ounce can chickpeas
- 4 scallions
- 1 egg
- 2 Tablespoons all-purpose flour
- 1 Tablespoon chopped fresh oregano
- 1/2 teaspoon ground cumin
- 1/4 teaspoon salt
- 2 Tablespoons extra-virgin olive oil
- 2 6-1/2-inch whole-wheat pitas
- 1/2 cup low-fat plain yogurt
- 2 Tablespoons tahini
- 1 Tablespoon lemon juice
- 1/3 cup chopped flat-leaf parsley
- 1/4 teaspoon salt

Direction

- To prepare burgers: Rinse chickpeas and place chickpeas, scallions, egg, flour, oregano, cumin and 1/4 teaspoon salt in a food processor. Pulse, stopping once or twice to scrape down the sides, until a coarse mixture forms that holds together when pressed. (The mixture will be moist.) Form into 4 patties
- Heat oil in a large non-stick skillet over medium-high heat. Add patties and cook until golden and beginning to crisp, 4 to 5 minutes. Carefully flip and cook until golden brown, 2 to 4 minutes more.
- Meanwhile, combine yogurt, tahini, lemon juice, parsley and 1/4 teaspoon salt in a

medium bowl. Divide the patties among the pitas and serve with the sauce.

36. Best Yet Turkey Burgers Recipe

Serving: 6 | Prep: | Cook: 25mins | Ready in:

Ingredients

- 1 lb. ground turkey
- 1lb. bulk turkey sausage
- 1 bunch green onions, minced (opt.)
- 1 pack saltine crackers
- 1 egg
- 3-5 Tablespoons A-1 sauce
- hamburger buns

Direction

- Mix thoroughly with hands.
- Shape into patties.
- Fry slowly.
- Eat on hamburger buns with ketchup, Worcestershire, or A-1.

37. Better Than Maid Rite Sandwiches Recipe

Serving: 4 | Prep: | Cook: 75mins | Ready in:

Ingredients

- 1 pound 85% lean ground beef
- ½ cup minced white onion
- California blend garlic powder, several shakes of it
- 1 cup chicken broth
- 1/3 cup Coca-Cola
- 1 Tbsp worcestershire sauce
- 1 Tbsp red wine vinegar
- 1 Tbsp spicy brown mustard.
- 1 Tbsp prepared yellow mustard

- 1/4 cup thinly sliced dill pickle slices
- 4 American or cheddar cheese slices, optional
- 4 hamburger buns

Direction

- Heat a cast iron skillet over medium-low heat. Add the ground beef and the minced onions, sprinkle with garlic powder and sauté for a couple of minutes. Flip the meat mixture in the skillet and sprinkle again with more garlic powder. Break up the meat as much as you can with a spatula. Soon as the meat has lost most of its pinkness – remove from the burner.
- In a 4 cup measuring cup, mix together the broth, Coca-Cola, vinegar, Worcestershire sauce and the brown mustard. Stir this mixture into the skillet and return the skillet to the burner. Bring to a boil, stirring often to break up the meat. Soon as the meat mixture reaches a boil, lower the heat to a simmer and continue cooking over low heat till the liquid has been absorbed, about 45 – 60 minutes. It is very important to slowly simmer the meat till all of the liquid is absorbed thus imparting all of the flavors into the meat.
- Split the hamburger buns or sandwich rolls, smear some yellow mustard on the inside of the upper buns. Spread a couple of thin pickle slices on the lower half of the buns. Spoon equal amount of the meat mixture over the lower bun halves, top with an optional slice of cheese then place the bun top on top.

38. Bison Blue Cheese Burgers Recipe

Serving: 4 | Prep: | Cook: 30mins | Ready in:

Ingredients

- 1lb Ground Bison Meat
- blue cheese Crumbles
- 1 yellow onion
- hamburger rolls (I used kaiser rolls)

- Veined Blue Cheddar Slices
- salt and pepper
- butter
- (Assorted condiments/toppings, I used Mayo, mustard, arugula)

Direction

- Mix Ground Bison with Blue Cheese Crumbles, Salt, and Pepper. Divide into 4 even sections and from patties.
- Cut onion in half, then slice (both halves) into 1/4 inch thick slices. Add butter to pan and caramelize the onions over med/low heat; approximately 10 minutes. Set aside.
- In separate pan (or on grill) cook Bison patties, flip, and add a slice of Veined Blue Cheddar to each patty, allow to slightly melt.
- Slightly toast rolls in oven or on grill. Spread desired condiments on rolls, place Bison patties on each roll, top with caramelized onions and arugula.
- Enjoy!

39. Bison Burger With Spicy Peanut Sauce Recipe

Serving: 4 | Prep: | Cook: 15mins | Ready in:

Ingredients

- peanut sauce
- 1/2 cup peanutbutter (natural or Organic PB)
- 3/4 cup coconut milk
- 1 tsp grated lime zest
- 2 tbsp soy sauce
- 1 tbsp sugar (organic, or brown sugar)
- 1 tsp grated ginger
- 1/4 tsp chilli flakes or suit to taste
- add all ingredients into pot on stove medium-low heat for 5-10 minutes
- add water to thin sauce if needed
- Bison meat (ground or hamburger)
- oil for frying
- 1.5 lbs ground bison

- 2-3 garlic (minced)
- 1 or 2 onions (chopped) and/or green onions
- 1 tbsp lime juice
- 1 egg (beaten)
- 1 tbsp chopped lemongrass (optional)
- 1 tbsp Thai curry paste
- 1/2 tsp sea salt
- 2 tbsp cilantro (chopped)
- 1/4 cup of rice flour (or wheat,buckwheat or other flour)
- 1 tbsp lemongrass (chopped and minced) optional

Direction

- Mix all the bison burger ingredients. I use my hands, either make burgers or meatballs. Heat pan on stove, medium heat
- Coat burger or meatball with rice flour then add to frying pan, maybe 6 minutes on each side
- When fully cooked, add to plate of brown rice and steamed vegetables
- Add warm spicy Peanut sauce
- Adapt to your own preference and enjoy

40. Bistro Burgers Recipe

Serving: 6 | Prep: | Cook: 17mins | Ready in:

Ingredients

- 2 T dry white wine, water, or chicken broth
- 1/4 t salt
- 1/4 t black pepper
- 1 lb ground chicken
- 1 lb ground pork
- 2 T creamy Dijon mustard
- 1 T snipped fresh chives
- 2 cloves garlic, minced
- 1 - 4 1/2 oz round brie cheese, rind removed and cut into 12 slices
- 6 slices French bread
- 6 tomato slices
- radicchio or green leaf lettuce

Direction

- In a large bowl combine wine, salt and pepper
- Add chicken and pork
- Mix well by hand
- Shape into 6 patties
- Chill for 30 minutes
- Meanwhile, for sauce, stir together mustard, chives and garlic; set aside
- Preheat grill to medium high
- Place patties over heat, and reduce to medium
- Cover and grill 7-9 minutes each side, turning only once, internal temp of 170
- Top each burger with 2 slices of cheese and grill uncovered 2 or 3 minutes more, until cheese melts
- Toast bread, and spread sauce on one side of each piece
- Add lettuce, tomato and burgers
- Serve open faced

41. Bistro Onion Burgers Recipe

Serving: 6 | Prep: | Cook: 10mins | Ready in:

Ingredients

- 1 1/2 lb. ground beef
- 1 pouch Campbell's® Dry onion soup and Recipe Mix
- 3 tbsp. water
- 6 Pepperidge Farm® Farmhouse Premium White rolls with sesame seeds, split and toasted
- lettuce leaves
- tomato slices

Direction

- MIX thoroughly beef, soup mix and water. Shape firmly into 6 patties, 1/2" thick each.
- COOK patties in skillet or on grill (my preference) 10 min. or until done.
- SERVE on rolls -homemade rolls are the best and heat them on grill for a few minutes. Top

with lettuce and tomato. And I like a thin slice of red onion and whatever your little heart desires.

42. Bit Of A Better Burger Recipe

Serving: 6 | Prep: | Cook: 10mins | Ready in:

Ingredients

- 1-1/2 pound lean ground beef
- 2 tablespoons red wine
- 3 tablespoon garlic-and-herb cheese
- 1 tablespoons shallots, finely chopped
- 1 clove garlic, finely minced
- salt and pepper to taste
- 2-4 dashes hot sauce, to taste
- 1 teaspoon italian seasoning
- 2 tablespoons grated parmesan cheese
- 1 teaspoon lime zest
- 12 slices French bread, toasted or 6 kaiser rolls
- Toppings of choice

Direction

- In a bowl, combine all ingredients.
- Form into 6 patties.
- Grill or fry on stovetop.
- Serve on toasted French bread or Kaiser rolls.
- Top with your favorite toppings: grilled onions are great on these.

43. Black Bean Burgers Recipe

Serving: 6 | Prep: | Cook: 10mins | Ready in:

Ingredients

- 2, 15 oz can black beans
- 1/2 cup chunky salsa (mild is to bland- use medium or hot)
- 1/4 cup yellow cornmeal
- 1/2 cup white or whole wheat flour

- 1 tsp cumin
- 1 clove garlic
- salt and pepper to taste

Direction

- Rinse and drain beans.
- Place in food processor and process until almost smooth.
- Add remainders and process well mixed
- Divide into 6 portions and make patties with your hands.
- Chill well.
- To prepare: heat some olive oil in skillet and cook until browned on both sides.
- Serve on buns with lettuce, tomatoes and onions.
- Note: add some fresh chopped parsley or cilantro f desired to the bean mixture.
- Also grills well, be sure to spray grill with Pam grilling oil to prevent burgers from sticking.
- Also may be prepared and reheated.

44. Black Bean Cakes Recipe

Serving: 6 | Prep: | Cook: 10mins | Ready in:

Ingredients

- 2 (15 ounce) cans black beans
- 6 tbsp salsa (also a little more to serve cakes with)
- 6 tbsp onions, finely diced
- 3/4 cup red bell peppers, finely diced
- 3 tbsp fresh cilantro, chopped
- 1 1/2 cups plain dry breadcrumbs
- 1/4 cup poblano peppers mild flavor (or 1 tbsp jalapeno, diced)
- 1 large clove of garlic, minced
- 2 tsp chipotle sauce (or 1/2 tsp hot sauce)
- 1 1/2 tbsp lemon juice
- salt and pepper, to taste
- tortilla chip breadING

- 1 1/2 cups tortilla chips, crushed (baked variety works well)
- 1 tsp ground cumin

Direction

- Place beans in a colander and rinse in cold water.
- Drain well, for at least 10 minutes.
- Add drained beans and all the other ingredients except for tortilla chip breading into a mixing bowl.
- Blend well, mashing some of the beans to form a thick mixture. Form into 6 patties and roll in tortilla breading.
- At this point you can cover and refrigerate until ready to heat.
- Heat skillet, sauté in just enough oil to brown cakes and heat through.
- Serve with a dab of salsa.

45. Black Eyed Pea Burgers Recipe

Serving: 4 | Prep: | Cook: 30mins | Ready in:

Ingredients

- 15 oz cooked black-eyed peas
- 1/2 cup chopped cauliflower, cooked very well
- 1/2 cup chopped broccoli, cooked very well
- 1/2 cup chopped cremini mushrooms
- 2 tablespoons cornmeal
- 2 tablespoons vegetable broth
- 4 cloves garlic, minced
- 1 tsp tamari
- 1/4 tsp cayenne
- 1/4 tsp chili powder
- 1/2 tbsp garlic powder
- 1/8 tsp black pepper
- 1/4 tsp paprika
- 1/4 tsp ground ancho powder
- 1/2 tbsp onion powder
- 1/8 tsp thyme

Direction

- Preheat your oven to 400 degrees F.
- Puree all ingredients together in a food processor.
- Form into 4 patties, cover and chill 1 hour.
- Lightly coat a baking sheet with cooking spray.
- Put the patties on the pan.
- Bake for 15 minutes, flip the patties, and continue baking for another 15 minutes.

46. Bloody Mary Burgers Recipe

Serving: 4 | Prep: | Cook: 10mins | Ready in:

Ingredients

- 1 lb premium ground chuck
- 2 to 3 tsp of Tobasco
- 4 to 6 shakes of Worchestershire sauce
- 2 Tbs ketsup
- 1 egg beaten
- 1 tsp horseradish
- 1 shallot minced
- 1 tsp celery salt
- 4 hamburger buns
- celery salad:
- 4 inner tender celery stalks with keaves from the celery heart
- 1 tsp fresh squeezed lemon juice
- 1 Tbs olive oil
- Optional seasonings and garnishes:
- green onions
- Old Bay Seasoning
- smoked clams (for a bloody caesar burger !)

Direction

- In a bowl gently combine the chuck, all the seasonings and ingredients and mix well.
- Divide into 4 patties
- Finely diced the celery and add the lemon juice and olive oil and set aside
- Grill the burgers to desired degree of doneness

- Place burgers on toasted buns and top each burger with the celery salad

47. Blue Cheese Burgers Recipe

Serving: 12 | Prep: | Cook: | Ready in:

Ingredients

- 3 pounds lean ground beef
- 4 oz crumbled blue cheese
- 12 hamburger buns or French rolls
- 1 tsp worcestershire sauce
- 1 tsp dry mustard
- 1/4 tsp hot pepper sauce
- 1/2 cup fresh chives, minced
- 1 1/2 tsp salt
- 1 tsp black pepper, coarsely ground

Direction

- Combine the ground beef, blue cheese, Worcestershire sauce, dry mustard, hot pepper sauce, chives, salt and pepper in a large bowl. Place, covered, in the refrigerator for 2 hours.
- Preheat grill on high heat. Gently create about 12 patties from the mixture.
- Oil the grate and grill patties 5 minutes per side, or until they're well done. Serve on rolls or buns.

48. Blue Ribbon Burgers Recipe

Serving: 6 | Prep: | Cook: 15mins | Ready in:

Ingredients

- 2 lbs ground beef
- 2 teaspoons worcestershire sauce
- 1/2 teaspoon salt
- 1/4 teaspoon garlic salt
- 1/4 teaspoon pepper
- 3 oz. Cream cheese; softened

- 2 Tablespoons Blue cheese; crumbled
- 4 ounces canned mushroom pieces

Direction

- Mix Meat, Worcestershire sauce and Seasonings.
- Shape the mixture into 12 thin patties, each about 4 inches in diameter.
- Mix the Cream cheese and the Blue cheese. Top each of the 6 patties with the cheese mixture, spreading to within 1/2 inch of the edge; press the mushrooms into the cheese.
- Cover each patty with one of the remaining patties, sealing the edges firmly.
- Broil or grill the patties 4 inches from the heat turning once, until the desired doneness is reached and the cheese is melted, about 10 to 15 minutes.

49. Bronco Burger Recipe

Serving: 8 | Prep: | Cook: | Ready in:

Ingredients

- 4 pounds ground beef
- 1/4 cup Fritos corn chips, crushed
- 5 fresh jalapeno peppers
- 1 egg
- 1 tbsp worcestershire sauce
- 1 teaspoon hot pepper sauce (e.g. Tabasco™)
- 1/4 cup steak sauce, (e.g. Heinz 57)
- 1/4 cup white onion, minced
- 1 tsp garlic salt
- 1 pinch oregano, dried
- 8 Pepper Jack cheese slices
- 8 large potato hamburger buns
- salt and pepper (to taste)

Direction

- Preheat a grill at high heat. When the grill becomes hot, add the jalapeno peppers and grill until blackened on each side. Place them into a plastic bag to sweat, and loosen the blackened skin. Rub the skin off, then seed (if preferred), and dice.
- Using your hands, combine the ground beef, egg, Fritos, Worcestershire sauce, hot pepper sauce, steak sauce, onion, garlic salt, oregano, salt and pepper in a large bowl. Separate into 8 balls, then flatten to form patties.
- Grill for 10-15 minutes, flipping once, until well done. (I always drink one beer, flip, drink another beer, and then remove from the grill). Place on buns and top each one with a slice of pepper jack cheese then pig out!

50. Brrgrr Licious Mushroom N Swiss Burgers With Garlic Herb Mayo Recipe

Serving: 6 | Prep: | Cook: 18mins | Ready in:

Ingredients

- BURGER
- 1.5 lbs 10% lean ground sirloin
- 1.5 lbs 15% lean ground beef
- Worcestershire
- liquid smoke
- seasoned Salt
- garlic pepper
- 1 T chopped garlic
- 1 packet dry Italian dressing mix
- 3 T grated parmesan
- TOPPING
- 1 large white or yellow onion, sliced thin
- 1 tub fresh mushrooms, wiped clean and sliced
- 1 T butter or margarine
- EVOO
- Worcestershire
- Splash jack Daniels
- 1/2 c grated swiss cheese (or slices)
- 1/2 c grated provolone cheese (or slices)
- garlic herb MAYO
- 1/2 C mayo

- 1 large clove garlic
- 1/2 T lemon juice
- zest from 1/2 lemon (1/4-1/2 t)
- 1/2 t fresh rosemary
- 1/2 T fresh oregano
- 1T fresh basil
- SERVE WITH
- Large deli sandwich buns
- Melted butter
- Thick slices tomato
- Thick sliced pepper bacon

Direction

- BURGERS
- Preheat grill to medium heat
- Mix all ingredients by hand in large mixing bowl
- Shape into 6 large patties (leaving edges uneven helps burger to cook more evenly inside)
- Grill 8-12 minutes per side to desired doneness
- TURNING ONLY ONCE
- TOPPING
- While burgers are grilling, drizzle sauté pan with evoo and add 1 T butter, Worcestershire, and splash Jack Daniels, if desired
- Sauté onions and mushrooms
- Fry slices of thick cut peppered bacon and crumble
- Mix bacon with mushrooms and onions
- MAYO
- Place mayo in a small food processor.
- Finely mince garlic, or press, and add to mayo.
- Add lemon zest then juice.
- Chop all herbs and add to mayo mixture.
- I chop everything first to assure it gets evenly chopped in the food processor. If you do it by hand, without a food processor, just finely chop everything, and make sure to press garlic so you don't get any big chunks.
- PUTTING IT TOGETHER
- Spread insides of buns with melted butter and place on grill for a couple of minutes, until lightly browned

- Top each burger while on the grill with onion/mushroom/bacon mixture, then each type of cheese
- Spread buns with mayo, top with burger and big slice of tomato

51. Bruschetta Burgers Recipe

Serving: 8 | Prep: | Cook: 3mins | Ready in:

Ingredients

- Bruschetta Burgers
- I1 lb lean ground beef
- 3 teaspoons montreal steak spice
- 1 egg
- 1/4 cup oatmeal
- 6 kaiser rolls or focaccia bread
- 1 tablespoon mayonnaise
- 1 tablespoon basil pesto
- mozzarella cheese
- 6-12 tablespoons tomato bruschetta topping

Direction

- Combine ground beef, steak spice (I use Montreal steak spice), egg and oatmeal. Form into patties. Barbeque patties over medium heat on barbeque turning frequently for approximately 5 minutes per side.
- Prepare buns or focaccia (focaccia is the most tasty for these burgers).
- On one half of the bun, spread the mayonnaise and top with mozzarella cheese. Heat bun until cheese is melted. Place the cooked burger patty atop the side of the bun with the mozzarella cheese on it. Top the burger patty with basil pesto 1-2 tbsp. to taste.
- 5Now you are ready to enjoy!

52. Buckeye Burger Recipe

Serving: 4 | Prep: | Cook: 20mins | Ready in:

Ingredients

- 1 lb ground chuck
- buns
- 1/2 envelope (1 oz size) dry onion soup mix
- 1.4 cup dry bread crumbs
- 2 tablespoons water
- lettuce
- slice tomato
- ketchup

Direction

- Mix together the beef, soup mix, bread crumbs and water.
- Form into 4 burgers.
- Grill till desired doneness.
- Serve on buns with lettuce, tomato and ketchup.

53. Buffalo Turkey Burgers Recipe

Serving: 4 | Prep: | Cook: 15mins | Ready in:

Ingredients

- Burgers
- 1 pound ground turkey (ground chicken would work as well)
- 1 egg
- 3/4 - 1 cup panko breadcrumbs
- 1/4 cup hot sauce (I used Frank's Red Hot)
- 1 tsp celery seed
- 1/2 tsp salt
- 1 tbsp vegetable oil
- To Serve
- 2 cups shredded cabbage
- 2 tbsp mayo
- 1 tbsp ranch dressing or Bleu cheese dressing
- 4 whole wheat buns

- 4 slices provolone cheese/4 oz. bleu cheese crumbles/4 slices sharp white cheddar
- 12 celery stalks, cut in half
- 24 baby carrots or about 6 carrots peeled & cut into sticks

Direction

- Burgers
- Combine ingredients in a bowl. Mix gently until just incorporated, do not over mix. Divide into 4 equal portions and form into patties.
- Heat oil over medium in a skillet. Place patties in skillet and cook for about 5 minutes on each side or until juices run clear and patties are done through.
- *Note: These may also be cooked on a grill or under broiler.
- To Serve
- Combine mayo with dressing of choice. Equally distribute mayo mixture on tops and bottoms of all 4 buns.
- Place cooked burger on dressed bottom bun. Top with cheese of choice, followed by cabbage and bun top.
- Serve with carrots & celery alongside.

54. Buffalo Burgers With Pickled Onions And Smoky Red Pepper Sauce Recipe

Serving: 4 | Prep: | Cook: 15mins | Ready in:

Ingredients

- Buffalo burgers with pickled onions and smoky red pepper sauce
- Active time: 1 hr Start to finish: 2 1/2 hr
- Servings: Makes 4 servings.
- IngredientsFor sauce
- 1 red bell pepper
- 1/2 cup low-fat buttermilk dressing
- 1 small garlic clove, chopped

- Rounded 1/4 teaspoon hot Spanish smoked paprika*
- 1/4 teaspoon salt
- For pickled onions
- 2 small red onions (1/2 lb total)
- 1/2 cup cider vinegar
- 1/4 cup sugar
- 1 teaspoon salt
- For burgers
- 1/4 teaspoon salt
- 1/4 teaspoon black pepper
- 1 lb ground buffalo**, formed into 4 (1/2-inch-thick) patties
- 4 English muffins, split in half
- Special equipment: about 20 wooden picks

Direction

- Preparation
- Make sauce:
- Roast bell pepper on rack of a gas burner over high heat, turning with tongs, until skin is blackened, 12 to 15 minutes. (Or broil pepper on a broiler pan about 5 inches from heat, turning occasionally, about 15 minutes.)
- Transfer to a bowl and cover tightly, then let stand 20 minutes. When cool enough to handle, peel pepper, discarding stem and seeds, and coarsely chop. Purée pepper in a blender with dressing, garlic, paprika, and salt until smooth, then transfer to a bowl and chill, covered, until ready to serve.
- Grill onions:
- Peel onions and trim root ends slightly, leaving onions whole, then halve lengthwise and cut halves lengthwise into 1/2-inch-thick wedges. Insert 1 wooden pick through each wedge to hold layers together while grilling, then put onions in a bowl.
- Heat vinegar, sugar, and salt in a small nonreactive heavy saucepan over moderate heat, stirring, until sugar is dissolved. Pour pickling liquid over onions, stirring occasionally to coat with liquid, and let stand 5 minutes (onions will brighten in color), then drain onions and pat dry.

- Prepare grill for cooking. If using a charcoal grill, open vents on bottom of grill, then light charcoal. Charcoal fire is medium-hot when you can hold your hand 5 inches above rack for 3 to 4 seconds. If using a gas grill, preheat burners on high, covered, 10 minutes, then reduce heat to moderate. Grill onions on a lightly oiled grill rack, covered only if using a gas grill, turning over once, until tender, about 5 minutes total. Remove and discard wooden picks.
- Grill burgers:
- Sprinkle salt and pepper on both sides of burgers, then grill burgers on lightly oiled grill rack, covered only if using a gas grill, turning over once with a spatula, 5 to 6 minutes total for medium-rare. Meanwhile, grill English muffins, turning over once with tongs, until toasted, about 3 minutes total. Serve burgers on muffins topped with sauce and onions.
- Cooks' note:
- If you aren't able to grill outdoors, you can use a hot well-seasoned ridged grill pan. Grill onions first, then burgers, then muffins, all over moderately high heat. (Burgers may take 1 minute longer than if cooked outdoors.) Lower heat during cooking as necessary.

55. Build A Better Burger Secret Sauce Recipe

Serving: 4 | Prep: | Cook: 10mins | Ready in:

Ingredients

- The meat: 80% lean, 20% fat, freshly ground chuck, not frozen
- 1 1/2 lbs per 4 burgers- approx 6 oz meat for each patty
- No fillers, herbs, onion or seasonings needed in meat
- The cheese if desired: American cheese, melts nicely- molten and seeping into the crags of the crisp patty, use no other fancy

- cheese
- The bun: soft yet sturdy and slightly sweet, like the potato bun- a moist warm wrapper for the meat
- The lettuce leaf : crisp like iceburg, won't get soft and soggy
- The onion slice : lay on the roll then add the hot burger it's fat soften the onion
- The tomato slice: ripe and juicy
- The pickle: briny, crisp and dill, nothing sweet, adds pucker and punch to the rich burger
- The sauce: Bon Appetit's recipe for special sauce for burgers:
- 1/2 cup mayonnaise
- 2 Tbs ketchup
- 1 Tbs grated onion
- 1 Tbs pickle relish: sweet or dill
- 2 tsp canned adobo sauce from canned chipotle chiles in adobo
- 1/8 tsp celery salt
- 1/8 tsp kosher salt

Direction

- Shaping the burgers: be gentle, lightly form a patty with cupped palms, 3/4 inch thick, about 4 inch patty; loosely formed is fine
- Make a small indentation in center with thumb because burgers contract when cooked and this helps them keep flat
- Season with salt and pepper- grill seasoned side down, then season the other side as you turn them
- Do not press on them with a spatula, this causes them to lose valuable juices
- Cook: gas grill with high heat or charcoal grill to medium high heat
- Grill: lightly charred about 4 minutes per side for medium rare
- Transfer burgers to buns
- Compose the burgers:
- Onion on the bottom of the bun, burger, cheese, lettuce, tomato, sauce
- Let stand 3 minutes before serving
- Enjoy!
- Sauce Recipe:

- Mix all: makes 1 cup

56. Bulgogi Inspired Beef Burgers Recipe

Serving: 4 | Prep: | Cook: 15mins |Ready in:

Ingredients

- 4 Sesame Seed buns, lightly toasted (or use lettuce wraps)
- 4 green onions
- 1 lrg. garlic clove, grated
- 2 tsp.'s grated fresh ginger
- 1 egg
- 2 tsp.'s water
- 2 tsp's of soy sauce
- 1/4-1/3 cup panko bread crumbs (or crushed saltine crackers)
- 1 tsp. toasted sesame oil
- 1/4 tsp. black pepper
- 1 pound lean ground beef
- -------Korean Style Pickled Veggies----
- 1/4 cup Each: vinegar, water, sugar
- 1/2 cup Each: thinly sliced radish, cucumber and matchstick carrots.
- pinch of salt
- ---------Sauce---------
- 1/4 cup mayo mixed with 1-2 tsps. of Srirracha sauce
- ~
- *This burger can be made so many ways by changing the toppings and sauce, here are a few ideas:
- Sauces: Korean BBQ sauce, Hoisin sauce, Thai Peanut sauce, Gochujang Mayo, Wasabi Mayo
- Toppings: Kimchi, matchstick bell peppers, coleslaw/Asian slaw, radish sprouts, bean sprouts, lettuce, tomato, cilantro, etc.

Direction

- Slice the green parts of the green onion and set aside for later. Mince the white and light green parts and add it to a large bowl. Add the minced garlic, ginger, egg, water, soy sauce, panko bread crumbs, sesame oil, black pepper and ground beef. Mix together with your hands and form into 4 patty's. (The amount of bread crumbs depends on the moisture content of your beef) Place them on a plate and wrap in plastic wrap, store in the fridge for at least an hour. The longer they sit the more flavor they will have.

- Pickled Veggies: Mix the vinegar, sugar and water together in a glass bowl. Heat in the microwave for 30 seconds, stir until the sugar is dissolved. Add a pinch of salt. Place the veggies in an air tight container, a non-reactive container like glass is best. Pour over the pickling liquid and let sit in the fridge for at least an hour before serving.
- Cook the burgers on a grill or pan over medium-high heat, approx. 5-6 minutes a side. (To your likeness of course!)
- Meanwhile mix the mayo with enough sriracha sauce to your taste. Place a generous dollop of sauce on your toasted sesame bun. Top with the burger, pickled veggies and green onions.
- Any leftover pickled veg can be added to some chopped lettuce, with the pickling liquid as a dressing with salt and pepper.
- Enjoy!

57. Bulls Eye Burgers Recipe

Serving: 4 | Prep: | Cook: 20mins |Ready in:

Ingredients

- 3/4c. soft bread crumbs (1 slice of bread)
- 1/4c. milk
- 1/2tsp. onion salt
- 1/4tsp. garlic salt
- Dash pepper
- 1lb. ground beef, or turkey
- 2 hard-cooked eggs
- hot chili sauce

Direction

- In a bowl combine bread crumbs, milk, onion salt, garlic salt, and pepper. Add ground meat; mix well. Shape meat mixture into 4 patties, 3/4 inch thick. Cut eggs in half lengthwise. Press one egg half, cut side up, into each meat patty.
- Cover.
- Bake at 350F. for 20 minutes.
- Meanwhile, in a small saucepan heat chili sauce.
- Serve with burgers.

58. Bun Less Portobello Shrimp Burgers Recipe

Serving: 10 | Prep: | Cook: 8mins |Ready in:

Ingredients

- 10 burger sized portobello mushrooms, cleaned, stemmed and gills removed
- 1 Tbl. butter
- 1/4 cup celery
- 1/4 cup green bell pepper, fine dice
- 3/4 cup yellow onion
- 1 1/2 tsp. salt
- 3/4 tsp. cayenne pepper
- 2 pounds of raw shrimp (get the best buy on any size)
- 1/4 pound ground pork
- 1 Tbl. hoisin sauce
- 2 tsp. garlic, chopped fine
- 1/4 cup scallions (green part only), chopped fine
- 5 water chesnuts, chopped
- 4 large eggs, beaten
- 1 cup dried plain bread crumbs
- 2 cups of panko bread crumbs (use regular if you must)
- 1/2 cup all-purpose flour
- 2 tsp. creole seasoning
- 2 Tbl. water

- oil for frying
- For special sauce:
- 1/4 cup sugar
- 1/2 cup water
- 2 Tbl. soy sauce
- 2 Tbl. rice wine vinegar
- 2 Tbl. ketchup
- 1 Tbl. fresh lemon juice
- 1/8 tsp. dark sesame oil
- 1 Tbl. dried mustard powder
- 2 tsp. hot water
- 1 tsp. chinese garlic and red chili paste.

Direction

- Prepare special sauce:
- Dissolve the sugar in water in a small bowl.
- Add soy sauce, rice wine vinegar, ketchup, lemon juice and sesame oil, mix well.
- Combine the mustard and hot water, mix well.
- Add your desired amount of mustard and chili paste to the sauce and store refrigerated until ready to use.
- Prepare burgers:
- Process the shrimp in a food processor until the texture of ground beef (not a paste), transfer to a mixing bowl.
- Pan fry the ground pork until it just changes color, add the hoisin sauce and stir to combine.
- Add the pork mixture to the shrimp and stir to combine.
- In a large skillet, melt the butter over medium heat.
- Add the onions, celery, green peppers, salt and cayenne.
- Cook, stirring, until soft (about 6 minutes).
- Add the shrimp and pork mixture and stir fry for 3 minutes.
- Transfer the mixture to a large bowl and allow to cool slightly.
- Add the garlic, scallions, 2 of the beaten eggs and 1 cup of plain bread crumbs.
- Add the water chestnuts.
- Stir to mix well.
- Divide the mixture among the Portobello caps.
- Put flour into a shallow dish and add 1 tsp. creole seasoning, mix well.

- Put the panko bread crumbs in another dish and add the remaining creole seasoning, mix well.
- Put the remaining beaten eggs in yet another bowl, add the water and beat slightly to combine.
- Heat the oil in a deep skillet to about 350 degrees.
- Carefully (as so not to lose the filling), dredge the stuffed caps in the flour first, then the egg, and finally the panko making sure to fully coat them.
- Carefully again place the caps 4 at a tie into the skillet and fry for about 6 minutes per side, or until golden and cooked through.
- Repeat the frying, draining previous batches on paper towels or brown paper sacks.
- Keep warm until you have finished all burgers. Serve with the special sauce.

59. Burger Heaven Casserole Serves 6 1 Cup Each Recipe

Serving: 6 | Prep: | Cook: 68mins | Ready in:

Ingredients

- 16 oz. extra lean ground beef (or turkey)
- 2 cups sliced raw potatoes
- 1 & 1/2 cups sliced carrots
- 1 cup chopped celery
- 1/2 cup chopped onion
- 1 cup frozen peas –thawed
- 1 cup frozen whole kernel corn – thawed
- 1 10 oz. can healthy Request tomato soup
- 1/2 cup beef broth
- 1 tsp. dried parsley flakes
- 1 can mushrooms (optional)
- salt and pepper
- In large skillet brown meat, onion & celery mixture and mushrooms. In slow cooker container - sprayed with butter flavored spray combine meat mixture, potatoes, carrots, peas, and corn. Stir in tomato soup, water, parsley

flakes and salt and pepper to taste. Cover and cook on low 6 to 8 hours.

- Serves 6 - (1 cup each)
- 5 points
- * You can also cook this in an electric fry pan or simmer on top of the stove.

Direction

- In large skillet brown meat, onion & celery mixture and mushrooms. In slow cooker container - sprayed with butter flavored spray combine meat mixture, potatoes, carrots, peas, and corn. Stir in tomato soup, water, parsley flakes and salt and pepper to taste. Cover and cook on low 6 to 8 hours.
- Serves 6 - (1 cup each)
- 5 points
- * You can also cook this in an electric fry pan or simmer on top of the stove.

60. Burger Pepperoni Recipe

Serving: 6 | Prep: | Cook: 10mins | Ready in:

Ingredients

- 1 pound ground beef
- 1/4 pound pepperoni sausage, minced
- 1/4 cup italian seasoned bread crumbs
- 1 clove garlic, minced
- salt and pepper to taste

Direction

- Preheat the grill for high heat.
- In a bowl, mix the beef, pepperoni, bread crumbs, garlic, salt, and pepper. Form into burger patties.
- Oil the grill grate. Place burger patties on the grill, and cook 5 minutes on each side, or until well done.

61. Burger Potato Bites Recipe

Serving: 8 | Prep: | Cook: 20mins | Ready in:

Ingredients

- 16 large frozen French-fried waffle-cut potatoes (1/3 of a 22-oz. pkg.)
- 1 lb. ground beef
- 2 to 3 tsp. grilling seasoning blend
- 4 slices cheddar cheese, cut into quarters (4 oz.)
- 4 cherry tomatoes, sliced
- mustard, ketchup, dairy sour cream, and/or dill pickle slices

Direction

- Preheat oven to 400 degrees F. Line a baking sheet with foil. Evenly space potatoes on baking sheet. Bake potatoes for 18 to 20 minutes or until crisp and lightly browned. Remove from oven. Adjust oven racks and preheat broiler.
- Meanwhile, in a medium bowl combine meat and seasoning. Form into sixteen 1-ounce mini burgers (about 2 tablespoons). In a 12-inch skillet cook burgers, uncovered, over medium-high heat for 5 minutes or until temperature registers 160 degrees F on an instant-read thermometer, turning burgers once halfway through cooking. Drain fat. Top each potato with a burger, cheese quarter, and tomato slice. Broil 4 to 5 inches from heat for 1 to 2 minutes or until cheese is melted and tomato begins to brown. Serve with mustard, ketchup, sour cream, and/or pickles. Makes 16 snacks.

62. Burgers With Sweet Chili Mayo Spread Recipe

Serving: 4 | Prep: | Cook: 8mins | Ready in:

Ingredients

- 1 pound ground turkey or ground chuck
- 1/4 cup chopped green onions
- 2 1/2 tablespoons chopped fresh cilantro
- 2 tablespoons light soy sauce
- 1 tablespoon sweet chili sauce
- 1 tablespoon peeled, finely chopped fresh ginger (or 1 Tsp gound)
- 1 teaspoon curry powder
- 1 teaspoon ground cumin
- 1 teaspoon granulated sugar
- 4 large sesame hamburger buns, toasted
- Toppings: shredded napa cabbage, bean sprouts, fresh cilantro, sliced tomatoes
- SWEET chili MAYO SPREAD:
- 1/2 cup mayonnaise
- 2 tablespoons sweet chili sauce
- 1 Tbs light soy sauce
- 1 teaspoon sesame oil

Direction

- Place turkey or chuck in large bowl
- Add green onions, chopped cilantro, soy sauce, chili garlic sauce, ginger, curry powder, cumin and sugar; mix well.
- Shape into 4 patties.
- Prepare Sweet Chili Mayo spread by whisking mayonnaise, sweet chili sauce, soy sauce and oil in small bowl; refrigerate.
- Grill or broil for 4 to 5 minutes on each side or until desired doneness.
- Spread Sweet Chili Mayo Spread on buns; top with burgers and toppings.
- Enjoy

63. Burgundy Burgers Recipe

Serving: 6 | Prep: | Cook: 15mins |Ready in:

Ingredients

- 1-1/2 pounds lean ground beef
- 1 small onion, finely chopped (about 1/4 cup)
- 1/4 cup Burgundy or other good red wine
- 1 tablespoon worcestershire sauce

- 2 cloves garlic, finely chopped
- salt and pepper to taste
- Kaier rolls to serve

Direction

- Brush your grill rack with vegetable oil.
- Heat up your grill.
- Mix beef, onion, wine, Worcestershire sauce, garlic, and salt and pepper to taste.
- Shape into 6 patties, about 3/4 inch thick.
- Grill patties, uncovered, about 4 inches from medium heat for 10-15 minutes.
- Turn just once and wait until it's no longer pink in the center and the juices run clear.
- Toast buns, if you'd like, before serving.
- Top with your favorite toppings and condiments.

64. Caesar Burgers Recipe

Serving: 4 | Prep: | Cook: 15mins |Ready in:

Ingredients

- 1 lb. lean ground round
- 2 Tbsp. chopped parsley
- 1/2 cup caesar salad dressing
- 2 Tbsp. parmesan cheese
- 1/2 tsp. seasoned salt
- 1/8 tsp. pepper
- 1 vidalia onion, cut into 1/4" slices
- 4 sandwich buns

Direction

- Prepare and heat grill. Combine beef, parsley, 3 Tbsp. salad dressing, Parmesan cheese, seasoned salt, and pepper and mix gently.
- Shape into four patties, each about 1/2" thick.
- Grill patties on covered grill 4-6" from heat for 12-15 minutes, until hamburgers are no longer pink in center. Turn once, brushing with remaining salad dressing. Grill onions for last 8 minutes of grilling time, brushing with some

of the dressing. Discard any remaining dressing. Serve on sandwich buns.

65. Cajun Burgers Recipe

Serving: 45 | Prep: | Cook: 10mins | Ready in:

Ingredients

- 2 lb. lean ground beef
- 1/2 cup chopped green bell pepper
- 1/2 cup chopped red bell pepper
- 1 large tomato chopped
- 1 small onion chopped
- 2 cloves garlic minced
- 1 egg or 1/4 cup non- fat yogurt
- 1/2 cup fresh coriander chopped
- 1 tsp. chopped jalapeno pepper
- 1/2 tsp. paprika
- 1/2 tsp. salt
- 1/2 tsp. black pepper

Direction

- In a big bowl mix together all the ingredients
- Make patties as thick as you like them
- You can grill the burgers or fry them
- If you fry them, dredge the patties in flour and then fry in skillet with 2 tbs. hot oil.

66. Cajun Tuna Burgers Recipe

Serving: 4 | Prep: | Cook: 20mins | Ready in:

Ingredients

- 1 can of tuna
- 1 med potato
- 1 egg
- cajun seasoning to your taste..(hot pepper flavor)
- onion, these are optional...japaleno pepper,or bell pepper, celery..garlic.

- flour (i put a little seasoning in the flour)
- one skillet
- cooking oil to fry.

Direction

- Boil the med potato then mash up in a bowl
- Beat the egg and add to potato
- Add seasoning and onions
- Then add tuna mash up into the potato
- Then make patties, roll in flour then fry until brown

67. California Burger Recipe

Serving: 4 | Prep: | Cook: 10mins | Ready in:

Ingredients

- 1 pound ground beef
- 4 sesame seed buns
- 1 pound mushrooms sliced and grilled
- 12 slices avocado
- 4 slices jack cheese
- 4 slices tomato
- 4 teaspoons thousand island salad dressing

Direction

- Cook burger to desired doneness.
- Pan toast rolls with small amount of butter then spread with Thousand Island dressing.
- Place grilled burger on roll and garnish.

68. Caprese Polenta Burgers With Vidalia Onions And Beef Bouillon On The Grill Recipe

Serving: 4 | Prep: | Cook: 45mins | Ready in:

Ingredients

- BURGERS:

- 1-1/2 lbs. ground beef (95% lean)
- 2/3 cup balsamic vinegar
- 1 package refrigerated prepared polenta (16-18oz.), cut into 8 slices
- 2 Tbs. olive oil
- salt and pepper to taste
- 1 package fresh mozzarella cheese (8oz.), cut into 8 slices
- 2 medium tomatoes, cut into 4 slices each
- Thinly sliced fresh basil
- VIDALIA ONIONS:
- 4 large vidalia onions
- 4 Knorr extra large beef bouillon cubes (these are worth buying – they're the best for this recipe!)
- 4 tablespoons butter
- 4 cloves of peeled garlic, each clove cut in half
- heavy duty aluminum foil (a must!)
- garlic croutons, optional
- grated swiss cheese, optional

Direction

- BURGERS:
- Bring vinegar to a boil in a 2-quart saucepan. Reduce heat; simmer, uncovered, 9-10 minutes or until reduced to 1/3 cup. Set aside.
- Meanwhile, lightly shape ground beef into 8, 1/2-inch thick, patties. Brush polenta slices with oil. Place patties in center of grid over medium, ash-covered coals; arrange polenta around patties.
- Grill patties and polenta, uncovered, 11-12 minutes (over medium-heat on preheated gas grill, for 9-11 minutes) or until patties are medium (160 degrees) doneness, not pink in center and juices show no pink color and polenta is heated through, turning once and basting patties with 2 Tbs. reduced vinegar after turning.
- Season burgers with salt and pepper, as desired.
- For each serving, layer 1 each polenta slice, burger, mozzarella slice and tomato slice. Drizzle with remaining vinegar and sprinkle with basil, as desired.
- VIDALIA ONIONS:

- Peel onions without cutting off the root end; cut off about 1 inch of the top of the onion.
- Removing as little as possible, cut the root end into a nice flat surface so the onion will remain upright while cooking.
- Using a potato peeler or knife, dig a small cone shaped section from the center of each onion (be careful not to cut through to the root end!)
- Cut the onion into quarters from the top down, stopping within an inch of the root end. Place a bouillon cube in the center of each onion, and place chunks of butter around the bouillon.
- If you are using the garlic, place 1 half in each of 2 quartered sections of the onion.
- Wrap each onion separately in heavy duty aluminum foil. Seal the foil well so moisture can't escape during baking, letting the yummy broth evaporate. Place the foil packages directly on the grill grate, or in a baking pan in a 400 degree oven. Bake until onions are soft, about 45 minutes to 1 hour.
- To serve, place each onion in an individual bowl and open foil package (don't burn yourself with the steam!). Remove onion and all the broth from inside the foil. Serve warm.
- To create instant onion soup, carefully open the tops of each foil packet when onions are done, throw in some croutons and top with grated Swiss cheese, then place the opened packets back on the grill (or in the oven) and continue to cook until the cheese melts (this should only take a few minutes).
- **serves 4 at 2 burgers each, onions serve 4**

69. Captain Neon Burgers Recipe

Serving: 4 | Prep: | Cook: 15mins |Ready in:

Ingredients

- 2 oz. cream cheese
- 2 oz. crumbled blue cheese
- 1/8 t. onion powder
- 1 T. chopped fresh parsley

- salt and pepper to taste
- 1 pound ground beef (I use 85% lean)
- 1-2 slices white bread
- milk
- salt and pepper
- Coarsely ground black pepper

Direction

- 1. In a small bowl, mash together cream cheese and blue cheese then stir in the onion powder and parsley. Taste and season with salt and pepper.
- 2. Moisten the bread in a bowl with enough milk to soften, and mash with a fork and then add the beef. Divide ground beef into 8 equal pieces. I first divide it into four pieces then divide each piece again. Form the pieces into balls then sprinkle the balls lightly with salt and pepper, rolling them around a bit to make sure all sides are covered. Flatten each ball to form thin patties of equal size. I find it easiest to form the patties on a sheet of waxed paper.
- 3. To fill burgers, place a tablespoonful of cream cheese mixture in the center of each of four patties. Spread the filling out evenly to within half an inch of the edge of each patty. Place the remaining patties on top to form four filled burgers. Gently press the edges of each burger together to form a seal.
- 4. Sprinkle burgers liberally with coarsely ground black pepper (optional).
- 5. Prepare your grill and cook burgers until the internal temperature reaches 160 degrees (USDA recommendation) or until desired degree of doneness. Let rest for ten minutes.
- 6. Serve with crisp bacon and lettuce. Enjoy!

70. Caribbean Burgers Recipe

Serving: 4 | Prep: | Cook: 8mins | Ready in:

Ingredients

- 1 1/2 pounds lean ground beef, chuck or turkey
- 4- teaspoons dry jerk seasonings (see my recipes)http://www.grouprecipes.com/83563
- 2- tablespoons ketchup
- 2- tablespoons honey-ginger dipping sauce
- 2- tablespoons vegetable oil
- 4 hamburger buns
- 4 slices cheddar cheese
- 4- slices cored fresh pineapple
- *********************************
- Honey- ginger Dipping sauce
- 1- 8 ounce can sweetened tamarind nectar
- 1- tablespoon honey
- 2- 3 inches fresh ginger peeled and grated
- 1- tablespoon soy sauce
- 1- tablespoon dry jerk seasoning
- 1- teaspoon cornstarch
- 1- teaspoon water
- in a small saucepan combine the tamarind nectar and honey
- bring to a boil and cook until reduced by 1/3
- stir in the ginger, soy sauce, dry jerk seasonng
- mix the cornstarch with the water to form a paste then stir into the tamarind mixture
- cook stirring constantly, until the sauce thickens 1-2 minutes
- serve hot or at room temperature
- store unused sauce in tightly sealed glass jar in the refrigerator use within 30 days ....

Direction

- Light a medium fire in a charcoal grill, or preheat a gas grill to 350 degrees f or heat a large skillet over medium- high heat
- Season the beef with the dry jerk seasoning and mix well
- Form into 4 equal patties
- In a small bowl, combine the ketchup and dipping sauce
- Oil the grills grids or heat oil in the pan over medium high heat
- Add the patties to the grill or pan and cook until browned, about 3-4 minutes each side if you are using a grill, grill the pineapple slices for about 1 minute per side

- Lightly toast the buns
- To serve place the meat patties on the buns and top each with 1 slice of cheese and 1 slice of grilled pineapple
- Dress with ketchup mixture and dipping sauce and whatever else you want on it
- Serve at once
- Serve 4

71. Catherines Ranch Burgers Recipe

Serving: 4 | Prep: | Cook: 8mins | Ready in:

Ingredients

- 1 pound ground beef (lean ground, chuck, whatever your favorite.)
- 3 Tablespoons Hidden Valley Ranch seasoning and salad dressing Mix (this is equal to a 1 oz packet.)
- You might also need: charcoal, hamburger buns, other condiments you like.

Direction

- Mix Dressing Mix and hamburger together gently.
- Form into 4 burgers and grill for about 8 -10 minutes for medium.
- Of course you can broil these in the oven or use any method you like.
- The taste is in the burger!

72. Charmoula Lamb Burgers Recipe

Serving: 4 | Prep: | Cook: 7mins | Ready in:

Ingredients

- 3   garlic cloves

- 11/2tsp ground cumin
- 1tsp   ground coriander
- 1tsp   paprika
- 1/2tsp   cinnamon
- 1/2tsp   cayenne pepper
- 1/3c   finely chopped cilantro
- 11/2lb   ground lamb (not lean)
- 4   6-7" pita pockets
- 1/4c   tapenade
- 1T   extra virgin olive oil
- 2tsp   fresh lemon juice
- 4   thick tomato slices

Direction

- Mince garlic and mash to a paste with 3/4tsp salt using the side of a heavy knife. Stir together garlic paste with the cumin, coriander, paprika, cinnamon, cayenne and the cilantro; sprinkle over lamb and mix until combined (do not overmix) Form lamb into 4 3/4" thick patties.
- Cut off enough from one side of each pita to leave a 5" opening. Stir together tapenade, olive oil and lemon juice.
- Oil grill and cook burgers over medium-high heat, turning once; about 6-7 minutes for medium rare; grill pitas.
- Spread patties with the tapenade mixture and slide into pitas with the tomato slices.

73. Cheddar Burgers And Crispy Oven Fries Recipe

Serving: 4 | Prep: | Cook: 25mins | Ready in:

Ingredients

- 2 tablespoons vegetable oil, plus more for baking sheet
- 3/4 cup cornflake crumbs (store-bought or crushed from 2 cups cornflakes)
- 1/8 to 1/4 teaspoon cayenne pepper
- coarse salt and ground pepper

- 1 1/2 pounds baking potatoes (about 3), well scrubbed and cut lengthwise 3/4 inch thick
- 1 1/2 pounds ground beef chuck
- 1 cup finely grated cheddar (2 ounces)
- 4 hamburger buns, split
- Burger sauce (see note, above)
- Garnishes, such as lettuce, sliced onion, sliced tomato, sliced pickles, ketchup, and mustard

Direction

- Preheat oven to 375 degrees. Brush a large rimmed baking sheet with oil; set aside.
- In a pie plate or shallow bowl, combine cornflake crumbs, cayenne, and 1 tablespoon salt. In a large bowl, toss potatoes with oil to coat. One or two at a time, dip potatoes in crumbs, turning to coat all sides; transfer to prepared baking sheet. Bake potatoes, turning once, until crispy on the outside and tender on the inside, 40 to 50 minutes. Remove from oven, and season with more salt.
- Meanwhile, in a medium bowl, combine beef, cheddar, 1 teaspoon salt, and 1/2 teaspoon pepper. With a fork, mix very gently to combine. Gently shape meat into 4 patties, each 4 inches in diameter and 1 inch thick; season with salt and pepper.
- Fifteen minutes before potatoes are finished baking, heat a large non-stick skillet over medium-high. Place burgers in skillet, and cook until browned on both sides and done to taste (4 to 6 minutes per side for medium-rare). Serve on hamburger buns with crispy oven fries.

74. Cheese Stuffed Burgers For Two

Serving: 4 | Prep: | Cook: 10mins | Ready in:

Ingredients

- 1 tablespoon finely chopped onion
- 1 tablespoon ketchup
- 1 teaspoon prepared mustard

- 1/4 teaspoon salt
- 1/8 teaspoon pepper
- 1/2 pound lean ground beef (90% lean)
- 1/4 cup finely shredded cheddar cheese
- 2 hamburger buns, split
- Optional: Lettuce leaves and tomato slices

Direction

- In a small bowl, combine the first 5 ingredients. Crumble beef over mixture and mix well. Shape into 4 thin patties. Sprinkle cheese over 2 patties; top with remaining patties and press edges firmly to seal.
- Grill burgers, covered, over medium heat 5-6 minutes on each side or until a thermometer reads 160°. Serve on buns, with lettuce and tomato if desired.
- Nutrition Facts
- 1 each: 357 calories, 15g fat (7g saturated fat), 84mg cholesterol, 787mg sodium, 25g carbohydrate (4g sugars, 1g fiber), 28g protein. Diabetic Exchanges: 3 lean meat, 1-1/2 starch, 1-1/2 fat.

75. Cheeseburger Sliders

Serving: 0 | Prep: | Cook: | Ready in:

Ingredients

- 1 pound ground beef
- ½ onion, chopped
- 2 tablespoons ketchup
- 3 teaspoons Dijon mustard, divided
- 3 teaspoons Worcestershire sauce, divided
- ½ teaspoon garlic powder
- 1 pinch salt and ground black pepper to taste
- 1 (12 count) package Hawaiian bread rolls
- 1 (8 ounce) package shredded Monterey Jack cheese
- ¼ cup butter
- 1 tablespoon brown sugar

Direction

- Preheat the oven to 350 degrees F (175 degrees C). Lightly grease an 11x7-inch baking dish.
- Heat a large skillet over medium-high heat. Cook and stir ground beef and onion in the hot skillet until meat is browned and crumbly, 5 to 7 minutes. Drain and discard grease. Stir in ketchup, 2 teaspoons Dijon mustard, 2 teaspoons Worcestershire, and garlic powder. Season with salt and pepper to taste.
- Cut rolls in half horizontally without separating each roll from one another. Place bottom halves in the prepared baking dish. Spread meat mixture on rolls, top with Monterey Jack cheese, and cover with roll tops.
- Combine butter, brown sugar, remaining Dijon mustard, and remaining Worcestershire in a microwaveable bowl; cover loosely and microwave until butter is melted, about 1 minute. Mix and pour mixture over the top of the rolls.
- Bake, covered, in the preheated oven for 15 minutes. Uncover and bake until cheese is melted and rolls are golden brown, about 10 minutes more.
- Nutrition Facts
- Per Serving:
- 453.3 calories; protein 25.1g 50% DV; carbohydrates 44.9g 15% DV; fat 14.1g 22% DV; cholesterol 90.4mg 30% DV; sodium 446.5mg 18% DV.

76. Cheesy Biscuit Burger Ring Recipe

Serving: 16 | Prep: | Cook: 45mins | Ready in:

Ingredients

- 1 pound lean ground beef
- 1 (1.25 ounce) package taco seasoning mix
- 1 (4.5 ounce) can chopped green chiles
- 1/2 cup water
- 1/4 cup refrigerated or frozen egg product, thawed
- 2 cups finely shredded mexican cheese blend
- 2 (16.3 ounce) cans buttermilk biscuits
- 1 cup thick 'n chunky salsa

Direction

- Heat oven to 375 degrees F.
- Spray fluted tube cake pan with non-stick cooking spray.
- Brown ground beef in large skillet over medium heat until thoroughly cooked, stirring frequently. Drain well.
- Add taco seasoning mix, chilies, water and egg product; mix well. Cook and stir 1 to 2 minutes or until mixture thickens.
- Stir in 1 cup of the cheese. Cool while shaping biscuits.
- Separate dough into 16 biscuits. Split each biscuit to make 32 rounds. Press out each biscuit half to form 4-inch round.
- Place 1 rounded tablespoon beef mixture in center of each round. Bring up sides of dough over filling; pinch edges to seal. Place, seam side down, randomly in sprayed pan.
- Bake at 375 degrees F for 33 to 43 minutes or until dark golden brown.
- Cool in pan for 5 minutes. If desired, line serving platter with leaf lettuce. Invert biscuit ring over lettuce.
- Immediately sprinkle with remaining 1 cup cheese.
- Let stand 5 minutes to melt cheese.
- Cut into slices.
- Serve with salsa.

77. Cheesy Burger Casserole Recipe

Serving: 6 | Prep: | Cook: 30mins | Ready in:

Ingredients

- 1 pound of ground beef (can sub. small cut stew meat)

- 1 bag of egg noodles
- 2 cans cream of mushroom soup
- 1 bag frozen or fresh cooked broccoli
- 1/2 pound of cheddar cheese, grated

Direction

- Preheat oven to 350 F.
- Cook noodles to desired doneness, as well as broccoli and ground beef (season to taste).
- Place noodles, broccoli, ground beef, and mushroom soup in 13 x9 casserole dish.
- Mix well.
- Sprinkle cheese over top of casserole.
- Bake uncovered 30 - 40 mins or until cheese is melted and bubbly.

78. Cheesy Spinach Burgers Recipe

Serving: 8 | Prep: | Cook: 10mins | Ready in:

Ingredients

- 2 lbs ground beef
- 1 envelope LIPTON RECIPE SECRETS onion soup mix.
- 1 pkg (10oz) frozen chopped spinach, thawed and squeezed dry.
- 1 cup shredded mozzarella cheese.

Direction

- In a large bowl, combine all ingredients; shape into 8 patties.
- Grill or broil or pan fry until done.
- Serve with lettuces or hamburger buns.

79. Cheesy Stuffed Chipotle Burgers With Salsa Mayo Recipe

Serving: 6 | Prep: | Cook: 30mins | Ready in:

Ingredients

- 2 1/2-3lbs ground red meat(your choice.... I usually use venison and beef)
- 1 can chipotles in adobo sauce
- about 6oz shredded Jack, cheddar or colby cheese
- 1/2 cup grated or dried minced onion
- 2T worcestershire sauce
- 1t smoked paprika
- kosher or sea salt and fresh ground pepper
- For salsa Mayo
- 1 heaping cup mayonnaise
- 1 can rotel style tomatoes, drained well
- few T fresh cilantro, chopped

Direction

- Mince chipotle peppers and mix all the adobo, and as many of the chopped peppers as you like (I used the whole little can) with the meat, cheese, onion, Worcestershire sauce, paprika and salt and pepper. Mix well as you would a meat loaf, but be gentle.
- Form into 1/4 or 1/3lb patties.
- Grill or broil for a few minutes, each side, until cooked through to your preference.
- Salsa Mayo
- Combine ingredients and refrigerate until ready to use.
- Serve burgers on buns with desired ingredients.

80. Chesapeake Bacon Cheese Stuffed Burgers Recipe

Serving: 6 | Prep: | Cook: 30mins | Ready in:

Ingredients

- 1 pound ground beef
- 1 pound ground pork
- 1 cup shredded sharp cheddar cheese
- 1/2 sweet onion, finely chopped
- 1/4 pound chopped hickory smoked bacon
- 1 tablespoon Old Bay Seasoning

- 1/2 teaspoon ground black pepper
- Burger buns
- Your favorite garnishes for burgers
- mustard, mayonnaise, lettuce, tomato, onion, and pickles

Direction

- In a pan fry bacon until crisp.
- Remove bacon from pan and slowly fry the onion in the bacon drippings for about 7 minutes or until softened.
- Allow the onion to cool and crumble bacon. In a bowl combine beef, pork, Old Bay, pepper, bacon, onion, and cheddar cheese mix thoroughly. Shape the meat into six 1" thick 1/3 lbs. patties. Let the flavors marry in the refrigerator for 1 hour. Grill, broil or pan fry until well done.

81. Chesapeake Bay Stuffed Burger Recipe

Serving: 4 | Prep: | Cook: 18mins | Ready in:

Ingredients

- 2 pounds ground chuck
- 1 1/2 cups crabmeat
- 4 Sesame seed buns
- 2 tablespoons chopped fresh cilantro
- 6 tablespoons saltines - crushed
- 2 tablespoons mayonnaise
- 1/2 tsp. Dijon mustard
- 1 teaspoon horseradish
- 1 teaspoon fresh lemon juice
- 1 teaspoon Old Bay Seasoning
- 1/2 tsp. garlic & herb salt Free seasonings
- 4 teaspoons finely chopped green onion
- 2 teaspoons minced ginger
- 1 tsp. fresh ground sea salt
- 1 tsp. fresh ground pepper
- Fresh green leaf lettuce
- fresh tomato slices

- Swiss cheese slices

Direction

- Season ground chuck with horseradish, garlic and herb seasonings, salt and pepper.
- Divide into eight, 1/4-pound patties about 1/4 inch x 5 inches.
- Make crab stuffing by combining crabmeat and remaining ingredients. (Leave the buns out though)
- Divide one cup stuffing between four of the patties.
- Flatten crabmeat slightly, leaving about 1/2 inch around edge.
- Place a remaining patty on top of each and crimp the edges with fork, once around on each side. (You might have to reshape the meat a bit)
- Grill on medium-high 15 to 18 minutes, adjusting time and temperature as needed.
- Top with Swiss cheese during the last 2 minutes of grilling.
- Serve on sesame seed buns and top with lettuce and tomato.
- Enjoy!

82. Chicago Pizza Burgers Recipe

Serving: 4 | Prep: | Cook: 15mins | Ready in:

Ingredients

- 1lb lean ground beef
- sandwich buns
- 1 cup(1/4lb) chopped pepperoni
- sliced mozzerella cheese
- 1/3 cup parmesan cheese
- couple pinchs of basil
- couple pinchs of orengano
- couple pinchs garlic powder
- pizza sauce
- tomatoe if desired

Direction

- Mix together the beef, pepperoni, parmesan cheese and seasoning.
- Form into 4 patties.
- Grill to desired doneness.
- Top with slice of mozzarella.
- Serve on a bun with pizza sauce and tomato if you desire.

83. Chickpea Burgers Recipe

Serving: 6 | Prep: | Cook: 8mins | Ready in:

Ingredients

- 2 c. cooked chickpeas, mashed
- 1 carrot, chopped finely
- 1 small onion, chopped finely
- 1/2 - 1 c. breadcrumbs (add more if you want a sturdier burger)
- 1 handful fresh parsley, chopped
- 1 egg, lightly beaten
- 1 t salt
- 2 T sesame seeds
- large dash red pepper flakes
- tomato, onion, and avocado for the burger!

Direction

- Combine all ingredients, mix well.
- Separate into six parts, and pat down into burgers
- Cook on a preheated non-stick skillet for about 4 minutes on each side, or until golden
- Serve on a roll with tomato, onion, and avocado.

84. Chickpea Flaxseed And Oatmeal Burgers With Tzatziki Recipe

Serving: 4 | Prep: | Cook: 10mins | Ready in:

Ingredients

- TZATZIKI:
- 1/2 medium cucumber, peeled, seeded, grated, and squeezed dry
- 1/4 cup fat-free plain yogurt
- 1/2 teaspoon minced garlic
- 1/8 teaspoon salt
- 1/8 teaspoon freshly ground black pepper
- BURGERS:
- 6 tablespoons flaxseed
- 1 can (15 1/2 ounces) chickpeas, rinsed and drained
- 1/4 cup rolled oats
- 2 cloves garlic
- 2 tablespoons water
- 1/4 cup chopped fresh mint
- 2 tablespoons lemon juice
- 2 teaspoons ground cumin
- 1 teaspoon salt
- 1/8 teaspoon freshly ground black pepper
- 1/4 cup panko bread crumbs
- 1 egg, lightly beaten
- 1 tablespoon olive oil
- 4 whole wheat hamburger buns
- 1 medium tomato, cut into 8 slices
- 1/2 cup alfalfa sprouts

Direction

- 1. To make the tzatziki: In a small bowl, combine the cucumber, yogurt, garlic, salt, and pepper. Cover and refrigerate while preparing the burgers. 2. To make the burgers: In a spice or coffee grinder, process 5 tablespoons of the flaxseed to a fine meal. In the bowl of a food processor, combine the chickpeas, oats, garlic, and water. Pulse until the mixture is coarsely chopped. Add the mint, lemon juice, cumin, salt, pepper, and flaxseed meal. 3. Pulse the food processor until the mixture is just combined. Divide the mixture into 4 equal portions and shape each into a 1/2"-thick patty. 4. Combine the bread crumbs and remaining flaxseed on a plate. Dip the burgers in the egg, then dredge in the bread crumb mixture. 5. In a large non-stick skillet, heat the oil over medium-high heat. Add the burgers and cook for 5 to 6 minutes per side, or until golden. 6. On the bottom of each bun, place 2 tomato slices and 2 tablespoons alfalfa sprouts. Place the burgers on top of the sprouts and top each burger with a slightly rounded tablespoon of the tzatziki.

85. Chile Pepper Burgers With Lime Mayonnaise Recipe

Serving: 8 | Prep: | Cook: 20mins | Ready in:

Ingredients

- 1/3 cup mayonnaise
- 1 teaspoon Dijon mustard
- 1 teaspoon lime juice
- 1/2 teaspoon grated lime peel
- 2 pounds lean ground sirloin
- 1/3 cup sliced green onions
- 3 tablespoons plain yogurt
- 2 tablespoons finely chopped jalapeno pepper
- 1/2 teaspoon salt
- 1/2 teaspoon pepper
- 8 ounces hot pepper cheese cut into 8 slices
- 8 kaiser rolls
- 2 cups hickory chips

Direction

- Place wood chips in large mixing bowl then cover with water and soak for 1 hour.
- In small mixing bowl combine mayonnaise, mustard, lime juice and lime peel.
- Cover with plastic wrap and chill.
- Combine beef, onions, yogurt, jalapenos, salt and pepper the shape into 8 patties.
- Drain hickory chips and sprinkle over hot coals then arrange patties on cooking grate.
- Grill covered for 15 minutes turning half way through cooking.
- Top each burger with 1 slice cheese then grill 2 minutes longer.
- Serve on rolls with your favorite condiments.

86. Chili Cheese Burgers Recipe

Serving: 6 | Prep: | Cook: 20mins | Ready in:

Ingredients

- 1&1/2 lbs. ground beef
- 1 ts.chili power
- 3/4 ts. salt
- 1/4 ts.pepper
- 6 slices of (6 slices of cheese any kind)
- 1 ts. worcestershire sauce
- 1/4 ts. garlic salt
- 1/4 ts. red pepper sauce (I use Franks Red Hot)
- 1 dash cayenne red pepper

Direction

- Mix all ingredients together except cheese slices
- Make 6 hamburger patties
- Turn once cook until done

87. Chipolte'n' Cheese Sliders Recipe

Serving: 12 | Prep: | Cook: 15mins | Ready in:

Ingredients

- 1 lb ground beef
- 1/2 med. onion,finely chopped
- 3 TB tomato paste
- salt and pepper
- 1 c mayonnaise
- 2 TB chipolte hot sauce,like Tobasco
- olive oil
- 12 dinner rolls,halved
- 12 leaves baby lettuce greens
- 3 med. tomatoes,cut in 1/2" slices

- fried onions,optional
- 12 mini slices med. cheddar cheese(or 6 reg. slices,halved)

Direction

- In med bowl, combine beef, onion, tomato paste, 2 tsp. salt and 1/4 tsp. pepper; use hands to mix. Makes 12 patties, about 2" wide.
- In small bowl, mix mayonnaise and chipotle hot sauce until well combined; set aside
- Lightly toast dinner rolls in toaster oven. Meanwhile, cook patties on med-high heat in olive oil in non-stick sauté pan or griddle, about 2 mins. a side.
- Spoon chipotle mayo onto the bottom buns. Top with a few leaves of baby greens, one slice of tomato, a meat patty and a slice of cheese; top with bun. Add fried onions, if so desired. Stick a long toothpick thru each slider; serve with extra chipotle mayo in bowl.

88. Chipotle And Pineapple Grilled Burger Recipe

Serving: 4 | Prep: | Cook: 25mins | Ready in:

Ingredients

- One can of pineapple slices
- 1 pound of beef
- 1/2 teaspoon of onion powder
- 2 chipotle peppers
- 1 tablespoon lime juice
- 1/4 teaspoon garlic powder
- mayonaise or salad dressing
- tomatoe slices
- lettuce
- 5-6 whole hamburger buns

Direction

- Peel and chop the onion. Dice the chipotle pepper, remove seeds if wanted. You can also put them in a food processor. Add the garlic

and lime juice to the onion and chipotle pepper mix. Then mix sauce with the pound of beef and form into 6 patties. Grill burgers and serve with a slice of pineapple, tomato slice and piece of lettuce. Spread mayonnaise on toasted buns. Serve warm and enjoy

89. Chipotle Burgers Recipe

Serving: 4 | Prep: | Cook: 10mins | Ready in:

Ingredients

- 1 lb. ground beef
- 1 chipotle in adobo, finely chopped with 1 tsp. of adobo sauce
- salt and pepper to taste
- 4 slices of pepper cheese (Use either pepper jack or as I've found recently, Land of Lakes pepper cheese)
- 4 hamburg buns
- Toppings
- sliced onion
- jalapeno rings
- sliced tomato
- sliced red onion
- sliced avocado
- Chipotle Aioli (posted)

Direction

- In mixing bowl, combine ground beef, chipotle, salt and pepper
- Form into 4 patties
- Grill over medium high heat until desired doneness
- Toast buns
- Add cheese to top of burgers when almost done
- Top with toppings
- Spread with Chipotle Aioli

90. Chipotle Burgers With Balsamic Onions And Chiptole Ketchup Recipe

Serving: 4 | Prep: | Cook: 10mins | Ready in:

Ingredients

- ONIONS:
- 1 pound red onions, or use Vidalia sweet onions like I did, cut crosswise into 1/3 to 1/2 inch thick rounds (thicker slices do not fall between the grill rack as easily)
- olive oil
- 3/4 t. coarse kosher salt
- 1/2 t. coarsely ground black pepper
- 2 T. Balasamic vinegar
- CHIPOTLE KETCHUP:
- 1 c. ketchup
- 1 1/2 t. chopped chiptole chiles from canned chiptoles in adobo plus 2 Tablespoons adobo sauce from can
- 2 t. (or more) balsamic vinegar
- BURGERS:
- 2 1/4 pounds ground beef (15% to 20% fat)
- Coarse kosher salt
- 6 Thick slices sharp cheddar cheese
- 6 large English muffins or hamburger buns, split, cut sides grilled
- 6 tomato slices (optional)
- 2 c. fresh spinach leaves, I used my home grown lettuce leaves

Direction

- For onions: Prepare barbecue (medium-high heat): Arrange onion rounds on baking sheet. Brush with oil; sprinkle with 3/4 teaspoon coarse salt and pepper. Transfer onion rounds (still intact) to grill rack; close cover. Cook until grill marks appear, about 4 minutes per side. Reduce heat or move onions to cooler part of grill. Close cover; cook until onions are tender, about 10 minutes. Transfer to medium bowl. Toss with vinegar. DO AHEAD: Can be made 3 days ahead. Cover; chill.
- For chipotle ketchup: Mix ketchup, chilies, adobo sauce, and 2 teaspoons vinegar in small bowl. Season with salt and more vinegar, if desired. Do ahead. Can be made 3 days ahead. Cover and chill.
- For burgers: Shape beef into six 1/2-inch thick patties. Sprinkle patties on both sides with coarse salt and pepper. Prepare barbecue (medium-high heat). Place burgers on grill. Close cover; cook burgers until bottoms start to darken and juices rise to surface, about 3 minutes. Turn burgers; cook to desired doneness, about 3 minutes longer for medium-rare. Top with onions and cheese. Close cover; cook until cheese melts. Place muffin bottoms on plates; spread with ketchup. Top with burgers, tomatoes, if desired, spinach, and muffin tops. Serve, passing remaining ketchup separately.

91. Chipotle Turkey Burgers Recipe

Serving: 4 | Prep: | Cook: 10mins | Ready in:

Ingredients

- * 1 pound ground turkey
- * 1/2 cup finely chopped onion
- * 1 chipotle chile in adobo sauce, finely chopped
- * 1/2 teaspoon garlic powder
- * 2 cloves garlic (minced)
- * 1 teaspoon onion powder
- * 1 teaspoon seasoned salt
- * 1/4 teaspoon black pepper
- * 4 slices mozzarella cheese (or pepperjack if you want to spice it up even more)
- * 4 hamburger buns, split and toasted
- * tomato, lettuce and onion to top

Direction

- Preheat grill to medium-medium high heat

- In a bowl combine ground turkey, garlic, chipotle chili, onion powder, seasoned salt, and black pepper
- Form 4 patties with mixture
- Place patties onto grill and cook about 3-5 minutes on each side or until the center is cooked through (no pink)
- Melt cheese on patties before you take them off the grill
- Place the cheesy patties on toasted buns with lettuce tomato and onion or any other toppings you choose.

92. Cilantro Burgers Recipe

Serving: 4 | Prep: | Cook: 20mins | Ready in:

Ingredients

- 1 1/2 pounds ground beef
- 1/4 cup of minced cilantro
- 1/2 cup of wasabi Mayo
- 1 tsp. cayenne pepper
- 1 tsp. Minced garlic (or garlic powder)
- 1/2 Minced roasted red peppers
- salt
- pepper
- Wheat hamburger buns
- provolone cheese
- Adjust seasoning to taste.

Direction

- Mix everything in a bowl but the bun, cheese, and mayo.
- Make 4 patties.
- Grill.
- At the end before they are done place the cheese on top of patties to melt.
- Place bun on grill until lightly toasted.
- Spread wasabi mayo on bun the put patty on buns.
- Enjoy!

93. Coconut Basil Chicken Burgers With Thai Peanut Pesto Recipe

Serving: 6 | Prep: | Cook: 8mins | Ready in:

Ingredients

- For the Asian pear Slaw:
- ---------------------------------
- 1 tablespoon fresh lime juice
- 1 teaspoon sugar
- 1 Asian pear, peeled and cut into thin matchsticks
- 1 medium carrot, peeled and cut into thin matchsticks
- For the Thai Peanut Pesto:
- ---------------------------------------
- 1/2 cup roasted and salted peanuts
- 1/2 cup fresh basil leaves
- 1/4 cup fresh cilantro leaves
- 2 tablespoons unsweetened shredded coconut
- 2 tablespoons roasted peanut oil
- 1/4 teaspoon sea salt
- 1/3 cup quartered cherry tomatoes
- For the Patties:
- ---------------------
- 1 (14-ounce) can unsweetened coconut milk
- 1 lime, zest grated
- 1 tablespoon fresh lime juice
- 1 teaspoon Thai red curry paste
- 2 pounds coarsely ground chicken thighs
- 1/2 cup chopped fresh basil leaves
- 1/2 cup panko (Japanese bread crumbs)
- 2 teaspoons sea salt
- vegetable oil, for brushing on the grill rack
- 6 seeded hamburger buns, split

Direction

- Prepare a medium-hot fire in a charcoal grill with a cover, or preheat a gas grill to medium-high.
- For the slaw:

94. Cola Burgers Recipe

Serving: 6 | Prep: | Cook: 15mins | Ready in:

Ingredients

- 1-1/2 pounds lean ground beef
- 1 egg
- 1/2 cup Coca-Cola®, divided
- 1/2 cup crushed saltines
- 3 tablespoons grated parmesan cheese
- salt and pepper to taste
- 6 tablespoons French dressing
- 1 small onion, diced
- 6 hamburger buns
- Toppings of choice

Direction

- In a bowl, combine egg, 1/4 cup Coca-Cola®, cracker crumbs, 2 tablespoons French dressing, parmesan cheese and salt and pepper.
- Add beef and mix well.
- Shape into 6 patties. (Mixture should be moist)
- Combine remaining cola and dressing and set aside.
- Grill patties uncovered for about 3 minutes.
- Brush with cola mixture and grill for 8-10 minutes longer, basting and turning occasionally.
- Top with your favorite toppings.

95. Crab Cake Sliders With Avocado Recipe

Serving: 4 | Prep: | Cook: 15mins | Ready in:

Ingredients

- 1 tablespoon unsalted butter
- 1 celery stalk, very finely chopped
- 1 tablespoon sweet red bell pepper, peeled and very finely chopped
- 2 tablespoons Best Foods mayonnaise
- 1 egg, lightly beaten
- ½ cup fresh bread crumbs (I used one mini brioche bun, crust removed, run thru food processor)
- ½ lb. fresh Dungeness crab meat
- 1 tablespoon each fresh chopped chives & parsley
- Cajun spice seasoning, to taste
- All purpose flour, for dusting
- oil & butter, for pan frying
- 4 miniature brioche buns
- Sauce:
- 3 tablespoons Best Foods mayonnaise
- 1 tablespoon ketchup
- 1 tablespoon sweet pickle relish
- A little fresh squeezed lemon juice
- Sugar, to taste
- Toppings:
- 1 medium ripe avocado, sliced (squeeze lemon juice on slices to prevent browning)
- 4 small inner leaves of red leaf lettuce (or other lettuce/mixed greens)
- 4 lemon wedges, for garnish

Direction

- In small sauté pan, melt butter and sauté celery and red bell pepper until soft. Put into a mixing bowl along with the remaining crab cake ingredients. When adding crab, be careful when folding it in, as to not break it up too much.
- Form into 4 patties (same diameter as the brioche buns you are using) . Refrigerate for at least an hour.
- Lightly dredge crab cakes in flour, patting off excess. Melt 1 tablespoon butter with about 1 tablespoon of oil in a non-stick pan. Fry crab cakes on each side until golden brown (about 2-3 minutes per side). Transfer crab cakes to a baking sheet and finish in the oven at 375 degrees for 10-15 minutes.
- Cut each bun in half and toast in a skillet. Spread sauce on buns, place crab cake on each,

top with avocado and a lettuce leaf. Place bun on top and skewer with bamboo skewer and lemon garnish.

96. Cream Cheese Jalapeno Hamburgers Recipe

Serving: 8 | Prep: | Cook: 30mins | Ready in:

Ingredients

- 2 c seeded and chopped jalapeno peppers
- 2 (8oz) cream cheese,softened
- 2 lbs ground beef
- 8 hamburger rolls,split

Direction

- Prepare grill for med. heat. When hot, lightly oil grates. In medium bowl, stir together the jalapenos and cream cheese.
- Divide the ground beef into 16 portions and pat each one to 1/4" thickness. Spoon some of the cream cheese mixture onto the center of 8 of the patties, pressing edges together to seal. Top with remaining patties, pressing edges to seal.
- Grill about 10 mins per side or till well done, taking care not to press on burgers as they cook. This will make the cheese ooze out. Serve on buns with favorite toppings.

97. Creole Crab Burgers Recipe

Serving: 4 | Prep: | Cook: 10mins | Ready in:

Ingredients

- 1 lb lump crabmeat, picked over
- ¼ cup mayonnaise
- 3 scallions, thinly sliced
- 1 large egg, lightly beaten
- 1 teaspoon worcestershire sauce
- ¾ teaspoon dry mustard
- ½ teaspoon cayenne
- 1¾ cups fine dry bread crumbs, divided
- ¾ cup vegetable oil
- 4 kaiser rolls or hamburger buns, split and toasted
- Accompaniments: tartar sauce; iceberg lettuce

Direction

- Stir together crabmeat, mayonnaise, scallions, egg, Worcestershire sauce, mustard, cayenne, ¼ teaspoon salt, and 3/4 cup bread crumbs in a bowl until just combined. Form into 4 (1-inch-thick) patties (3½ inches in diameter; patties will be soft but will firm up when fried). Spread remaining cup bread crumbs on a plate, then dredge patties in crumbs, knocking off excess, and transfer to a platter. Heat oil in a 12-inch heavy skillet over medium heat until it shimmers, then fry patties, turning over once, until golden, 5 to 6 minutes total. Transfer to paper towels to drain.
- Assemble burgers with buns and accompaniments.
- Note: Patties can be formed, without bread crumb coating, 12 hours ahead, and chilled, covered. Dredge in bread crumbs just before frying.

98. Crockpot Burger Heaven Casserole Recipe

Serving: 4 | Prep: | Cook: 360mins | Ready in:

Ingredients

- 16 oz. extra lean lean ground beef (or turkey)
- 2 C. sliced raw potatoes
- 1 1/2 C. sliced carrots
- 1 C. chopped celery
- 1/2 C. chopped onion
- 1 C. frozen peas, thawed
- 1 C. frozen whole kernel corn, thawed

- 1 (10 oz.) can Healthy Request tomato soup
- 1/2 C. water
- 1 tsp. dried parsley flakes
- 1 can mushrooms
- Salt and pepper

Direction

- Spray a crockpot container with butter flavor spray.
- In large skillet brown meat, onion and celery mixture and mushrooms.
- In crock pot container Mix together meat mixture, potatoes, carrots, peas and corn. Stir in tomato soup, water, parsley flakes and salt and pepper to taste.
- Cover and cook on LOW for 6 to 8 hr.

99. Cuban Burgers With Mojo Sauce Recipe

Serving: 4 | Prep: | Cook: 15mins |Ready in:

Ingredients

- 1 pound ground beef
- 1 teaspoon garlic powder
- 1/2 teaspoon ground cumin
- 4 thin slices cooked ham
- 4 slices provolone cheese
- 4 rolls or buns split and toasted
- 2 whole dill pickles sliced horizontally into 8 slices
- 4 slices red onion
- 4 slices tomato
- Sauce:
- 6 cloves garlic minced
- 2 tablespoons olive oil
- 1/3 cup orange juice
- 1/3cup lemon juice
- 1 teaspoon ground cumin
- 1/2 teaspoon salt
- 1/2 teaspoon freshly ground black pepper

Direction

- Combine beef, garlic powder, cumin and 1/2 teaspoon each salt and pepper.
- Shape into four patties then grill over medium coals for 18 minutes turning once.
- Top each with a slice of ham and cheese then cover and grill 30 seconds to allow cheese to melt.
- Serve on rolls with pickle onion and tomato and drizzled with sauce.
- Cook garlic in olive oil over medium heat until just starting to brown.
- Remove from heat then carefully add orange juice, lemon juice, cumin, salt and pepper.
- Bring to boiling then reduce heat and simmer uncovered 5 minutes.
- Remove from heat and cool then whisk before serving.

100. Cubano Style Burgers Recipe

Serving: 4 | Prep: | Cook: 20mins |Ready in:

Ingredients

- FOR THE MUSTARD RELISH:
- 1/4 c. prepared yellow mustard
- 1/4 c. dill pickle relish
- 2 T. minced onion
- 2 T. diced pickled jalapeno (regular jalapeno from slices in a jar works fine too)
- 1 T. honey
- FOR THE BURGERS:
- Mix 1/2 lb. ground turkey or pork WITH 1/2 lb. ground beef
- (You can use 1 lb. ground pork or ground turkey instead of the mix)
- salt and pepper
- 4 slices deli-sliced ham
- 4 slices Swiss cheese
- 4 onion hamburger buns, buttered

Direction

- Preheat one side of grill to medium-high and the other side to low.
- COMBINE ingredients for the relish in a bowl; set aside.
- DIVIDE the ground turkey and hamburger mix into 4 equal portions. Shape each portion into a patty slightly larger than the bun to allow for shrinkage. Season patties with salt and pepper and coat both sides of each one with non-stick spray.
- GRILL burgers, covered, over medium-high heat until cooked through, 3 minutes per side. Top each burger with a slice of ham and a slice of cheese. Grill, covered, until cheese is melted, 1-2 minutes more. Remove burgers from the grill and tent with foil.
- GRILL buttered buns, covered, over low heat until lightly toasted, 1-2 minutes. To serve, place burgers on buns, and top with mustard relish.

101.   Curried Pork Burgers

Serving: 5 | Prep: | Cook: 20mins |Ready in:

Ingredients

- 1 pound lean ground pork
- ½ cup crumbled feta cheese
- ½ cup chopped fresh cilantro
- 2 tablespoons curry paste
- 2 cloves garlic, minced
- 2 teaspoons minced fresh ginger
- 1 teaspoon ground cumin
- ¼ teaspoon salt
- ¼ teaspoon ground black pepper

Direction

- Preheat a grill for medium-high heat and lightly oil the grate.
- Mix pork, feta cheese, cilantro, curry paste, garlic, ginger, cumin, salt, and black pepper in a bowl. Divide mixture into fourths and form a

burger from each portion. Refrigerate for 10 minutes (up to 4 hours).
- Place burgers on preheated grill, close lid, and grill until an instant-read meat thermometer inserted sideways into the center of a burger reads 160 degrees F (70 degrees C), about 5 minutes per side.
- Nutrition Facts
- Per Serving:
- 268.8 calories; protein 21.4g 43% DV; carbohydrates 3g 1% DV; fat 18.4g 28% DV; cholesterol 98.7mg 33% DV; sodium 561.9mg 23% DV.

102.   Denver Mile High Taco Burger Recipe

Serving: 4 | Prep: | Cook: 10mins |Ready in:

Ingredients

- 1 pound lean ground beef
- 1 (1 ounce) envelope taco seasoning mix
- Sliced monterey jack cheese with hot peppers (pepper jack)
- 4 sandwich buns
- Shredded lettuce
- Sliced tomato
- Mustard, to taste
- catsup, to taste
- mayonnaise, to taste
- tortilla chips

Direction

- Mix together ground beef and seasoning mix in a medium bowl. Form 4 patties. Grill to desired doneness. Place cheese on each burger and heat briefly to soften cheese. Serve burgers in buns with lettuce, tomato, condiments and chips.

103. Devilfrogs Devilishly Delicious Devilicious Veggie Burgers Recipe

Serving: 6 | Prep: | Cook: 30mins | Ready in:

Ingredients

- 1 cup dry TVP (textured vegetable protein)
- 3/4 cup very hot water
- 1 cup shredded zucchini
- 1 teaspoon kosher salt
- 4 tablespoons olive oil
- 1/2 cup minced yellow onion
- 1 medium clove garlic, minced
- 3/4 cup shredded carrot
- 1/3 cup peeled, shredded red beet
- 1/4 cup plus 2 tablespoons sunflower seeds
- 2 teaspoons tomato paste
- 2 teaspoons dry mustard, such as Colman's
- 1 1/2 cups cooked short-grain brown rice (about 3/4 cup dry)
- 2/3 cup cooked brown lentils (about 1/4 cup dry)
- 2 tablespoons minced Italian parsley leaves
- 1 tablespoon dried thyme
- 1 cup coarse whole-wheat panko, such as Ian's
- 3/4 cup sliced cremini mushrooms
- 1 large egg
- 1 large egg white
- 3 tablespoons tamari or soy sauce
- 1/4 teaspoon freshly ground black pepper
- 6 whole-wheat hamburger buns, for serving

Direction

- In a medium bowl, combine dry TVP with hot water. Stir and set aside until ready to use.
- Toss zucchini with 1/2 teaspoon of the salt and put in a colander or strainer set over a bowl to drain, at least 10 minutes. Squeeze zucchini mixture to release excess water and set aside, discarding the liquid.
- Heat 1 tablespoon of the olive oil in a small frying pan over medium heat. When oil is hot, add onion and garlic, and sauté until vegetables are soft and translucent, about 5 to 6 minutes.
- In a large mixing bowl, combine 1 cup of the soaked TVP mixture, zucchini, carrot, beet, 1/4 cup of the sunflower seeds, tomato paste, dry mustard, 3/4 cup of the brown rice, 1/4 cup of the lentils, parsley, thyme, and 1/2 cup of the panko. Add the sautéed onion and garlic, and mix well; set aside.
- Heat 1 tablespoon of the olive oil in the same frying pan over medium-high heat. Add mushrooms and sauté, stirring occasionally, until tender and nicely browned, about 5 minutes. Remove from heat.
- Transfer sautéed mushrooms to the bowl of a food processor; add egg, egg white, tamari, pepper, and the remaining salt, TVP, lentils, brown rice, sunflower seeds, and panko. Process until mixture is well combined and uniform, about 30 to 45 seconds. (Mixture will not be smooth.)
- Add puréed mushroom mixture to reserved vegetable mixture and combine well (using your hands works best). Form mixture into 6 patties (about 3/4 cup each) and place them on a baking sheet. Heat remaining 2 tablespoons olive oil in a large non-stick frying pan over medium-high heat. Add 3 patties to the pan and brown on one side, about 6 to 7 minutes; flip burgers and continue cooking until crispy and heated through, about 5 to 6 minutes more. Repeat with remaining patties and serve in whole-wheat buns with your favorite toppings

104. Dirty Bird Burgers Recipe

Serving: 8 | Prep: | Cook: 15mins | Ready in:

Ingredients

- 2 lbs lean ground turkey
- 2 packets (1 oz) dry ranch dressing mix
- 1 egg
- 1 cup fat free shredded mozzarella cheese

- 1/2 cup crushed cheese flavored crackers
- 1 tbs onion salt
- pepper (to taste)
- 3-4 tbs olive oil

Direction

- Place turkey meat in bowl & add in ranch, egg, cheese crackers, mozzarella cheese, onion salt & pepper. Mix thoroughly.
- Form meat into patties.
- Lightly brush olive oil over patties before placing on the grill to prevent sticking.
- Cook on preheated grill for 15 minutes.

105.   Dominican Chimi Burger Recipe

Serving: 4 | Prep: | Cook: 15mins | Ready in:

Ingredients

- 1 1/4 lbs ground beef chuck
- 1 medium onion, finely chopped
- 1/2 of a large red bell pepper, diced
- 2 garlic cloves, minced
- 1/3 cup chopped cilantro
- 1 tsp dried oregano
- 2 tsp soy sauce
- 1 T worcestershire sauce
- salt and pepper
- 4 good quality hamburger buns, split
- 2 cups thinly sliced cabbage
- 1 carrot, coarsely grated
- 1 small red onion, cut into rings
- 1 tomato, sliced 1/4 inch thick
- 2 T ketchup
- 2 T mayonnaise
- 1 T yellow prepared mustard

Direction

- Mix together beef, onion, bell pepper, garlic, cilantro, oregano, soy sauce, Worcestershire sauce, a pinch of salt and pepper.

- Form into 4 patties.
- Heat a large griddle or 12-inch heavy skillet over medium heat until hot, then lightly toast buns.
- Oil griddle or pan, then cook patties, turning once, about 8 minutes total for medium rare.
- Transfer to buns.
- Mix together cabbage, carrot, and a pinch of salt. Then cook on same griddle turning occasionally, until slightly wilted, about 2 minutes. Divide among burgers.
- Oil griddle again, then sear onion and tomato, turning once, until slightly charred, about 2 minutes total. Divide among burgers.
- Stir together ketchup, mayo and mustard, then top burgers with sauce.

106.   Dominican Chimichurri Burgers Recipe

Serving: 4 | Prep: | Cook: 12mins | Ready in:

Ingredients

- Burgers:
- 1 1/4 pound ground beef chuck
- 1 medium onion, finely chopped
- 1/2 large red bell pepper, diced
- 2 garlic cloves, minced
- 1/3 cup chopped cilantro
- 1 teaspoon dried oregano
- 2 teaspoons soy sauce
- 3/4 teaspoon dried crushed red pepper
- 1/2 teaspoon ground cumin
- 1 tablespoon worcestershire sauce
- scant 1/2 teaspoon salt
- 1/2 teaspoon pepper
- ****
- Burger Topping:
- 2 cups thinly sliced cabbage
- 1 carrot, coarsely grated
- 1 small red onion, cut into rings
- 1 tomato, sliced 1/4 inch thick
- ****

- Burger Sauce:
- 2 tablespoons ketchup
- 2 tablespoons mayonnaise
- 1 tablespoon yellow mustard
- ****
- 4 hamburger buns, split, lightly brushed with olive oil and lightly toasted

Direction

- For Burgers:
- Mix together beef, onion, bell pepper, garlic, cilantro, oregano, soy sauce, Worcestershire sauce, crushed red pepper, cumin, a scant 1/2 teaspoon salt and 1/2 teaspoon pepper.
- Form into 4 (4 1/2-inch-wide) patties.
- Heat a large griddle or 12-inch heavy skillet over medium heat until hot, then lightly toast buns.
- Oil griddle, then cook patties, turning once, about 8 minutes total for medium-rare. Transfer to buns.
- ****
- For Burger Topping:
- Mix together cabbage, carrot, and 1/4 teaspoon salt, then cook, turning occasionally, until slightly wilted, about 2 minutes. Divide among burgers.
- Oil griddle again, then sear onion and tomato, turning once, until slightly charred, about 2 minutes total. Divide among burgers.
- ****
- For Sauce:
- Stir together ketchup, mayonnaise, and mustard, then top burgers with sauce.

---

107.   Doublebatch Chickpea Cutlets Recipe

Serving: 8 | Prep: | Cook: 30mins | Ready in:

Ingredients

- 1 16 oz can chickpeas, drained and rinsed
- 1/4 cup extra virgin olive oil
- 1 cup vital wheat gluten
- 1 cup plain breadcrumbs
- 1/2 cup vegetable broth or water
- 1/4 cup soy sauce
- 1 teaspoon dried thyme
- 1 teaspoon paprika
- 1/2 teaspoon dried sage
- olive oil for pan frying
- Optional ingredients:
- 4 cloves garlic, pressed or grated with a Microplane grater
- 1 teaspoon grated lemon zest

Direction

- In a mixing bowl, mash the chickpeas together with the oil until no whole chickpeas are left. Use an avocado masher or a strong fork. Alternately, you can pulse the chickpeas in a food processor. We're not making hummus here, so be careful not to puree them, just get them mashed up. You can also sneak the garlic cloves in here instead of grating them, just pulse them up before adding the chickpeas. If using a food processor, transfer to a mixing bowl when done.
- Add the remaining ingredients and knead together for about 3 minutes, until strings of gluten have formed.
- Preheat a large heavy-bottomed skillet over low-medium heat. Cast iron works best. If you have two pans and want to cook all the cutlets at once then go for it, otherwise you'll be making them in two batches.
- Divide the cutlet dough into 2 equal pieces. Then divide each of those pieces into 4 separate pieces (so you'll have 8 all together). To form cutlets, knead each piece in your hand for a few moments and then flatten and stretch each one into a roughly 6 by 4 inch rectangular cutlet shape. The easiest way to do this is to form a rectangle shape in your hands and then place the cutlets on a clean surface to flatten and stretch them.
- Add a moderately thin layer of olive oil to the bottom of the pan. Place the cutlets in the pan and cook on each side for 6 to 7 minutes. Add

more oil, if needed, when you flip the cutlets. They're ready when lightly browned and firm to the touch. I've found that they cook more thoroughly if I cover the pan in between flips. I also use my spatula to press down on them while they're cooking, that way they cook more evenly.

108.   Down South Burger Recipe

Serving: 6 | Prep: | Cook: 15mins | Ready in:

Ingredients

- 2 pounds lean ground beef
- 3 tablespoons Tabasco chipotle pepper sauce divided
- 1 teaspoon salt
- 1/2 cup mayonnaise
- 6 slices pepper jack cheese
- 6 hamburger buns
- 6 red onion slices
- 6 tomato slices
- 1 ripe avocado peeled pitted and cut into slices
- 6 lettuce leaves

Direction

- Combine beef, 2 tablespoons pepper sauce and salt in large bowl and mix well. Shape into 6 patties. Combine mayonnaise with remaining chipotle pepper sauce and mix well then set aside. Grill hamburger patties to desired doneness then place cheese slices on burgers and continue cooking just until cheese melts. Spread mayonnaise mixture on each cut side of buns. Top bottom half with burger, onion slice, tomato slice, avocado slices and lettuce leaf. Cover with bun top. Repeat for remaining burgers.

109.   Dried Tomatoe Burgers Recipe

Serving: 8 | Prep: | Cook: 14mins | Ready in:

Ingredients

- 2 pounds lean ground beef
- 2 tablespoons finely chopped, drained, oil-packed dried tomatoes
- 2 teaspoons finely shredded lemon or lime peel
- 1 teaspoon salt
- 1/2 teaspoon pepper
- 1/2 cup light mayonnaise dressing or salad dressing
- 1/4 cup snipped fresh basil
- 2 jalapeno peppers, seeded and finely chopped
- 8 onion hamburger buns
- 2 cups lightly packed arugula or spinach leaves

Direction

- Combine beef, tomatoes, lemon or lime peel, salt, and pepper in a medium bowl; mix lightly but thoroughly.
- Shape into eight 1/2-inch-thick patties. Grill patties on the rack of an uncovered grill directly over medium heat for 14 to 18 minutes
- Meanwhile, combine the light mayonnaise or salad dressing, basil, and jalapeno peppers in a small bowl; mix well.
- During the last 1 to 2 minutes of grilling, place buns, cut sides down, on grill rack to toast. Place burgers on bottom halves of buns. Top with the mayonnaise dressing mixture and spinach.
- Add the bun tops.

110. EXTRAVAGANT MARINATED BURGERS Recipe

Serving: 4 | Prep: | Cook: 15mins | Ready in:

Ingredients

- 1 lb ground beef
- 3 Tbsp lemon juice
- 1 1/2 tsp seasoned Salt
- 1 Tbsp worcestershire sauce
- 1 Tbsp soy sauce
- 2 tbsp BBQ sauce
- 1 tbsp olive oil
- 1/2 Cup beef stock
- 1/4 tsp garlic salt
- 1 tsp vinegar

Direction

- Take ground beef and shape meat into round patties, 3/4" thick.
- Mix remaining ingredients.
- Place patties in a covered container and pour the marinade mixture over them.
- Cover tightly and refrigerate 12 hours or overnight.
- Turn the patties frequently.
- Remove patties from marinade and sear over high heat to seal in the juices, then turn down heat and cook until juices run clear. About 15 minutes.
- Top with desired hamburger fixins'

111. East Meets West Vietnamese Pork Burgers Recipe

Serving: 4 | Prep: | Cook: 10mins | Ready in:

Ingredients

- 1 lb. lean ground pork

- 3 garlic cloves, chopped
- 2 green onions, chopped
- 2 teaspoon soy sauce
- 2 teaspoon peanut or other mild vegetable oil
- pinch of sugar
- a few drops Tabasco sauce, or a pinch of cayenne pepper
- hoisin sauce
- large whole green lettuce leaves – romaine works well
- ½ cup or so of roasted peanuts, coarsely ground
- a handful of cilantro, coarsely chopped

Direction

- Mix meat with garlic, onions, soy sauce, peanut oil, sugar and Tabasco or cayenne.
- Form into patties and grill until cooked through.
- Serve each grilled patty spread with hoisin sauce, wrapped in a leaf of lettuce, sprinkled with peanuts and cilantro.
- These are delicious exactly as described, however, you could spread the hoisin sauce inside a pita bread and insert the patties into it along with the lettuce for a more conventional burger experience.

112. Easy Chicken Fried Burgers Recipe

Serving: 8 | Prep: | Cook: 8mins | Ready in:

Ingredients

- 8-10 Frozen burger patties
- salt pepper
- 1 cup flour
- 1 sleeve of saltine crackers crushed into 1/2 inch pieces
- 2 eggs
- 1 cup milk
- oil -1 inch in bottom of skillet

Direction

- Salt and pepper burgers to your taste, dip in well beaten egg and milk mixture then into flour and cracker mixture then fry in oil in frying pan.
- Don't let oil get really hot because it will ruin the taste.
- Brown 5-6 minutes on each side and put into glass pan and into 350 degree oven for 10-15 minutes to continue cooking.
- Let "steaks" drain on paper towel before serving after removing from oven.
- FOR GRAVY
- When the last of the "steaks" are in the oven...Add 2-3 Tablespoons of Flour, 1/2 teaspoon of salt and 1/2 teaspoon of pepper and I-2 chicken bouillon cubes into skillet.
- Let flour and oil brown for 3-4 minutes, constantly stirring
- Then add 2-3 cups of milk and stir constantly until thickened into Chicken Fried Burger Gravy.
- Serve Gravy with Mashed Potatoes or over the chicken fried burgers.

113.   Elvis Burger Recipe

Serving: 4 | Prep: | Cook: 10mins | Ready in:

Ingredients

- 1 dried red chilli
- • 1/2 a red onion, peeled and finely chopped
- • a sprig of fresh tarragon, leaves picked and chopped
- • 1 large egg
- • a handful of breadcrumbs
- • 1 teaspoon Dijon mustard
- • 2 tablespoons freshly grated Parmesan
- • a good pinch of ground nutmeg
- • 2lbs beef mince
- oil, for frying
- • salt and freshly ground black pepper
- lettuce

- tomato slices
- 4 large rolls or baps
- slices of gherkin

Direction

- Grind up the red chilli in a pestle and mortar
- Mix it in a bowl with the onion, tarragon, egg, breadcrumbs, mustard, Parmesan, nutmeg and beef.
- Shape into four patties and refrigerate for half an hour or so to give them a chance to firm up slightly.
- When you're ready to cook the burgers, get a frying or griddle pan nice and hot. Brush the pan with a little oil, season the burgers generously with salt and pepper, and cook them for 10 minutes, turning them carefully every minute or so, until they're nice and pink and juicy, or longer if you like them well done. Make sure they don't break up as you turn them.

114.   Fajita Burger Wraps Recipe

Serving: 4 | Prep: | Cook: 30mins | Ready in:

Ingredients

- 1 pound lean ground beef (90%)
- 2 T. Fajita seasoning
- 2 t. canola oil
- 1 each medium green and sweet red peppers, cut into thin strips
- 1 medium onion, halved, sliced
- 4 flour tortillas (10 inch)
- 3/4 cup shredded cheddar cheese

Direction

- 1) In large bowl, combine beef and seasoning mix, mixing lightly but thoroughly. Shape mixture into four 1/2 inch thick patties.

- 2) In large skillet heat oil over medium heat. Add burgers, cook 4 minutes on each side. Remove from pan. In same skillet, add peppers and onions, cook and stir 5-7 minutes or lightly browned and tender.
- 3) On center of each tortilla place 1/2 cup pepper mixture, one burger and 3 T. Cheese. Fold sides of tortilla over burger, fold top and bottom to close, forming square.
- 4) Wipe skillet clean. Add wraps seam side down, cooking over medium heat 1-2 minutes on each side or until golden brown and when thermometer inserted into beef reads 160 F.

115.   Fajita Burgers Recipe

Serving: 4 | Prep: | Cook: 20mins |Ready in:

Ingredients

- 1 tablespoon olive oil
- 1 small red onion chopped
- 1 small green bell pepper chopped
- 1 garlic clove minced
- 1-1/4 pounds ground chicken or turkey
- 1 tablespoon lime juice
- 1 teaspoon chili powder
- 1 teaspoon salt
- 4 flour tortillas
- 1 cup salsa
- guacamole

Direction

- Prepare a hot fire in a grill.
- In large skillet heat oil then add onion and pepper then cook over medium heat 4 minutes.
- Add garlic and cook 1 minute then remove from heat and let cool slightly.
- In medium bowl combine cooked vegetables, ground chicken, lime juice, chili powder and salt.
- Using wet hands form into 4 ovals about 2" wide and 4-1/2" long.

- Place patties in center of oiled grill set 6" from coals.
- Cook turning once until browned about 4 minutes.
- Transfer burgers to outside edge of grill and continue grilling turning once for 10 minutes.
- Meanwhile wrap tortillas in aluminum foil and place on sides of grill to heat through.
- Place warm tortillas and bowls of salsa and guacamole on table.
- Place burgers on a tortilla then top with salsa and guacamole and roll up.

116.   Fajita Burgers Recipe

Serving: 4 | Prep: | Cook: 15mins |Ready in:

Ingredients

- 1 tsp each cumin and chili powder
- 1 pkg (16 oz) ground chicken burgers
- 1 bell pepper,quartered
- 4 burrito-size flour tortillas
- 2 Tbs oil
- 8 med. leaves of romaine lettuce
- Accompaniments: lime wedgrs,sour cream,sliced avocado,salsa

Direction

- Heat grill. Mix cumin and chili powder. Sprinkle burgers with 1 tsp. spice mixture
- Grill pepper, turning as needed 12 mins or till charred and crisp-tender Grill burgers as pkg. directs till cooked through.
- Brush 1 side of each tortilla with oil. Sprinkle oiled side with remaining spice mixture. Grill 1 to 2 mins, turning once, until grill-marked. Transfer to serving plates.
- For each fajita: Slice one of pepper quarters. Put 2 lettuce leaves, a burger and the pepper slices on half of the oiled side of tortilla. Fold over other half. Serve with accompaniments.

117. Family Favorite Burgers And Quick Meatball Recipe

Serving: 6 | Prep: | Cook: 10mins | Ready in:

Ingredients

- 1 1/2 pounds lean ground beef
- 1/2 cup soft bread crumbs
- 1/3 cup milk
- 1/3 cup tomato ketchup
- 1 teaspoon salt
- 2 teaspoons prepared horseradish
- 2 teaspoons worcestershire sauce
- 1 tablespoon prepared mustard
- 6 hamburger buns

Direction

- Mix together ground beef, soft bread crumbs, milk, ketchup, salt, horseradish, Worcestershire sauce, and prepared mustard.
- Shape into 6 patties, each about 3/4-inch thick.
- Broil 4 inches from the heat, turning once, until done, about 10 to 15 minutes.
- Serve on hamburger buns.
- ****************************
- Fast Sauce for Meatballs
- ****************************
- Heat 1 cup of grape jelly and 1 cup of cocktail sauce in a medium saucepan and cook on a low heat. Stir mixture constantly until it bubbles. Pour over meatballs.

118. Fat Planet Veggie Burger Recipe

Serving: 0 | Prep: | Cook: 30mins | Ready in:

Ingredients

- 2-3 cups garbanzo beans boiled til soft
- 1 bell pepper diced
- 2 carrots diced
- 2 celery ribs diced
- 1 med onion dices 4 cloves of garlic minced
- 4 tblsp olive oil
- salt and pepper to taste
- 1 tblsp mustard
- 1 tblsp ketchup
- 1/4 tsp chili powder
- 1/4 tsp paprika
- 1 egg
- 1/2 cup rolled oats or bread crumbs
- eat on a good bun with a slice of your favorite cheese mine is tilamook chedder, ketchup and honey mustard are yummy too

Direction

- Sauté all the veggies in the olive oil until slightly brown and "roasted" looking and smelling
- Add the spices and seasonings turn off the heat and let cool
- Once cool add the egg and oats
- Smash the cooled veggie mix until uniform and it can form a patty
- Form into patties as big as you want, remember no guilt in veggies!
- Sauté in olive oil until a light brown and crusty. Add slice of cheese or soy cheese and let melt and serve! Great with avocado tomato onion bacon cheese

119. Feasty Boys Bodacious Burgers Recipe

Serving: 8 | Prep: | Cook: 15mins | Ready in:

Ingredients

- 3 lbs. ground beef (15% lean)
- 1 cup yellow onion, chopped
- 1 cup bell pepper, chopped
- 1/2 cup cooked bacon, chopped
- 1 raw egg, gently whisked

- 1 tsp. granulated salt
- 1 tsp. ground black pepper
- 1/2 tsp. garlic powder
- Your favorite cheese slices: Cheddar, Provolone, pepper Jack, Swiss, etc.
- Big deli burger rolls
- Real Mayo, tomato, Brown mustard, romaine lettuce, Good qaulity dill pickles

Direction

- Preheat grill to medium-high heat.
- In a medium-sized bowl, combine ground beef, onion, peppers, bacon and seasoning.
- In a separate small dish, gently whisk egg, breaking the yolk and mixing.
- Pour raw egg over meat mixture.
- Gently mix the ingredients together.
- When thoroughly mixed, form into fairly loosely packed patties.
- Place burgers on grill and cook approximately 10 to 15 minutes, turning only once.
- Once grilled to desired doneness, apply cheese if desired and allow to melt.
- Remove burgers from grill and allow to cool for approximately five minutes. (This allows all the juices to gradually settle into the burger for enhanced taste.)
- Place burger on toasted bun and top with your favorite condiments.

---

120.   Fozz Burgers Recipe

Serving: 4 | Prep: | Cook: 30mins | Ready in:

Ingredients

- 2 pounds lean ground beef
- 1/2 pound lean ground pork
- 1 tablespoon snipped fresh chives
- salt and black pepper to taste
- 2 tablespoons soy sauce
- 1 tablespoon olive oil
- 4 to 6 tablespoons crumbled blue cheese
- 1 ripe avocado sliced into 8 slices

- 8 slices bacon
- 4 slices of tomato
- lettuce
- sliced onion for sauteing (about 1/2 medium onion)
- cilantro mayo:
- 3/4 cup mayo
- 3/4 cup loosely packed cilantro leaves finely chopped
- 1 tablespoon fresh lemon or lime juice
- 1 teaspoon light soy sauce
- 1 or 2 small cloves of garlic minced
- 4 Burger buns

Direction

- Combine all the ingredients for mayo and set aside
- Combine the beef, pork, chives, salt, pepper, soy sauce and olive oil in a large mixing bowl and mix well. Shape the mixture into 4 patties. Then, make a pocket in the center of each patty and fill each with a tablespoon of the blue cheese. Close the pocket by pinching the meat together. Grill each Patty about 5 minutes on each side, do not press them flat. This can be done in a skillet also.
- While they are cooking. In a skillet on the stove or grill cook bacon to desired texture, pour off some of the drippings and add onions and sauté until lightly brown. Place buns on the grill or in the oven, lightly toast.
- To complete burger, spread some of the mayo on each side of the bun. Place a patty with some sautéed onions on the bottom bun, top with two slices of Bacon, 2 slices of avocado, tomato and lettuce. Slap on the lid and enjoy.

121. GORGONZOLA STUFFED BEEF BURGERS W SAUTEED WILD MUSHROOMS And CARAMELIZED RED ONION MARMALADE Recipe

Serving: 4 | Prep: | Cook: 30mins | Ready in:

Ingredients

- BURGERS:
- 2 lbs ground beef
- 1/2 tsp freshly ground black pepper
- 1 1/2 tsp salt
- 1/2 cup crumbled gorgonzola cheese
- SAUTEED MUSHROOMS:
- 3 Tbs unsalted butter
- 1 medium shallot, minced
- 2 cloves garlic, minced
- 2 tsp minced fresh thyme
- 1/2 ounce dried porcini mushrooms, soaked in one cup of hot water for 20 minutes, squeezed dry and minced (save the soaking liquid!)
- 1/2 lb shiitake mushrooms, stems removed and thinly sliced
- 1/2 lb cremini mushrooms, sliced
- 3 Tbs brandy or cognac
- salt and freshly ground black pepper, to taste
- red onion MARMALADE:
- 4 large red onions, thinly sliced
- 1/2 cup olive oil
- 1/4 cup brown sugar
- 2 Tbs red wine vinegar
- 2 Tbs heavy whipping cream
- salt and freshly ground black pepper, to taste
- 4 toasted onion or poppy seed rolls

Direction

- 1. Prepare beef patties: In a mixing bowl, gently combine beef with salt and pepper. Divide meat into 8 equal portions. Quickly form each portion into a flat patty, handling the meat as little as possible. Sprinkle 4 of the patties with two Tablespoons of the gorgonzola cheese. Top with the remaining four patties of beef and pinch the sides together to form a seal, indent the center. Refrigerate for 20 minutes, then set out at room temperature until ready to grill.
- 2. Prepare mushrooms: Heat butter in a large frying pan until melted. Add shallot, garlic & thyme and sauté for 3 minutes or until the shallot is tender. Add all of the mushrooms and season with salt and pepper. Sauté over medium-high heat until the mushrooms begin to brown. Remove the pan from heat and add brandy and reserved mushroom-soaking liquid. Continue to cook this mixture until all of the liquid has evaporated and the mushrooms are tender.
- 3. Prepare onion marmalade: In a large sauté pan, heat oil until hot but not smoking. Add the onions, cover and cook over medium-low heat until onions are very soft and golden brown, about 25 minutes. Raise the heat to medium-high and add the vinegar and brown sugar. Cook until the liquid has almost evaporated and a thick syrup has formed. Add the heavy cream, salt and pepper to taste.
- 4. Grill the burgers: Place one burger on each bun and top with one Tablespoon of the marmalade and a heaping spoonful of the sautéed mushrooms.

122. Game Day Burgers Recipe

Serving: 10 | Prep: | Cook: 25mins | Ready in:

Ingredients

- 2 lbs lean ground beef
- 1/2 green bell pepper
- 1/2 red bell pepper
- 1/2 orange bell pepper
- 1 large onion(more or less to taste)
- 4 tbsp ground garlic(more or less to taste)

- 2 egg whites
- 1/2 cup seasoned bread crumbs
- olive oil
- 4 jalapeno peppers
- 2 ancho chiles
- 1 tbsp blairs death rain dry rub(http://extremefood.com/product.php?id=15)
- sliced monterey jack cheese
- hamburger buns

Direction

- Chop up the peppers and sauté them in olive oil for a few minutes before adding the onions
- Add the onions midway through and sauté with peppers till they become translucent
- Add all the ingredients into a large bowl and mix well
- Take a handful of the mixture and shape into a patty, continue till you are done with the mixture, this got me 10 good sized burgers
- Grill them on the barbecue, or on your George Foreman grill to the desired, add a slice of Monterey jack if desired
- Place cooked burger on a bun with condiments (I like mine with a bit of mayo)

---

123. Garbanzoe Oat Patties Recipe

Serving: 0 | Prep: | Cook: 90mins | Ready in:

Ingredients

- ingredients to blend
- 2 cups cooked garbanzoes (soak 1 cup to get 2 cups)
- 2 cup water
- 1 tablespoon soy sauce
- 3 tablespoons olive oil
- 3 cloves garlic
- other ingredients
- 1 onion, finely chopped
- 3 tablespoons tahini

- dry ingredients
- 2 1/2 cups rolled oats
- 2 tablespoons nutritional yeast
- 1 tablespoon parsley
- 1 tablespoon chili powder
- 1 tablespoon curry powder
- 1 teaspoon dried mustard
- 1/2 teaspoon sage
- 1/2 teaspoon thyme
- 1/2 teaspoon marjoram
- 1/2 teaspoon paprika
- 1/2 teaspoon basil
- 1/2 teaspoon powdered celery
- 1/4 teaspoon turmeric
- pinch of oregano
- pinch of savory

Direction

- 1. In large bowl, mix oats and herbs
- 2. Combine garbanzos in blender with water, soy sauce, oil, and garlic
- 3. Stir in tahini and chopped onion
- 4. Stir liquid ingredients into dry ingredients and let stand at least 15 minutes
- 5. Form into patties and fry in an oiled pan until lightly browned

---

124. Garlic Lovers Burger Recipe

Serving: 46 | Prep: | Cook: 6mins | Ready in:

Ingredients

- * 2 pounds ground beef
- * 1 tablespoon worcestershire sauce
- * 4 cloves garlic, minced
- * 1/2 cup minced onion
- * 1 teaspoon salt
- * 1/2 teaspoon ground black pepper
- * 1 teaspoon italian seasoning

Direction

- Combine all ingredients in a bowl and make patties (the size of the patties determines the servings. This can be up to you.)
- Refrigerate for a couple hours
- Grill burgers to desired doneness.
- Serve with lettuce tomatoes, cheese, chipotle mayo, or anything you like!

125. Glazed Bacon And Stuffed Cheese Burgers Recipe

Serving: 4 | Prep: | Cook: 20mins | Ready in:

Ingredients

- 3 tablespoons dark brown sugar
- 1-1/2 teaspoons paprika
- 1/2 teaspoon garlic powder
- 1/2 teaspoon ground cumin
- 1/4 teaspoon chipotle powder
- 1/4 teaspoon salt
- 1/4 teaspoon freshly ground black pepper
- 1 pound ground beef
- 1/2 cup shredded sharp cheddar cheese
- 6 slices bacon cooked and crumbled
- 4 poppy seed hamburger buns

Direction

- Preheat grill to medium.
- Combine sugar, spices, salt and pepper then set aside.
- Form beef into 8 equal patties.
- Toss cheese and crumbled bacon together and place an equal amount on 4 of the patties.
- Place remaining patties over cheese and bacon and pinches edges to seal.
- Generously pat each burger with the reserved spice mixture then grill 5 minutes per side.
- Serve on buns with your favorite condiments.

126. Gobblin' Good Turkey Burgers Recipe

Serving: 8 | Prep: | Cook: 30mins | Ready in:

Ingredients

- 3 lb ground turkey
- 1 well beaten egg
- 1/2 c italian style bread crumbs
- 1 t dry mustard
- 1 T celery flakes
- 1 packet dry ranch mix
- 1/2 c shredded cheese (I use colby/monterrey jack...any will work)
- 2 T Lea and Perrins chicken marinade (same as white wine worcestershire)
- salt and pepper
- TOPPINGS:
- Mayo, spicy mustard, tomato, romaine lettuce, good dill pickles, sliced red onion

Direction

- Preheat gas grill to med heat
- Line large baking sheet with parchment paper
- Mix all ingredients together by hand in large mixing bowl
- Shape into 8 large patties, laying each patty on parchment paper
- Spray grill grate with Pam, and lay burgers on grill using spatula.
- Grill about 8 minutes per side (165 internal temp)
- Serve with desired garnishes
- Top with slices of Swiss or cheddar if desired
- * Ground turkey tends to make a "wet" type patty. Different consistency than beef. However, when I don't add the eggs and breadcrumbs they tend to turn out too dry *

127. Good Ol' Burger

Serving: 0 | Prep: | Cook: | Ready in:

Ingredients

- 1 large egg, lightly beaten
- 1/4 cup dry red wine or beef broth
- 1 tablespoon chili sauce
- 1/4 teaspoon Italian seasoning
- 1/4 teaspoon pepper
- 1 pound ground beef
- 4 hamburger buns, split
- 4 lettuce leaves
- 4 slices tomato
- 4 slices onion

Direction

- In a large bowl, combine the first five ingredients. Add beef; mix lightly but thoroughly. Shape into four 1/2-in.-thick patties.
- Grill burgers, covered, over medium heat 5-7 minutes on each side or until a thermometer reads 160°.
- Grill buns over medium heat, cut side down, 30-60 seconds or until toasted. Serve burgers on buns with lettuce, tomato and onion.
- Nutrition Facts
- 1 burger: 364 calories, 16g fat (6g saturated fat), 123mg cholesterol, 349mg sodium, 25g carbohydrate (5g sugars, 2g fiber), 26g protein.

128. Gorgonzola Burger Mushrooms And More Recipe

Serving: 3 | Prep: | Cook: 15mins | Ready in:

Ingredients

- hamburger
- gorgonzola (crumbled)
- granulated onion
- granulated garlic
- Lawry's seasoned Salt
- pepper
- mushrooms
- brussel sprouts

- butter
- Good seasons vegetable Supreme

Direction

- Sauté mushrooms in butter with granulated garlic (a lot for me) and salt. Once cooked, cover to keep warm.
- Cut Brussels sprouts in half and boil until tender. Drain and cover to keep warm.
- Divide hamburger and spread out each amount
- Apply granulated garlic and onion liberally (see pics)
- Apply Lawry's to taste
- Apply pepper to taste
- Sprinkle on gorgonzola cheese
- Mush the meat, seasoning and cheese together. Don't overwork the meat or it becomes tough.
- Grill 3-4 minutes per side over open flame (that is how I grill).
- Place burger on plate, cover with mushrooms, and Brussels sprouts on the side and sprinkle with Vegetable Supreme. A great tasting dinner.

129. Gourmet Burger Recipe

Serving: 4 | Prep: | Cook: 30mins | Ready in:

Ingredients

- 1kg good quality minced beef (ground chuck is best)
- 1 small red onion, grated
- 2 garlic cloves, crushed
- 1/2 cup of fine breadcrumbs
- 1 egg, beaten
- 2 tsp of lemon juice
- 2 tbsp of fresh rosemary, chopped
- 2 tbsp of fresh thyme, chopped
- 1 tbsp of fresh parsley, chopped
- 1 tsp Dijon mustard
- 1 tsp dried chilli flakes
- Good pinch of salt and ground pepper

Direction

- 1. Mix all of the ingredients together in a large mixing bowl. Only mix the ingredients until combined. Over handling will make the burgers tough.
- 2. Make four balls of equal size and flatten down into burger shaped patties.
- 3. Heat a small amount of oil in a pan to a medium heat and fry the patties for around 4 minutes on each side depending on their thickness and the temperature of the pan. Avoid pressing down on the patties, you want to keep as much of the juice in as possible!
- 4. Serve in a very lightly toasted bun with lettuce and lemon mayonnaise - Perfect!

---

130. Gourmet Burgers Recipe

Serving: 4 | Prep: | Cook: 7mins |Ready in:

Ingredients

- 1-1/2 Ibs. extra lean ground beef
- 2 cloves garlic, minced or pressed
- 1/2 cup chopped fresh parsley
- 1 Tbsp. coarsely cracked black pepper
- 1 tsp. coarse salt
- 3 Tbsp. dry red wine
- 1/4 cup beef broth

Direction

- In a large bowl, blend the beef with garlic and parsley. Divide mixture into 4 parts. Shape each into a thick patty.
- Press patties into the black pepper, coating them evenly on both sides.
- Sprinkle salt on surface of a wide, cast-iron skillet. Turn heat on high until skillet begins to smoke.
- Add the meat patties. Pan-broil 1 minute on each side. Reduce heat to medium. Cook 2 to 5 minutes longer depending on how well you want the meat to be done.

- Remove patties to warm plates. Keep warm.
- Add wine and broth to pan. Boil, stirring, until reduced to 1/4 cup. Spoon over meat.

---

131. Greek Burgers Recipe

Serving: 4 | Prep: | Cook: 20mins |Ready in:

Ingredients

- ground beef(can use ground lamb)
- 1 tbs cumin
- 1 tbs season salt (I used Emeril's essence powder)
- 1 tbs lemon pepper
- 1/2 cucumber sliced(i used Persian cucumbers)
- 6 cherry tomatoes halved
- 1/2 small red onion chopped (soak in cold water for about 10 min.)
- fresh mint leaves diced
- Greek kalamata olives sliced
- 1 tbs balsamic vinegar
- 1tps olive oil
- feta cheese
- Greek yogurt (I used Greek honey yogurt)
- pocket pita bread

Direction

- Mix the cumin season salt and lemon pepper with the ground meat
- Make hamburger patties with it and grill
- Or you can just ground the meat and spoon it into the pita
- In a medium sized bowl mix sliced cucumbers, red onion, tomatoes, mint and olives
- Add a little kalamata olive juice and balsamic vinegar and olive oil
- Let cucumber sit for 10 min
- Heat the pita pockets cut open top so you can stuff
- Add the meat then the cucumber slaw feta cheese and top it off with
- Greek yogurt

lettuce, meat and chopped tomatoes. Serve with Yogurt Sauce. (Try a small squeeze of lemon or even lime in your yogurt sauce!)

132.   Greek Burgers With Yogurt Sauce Recipe

Serving: 4 | Prep: | Cook: 8mins |Ready in:

Ingredients

- Burgers:
- 1 lb ground beef
- 2 tsps ground cumin
- 1 T chopped fresh oregano or 1 tsp dried leaf oregano
- 1/2 tsp salt
- Dash of ground red pepper
- Dash of black pepper
- 2 T red wine
- pita bread
- lettuce
- chopped tomatoes
- yogurt Sauce:
- 2 cups plain yogurt
- 1 cup chopped red onion
- 1 cup chopped cucumber
- 1/4 cup chopped fresh mint or 1 1/2 T dried leaf mint
- 1 T chopped fresh marjoram or 1 tsp dried leaf marjoram

Direction

- Prepare Yogurt Sauce:
- Combine Yogurt Sauce ingredients in small bowl. Cover; chill up to 4 hours before ready to serve.
- For the burgers:
- Soak 4 bamboo skewers in water. Combine meat, seasonings and wine in medium bowl; mix lightly. Divide mixture into eight equal portions; form each portion into an oval, each about 4 inches long. Cover; chill 30 minutes.
- Preheat grill. Insert skewers lengthwise through centers of ovals, placing 2 on each skewer. Grill about 8 minutes or to desired doneness, turning once. Fill pita bread with

133.   Greek Feta Burgers Recipe

Serving: 4 | Prep: | Cook: 15mins |Ready in:

Ingredients

- For Burgers:
- 1 (10-ounce) package frozen chopped spinach, thawed, drained, and squeezed dry
- 1 tablespoon lemon juice
- 1/4 teaspoon pepper
- 1 egg white, lightly beaten
- 3/4 pound lean ground lamb
- 1/2 cup (2 ounces) crumbled feta cheese
- 1/4 cup chopped fresh mint or 4 teaspoons dried mint flakes
- ~~~~
- cooking spray
- 4 (1 1/2-ounce) hamburger buns with onions
- 1/2 cup diced tomato
- ~~~~
- cucumber-Dill Sauce :
- 1/4 cup diced seeded peeled cucumber
- 1/4 cup plain low-fat yogurt
- 1/2 teaspoon chopped fresh or 1/8 teaspoon dried dill
- 1 small garlic clove, minced

Direction

- Make Burgers:
- Combine first 4 ingredients in a bowl; stir well. Add lamb, cheese, and mint; stir well. Divide mixture into 4 equal portions, shaping into 1/2-inch-thick patties.
- Prepare grill. Place patties on grill rack coated with cooking spray; grill 5 minutes on each side or until done.

- Place patties on bottom halves of buns; top each with 2 tablespoons tomato, 2 tablespoons Cucumber-Dill Sauce, and top half of bun.
- ~~~~
- Make Cucumber-Dill Sauce:
- Combine all ingredients in a bowl, and stir well.

---

134. Greek Lamb Burgers Recipe

Serving: 6 | Prep: | Cook: 12mins | Ready in:

Ingredients

- Burgers
- 1/2 C (2 ounces) crumbled feta cheese
- 1 tbl chopped fresh rosemary
- 2 tsp grated lemon rind
- 2 tsp chopped fresh oregano
- 1/2 tsp salt
- 3 garlic cloves, minced
- 3/4 lb lean ground lamb
- 3/4 lb lean ground turkey breast
- cooking spray
- 3 (6 inch) pitas, cut in half
- 6 Tbl tzatziki sauce
- Sauce
- 3/4 C plain low fat yogurt
- 2 Tbl grated, peeled and seeded cucumber
- 1 1/2tsp minced onion
- 1/8 tsp salt
- 1/8 tsp freshly ground pepper
- Combine all ingredients
- Refrigerate in air-tight container for up to 2 days
- Yield about 3/4 C

Direction

- Prepare grill
- Combine first 8 ingredients
- Divide mixture into 6 equal portions, shaping into 1/2 thick burgers

- Place patties on grill rack coated with cooking spray or brushed with oil
- Grill 6 minutes on each side or until thermometer registers 165
- Remove from Grill; let rest 5 minutes
- Place 1 patty in each pita half; drizzle with 1 tbsp. Tzatziki sauce
- Tuck tomato slices and lettuce into pitas, if desired

---

135. Greek Turkey Burgers Recipe

Serving: 4 | Prep: | Cook: 15mins | Ready in:

Ingredients

- 1lb ground turkey
- 1 6 oz package crumbled feta cheese
- 1 tsp dried marjoram
- 3/4 tsp dried oregano
- 1/2 tsp garlic powder
- salt and pepper to taste
- olive oil (optional)

Direction

- Combine all ingredients except olive oil in a bowl.
- Using your hands, mix all ingredients together well so that they are mixed evenly.
- Heat a pan over medium-high heat.
- Form burger mixture into 4 patties
- If you feel you'll need lubrication, drizzle a little olive oil in your heated pan.
- Place patties in heated pan (as many as comfortably fit)
- Flip after 2 to 3 minutes.
- Let cook for one more minute, turn the heat to medium low and put a lid on the pan.
- Cook for around 7 minutes or until you feel they're done. Searing the top and bottom and then cooking on low heat with a covered pan will allow the inside to cook fully without drying out the burger.

- To serve, I enjoy these on whole wheat buns. If you're feeling adventurous, I highly suggest spreading a little Greek yogurt on instead of mayonnaise.

136. Grill Denver Mile High Taco Burger Recipe

Serving: 4 | Prep: | Cook: 12mins | Ready in:

Ingredients

- 1 pound lean ground beef
- 1 (1 ounce) envelope taco seasoning mix
- Sliced Monterey jack cheese with hot peppers (pepper jack)
- 4 sandwich buns
- Shredded lettuce
- Sliced tomato
- Mustard, to taste
- Ketchup, to taste
- Mayonnaise, to taste
- Tortilla chips

Direction

- Mix together ground beef and seasoning mix in a medium bowl. Form 4 patties. Grill to desired doneness. Place cheese on each burger and heat briefly to soften cheese. Serve burgers in buns with lettuce, tomato, condiments and chips

137. Grilled Beef Burgers Two Recipe

Serving: 6 | Prep: | Cook: 15mins | Ready in:

Ingredients

- 1/4 Cup onion,chopped
- 4 cloves garlic,minced

- 2 Tablespoons tomatoe Paste
- 1/2 teaspoon rosemary,crushed
- 1/4 teaspoon allspice
- 1/2 teaspoon salt
- 1/2 teaspoon pepper
- 2 Pounds of Good ground round
- 2 Cups of Dark Strong beer

Direction

- Mix everything together, except the beer.
- Shape into patties about 1" thick.
- Place in shallow pan.
- Pour beer over patties, cover, refrigerate for 8 or up to 24 hours.
- Grill burgers for about 20 minutes.
- Serve with a mustard sauce:
- 3 Tablespoons Stone ground mustard
- 1 Tablespoons Beer
- 1 teaspoon Worcestershire Sauce
- Mix and spread on toasted bun, top with beef patties.

138. Grilled Cuban Style Burgers With Grilled Ham & Cheese Recipe

Serving: 4 | Prep: | Cook: 30mins | Ready in:

Ingredients

- Patties
- 1 pound freshly ground sirloin
- 1 teaspoon minced garlic
- 1 teaspoon chile powder
- 1 teaspoon ground cumin
- 2 tablespoons chopped cilantro
- 5 dashes tabasco Pepper Sauce
- Kosher salt
- Freshly ground black pepper
- Vegetable oil, for brushing on the grill rack
- 4 slices baked ham
- 4 thick slices Monterey Jack cheese

- 4 large sesame seed buns, split and brushed with butter
- Mustard-Pickle Spread
- 1/4 cup dill pickle relish
- 1/4 cup yellow American mustard
- 1/4 cup spicy brown mustard

Direction

- 1. Prepare a medium-hot fire in a charcoal grill with a cover, or preheat a gas grill to medium-high.
- 2. To make the spread, combine the relish and mustards in a small bowl and stir to blend.
- Set aside.
- 3. To make the patties, combine the sirloin, garlic, chili powder, cumin, cilantro, and pepper sauce in a large bowl and season with salt and pepper. Handling the meat as little as possible to avoid compacting it, mix well. Divide the mixture into 4 equal portions and form the portions into patties to fit the buns.
- 4. When the grill is ready, brush the grill rack with vegetable oil. Place the patties on the rack, cover, and cook, turning once, until done to preference, 5 to 7 minutes on each side for medium. Just before the patties are done, turn a second time and place a ham slice and a cheese slice on top of each patty. During the last few minutes of cooking, place the buns, cut side down, on the outer edges of the rack to toast lightly.
- 5. To assemble the burgers, spread the pickle spread over the cut sides of the buns. On each bun bottom, place a patty. Add the bun tops and serve.

---

139.   Grilled French Onion Burgers Recipe

Serving: 6 | Prep: | Cook: 10mins | Ready in:

Ingredients

- 2 pounds ground beef

- 1 envelope (about 1 1/2 ounces) onion soup mix
- 8 ounces French onion dip (1 cup)
- 1/2 cup plain bread crumbs
- 1/8 teaspoon pepper
- lettuce leaves
- 8 slices tomato
- 8 kaiser rolls, split and toasted
- ketchup, if desired
- pickle planks, if desired

Direction

- Heat coals or gas grill for direct heat.
- Mix beef, soup mix (dry), onion dip, bread crumbs and pepper.
- Shape mixture into 8 patties about 3/4 inch thick.
- Grill patties uncovered 4 to 6 inches from medium heat 10 to 15 minutes, turning once, until meat thermometer inserted in center of patties reads 160F.
- Place lettuce leaves and tomato slices on bottom halves of rolls;
- Top with burgers, ketchup and pickles.
- Top with remaining roll halves.

---

140.   Grilled Gorganzola Stuffed Sirloin Burgers Recipe

Serving: 2 | Prep: | Cook: 20mins | Ready in:

Ingredients

- 1 pound ground sirloin
- 3 green onions, thinly sliced
- 4 tablespoons crumbled gorganzola cheese
- 1 egg, beaten
- 2 tablespoons balsalmic vinegar
- 3/4 teaspoon garlic powder
- 1/2 teaspoon coarse ground black pepper
- sea salt to taste
- 1/2 red pepper flakes
- 2 gourmet buns, of choice, split

- 3 teaspoons hot sauce
- 3 tablespoons butter, room temperature
- 2 slices of Walla Walla sweet onion
- 2 butter lettuce leaves

Direction

- Combine ground sirloin, green onions, egg, balsamic vinegar, garlic powder, black pepper, salt, and red pepper, mix until just combined. Set aside. Prepare BBQ over medium-high heat. Shape burger into 4 equal patties and indent the middle of each patty. Place 2 tablespoons of the gorgonzola cheese in the divet of 2 of the patties. Place 2 patties together and seal the edges. Grill until desired color. Meanwhile, combine hot sauce and butter in a small bowl and spread on the top part of the split buns. Place buns, butter-side down on grill the last 2-3 minutes of grilling time. Put burger on bottom bun, top with a slice of Walla Walla sweet onion and a leaf of butter lettuce.

141.   Grilled Gyro Burgers Recipe

Serving: 6 | Prep: | Cook: 15mins | Ready in:

Ingredients

- INGREDIENTS
- 2 (8 ounce) containers plain yogurt, divided
- 1 (1 ounce) package dry Ranch-style dressing mix
- 1 cucumber, peeled, seeded, and chopped
- 1 1/2 pounds ground beef
- 1/4 cup diced onion
- 6 pita bread rounds
- 2 cups torn lettuce leaves
- 1 tomato, seeded and diced

Direction

- DIRECTIONS

- In a medium bowl, combine 1 container of plain yogurt with the envelope of ranch dressing mix. Remove half of the mixture to another bowl. Into one of the bowls, add the remaining container of plain yogurt and diced cucumber; mix well. Cover and refrigerate. Preheat grill and lightly oil grate.
- Mix the ground beef and 1/4 cup onion into the remaining half of the yogurt mixture. Shape into 6 hamburger patties.
- Grill patties on medium heat for 7 minutes each side, turning once.
- Cut off 1/4 end of the pita pockets and fill with torn lettuce, grilled burger, creamy cucumber sauce and diced tomatoes.

142.   Grilled Hawaiian Honey Burgers Recipe

Serving: 8 | Prep: | Cook: 10mins | Ready in:

Ingredients

- 2 pounds ground beef
- ½ cup honey
- ¼ teaspoon ground cinnamon
- ¼ teaspoon paprika
- ¼ teaspoon curry powder
- 1/8 teaspoon ground ginger
- 1/8 teaspoon ground nutmeg
- ¼ cup soy sauce
- 1 can (23 ounces), sliced pineapple, drained
- 8 hamburger buns, split and toasted
- lettuce leaves, optional

Direction

- In a bowl, combine first 7 ingredients; mix well. Shape into eight ¾-inch thick patties.
- Grill the burgers, uncovered, over medium hot coals for 3 minutes on each side. Brush with soy sauce. Continue grilling for 4 to 6 minutes, or until juices run clear, basting and turning several times.

- During the last 4 minutes, grill the pineapple slices until browned, turning once.
- Serve burgers and pineapple on buns with lettuce, if desired.

143. Grilled Mexi Burgers Recipe

Serving: 4 | Prep: | Cook: 20mins | Ready in:

Ingredients

- 1 pound lean ground beef
- 1/3 cup crushed nacho flavored tortilla chips
- 1/3 cup salsa
- 3 tablespoons chopped cilantro (optional)
- 2 tablespoons chopped onion
- 1 teaspoon ground cumin
- 4 slices of pepperjack cheese
- your favorite guacamole
- lettuce leaves
- sliced tomatoes
- 4 warm hamburger buns

Direction

- Prepare your grill for grilling
- Mix first six ingredients together until well blended
- Form into four patties
- Place on grill over medium heat
- Grill to desired doneness turning once about 10 minutes
- Add cheese slices for one to two minutes until cheese begins to melt
- Serve on warm buns topped with guacamole, lettuce, and sliced tomatoes.

144. Grilled Pepper Turkey Burgers Recipe

Serving: 7 | Prep: | Cook: 15mins | Ready in:

Ingredients

- 1-1/2 pounds ground turkey
- 1 egg beaten
- 1 clove minced garlic
- 1/4 cup finely chopped red bell pepper
- 1/4 cup finely chopped green bell pepper
- 2 tablespoons finely chopped jalapeno pepper
- 2 tablespoon finely chopped green onion
- 1/4 cup soy sauce
- 1 tablespoon worcestershire sauce
- 1 tablespoon roasted garlic Montreal chicken seasoning
- 1 teaspoon ground black pepper

Direction

- Blend well by hand the meat, garlic, peppers and onion in a mixing bowl.
- Form into seven patties.
- Coat grill with cooking spray.
- Grill burgers pouring sauces and seasonings over.
- Sprinkling seasonings on each side of burgers while grilling.
- Serve on French rolls or hamburger buns.

145. Grilled Portobello Burger Recipe

Serving: 4 | Prep: | Cook: 10mins | Ready in:

Ingredients

- 4 big portobello mushrooms
- 1/4 cup of balsamic vinegar
- 2 tbsp of olive oil
- 1 minced clove of garlic
- 1/4 tsp of dried oregano
- 1/4 tsp of dried basil
- 1/4 tsp of dried mint
- 4 slices of provolone cheese
- 4 1/4 inch thick slices of red onion, with a skewer run through to hold together
- shredded romaine

- 4 sandwich buns-I prefer onion buns or square asiago buns (think Panera)
- Purchased roasted red pepper hummus

Direction

- Mix vinegar, herbs, and oil together with the garlic in a recloseable plastic bag.
- Add Portobello mushrooms and marinate for at least 15 minutes.
- Run a two skewers through the red onion slices to hold in place.
- Prepare medium hot charcoal fire.
- Grill Portobello mushrooms five minutes per side along with the onions.
- Brush generously with extra marinade while grilling.
- Top mushrooms with cheese and melt.
- Toast buns, add a smear of hummus to the bottom bun.
- Put a little bed of shredded lettuce on hummus.
- Top with mushrooms/cheese and grilled onion.
- Add top toasted bun.

146. Grilled Portobello Burgers With Roasted Red Peppers Recipe

Serving: 4 | Prep: | Cook: | Ready in:

Ingredients

- 4 large Portobello mushrooms, 5-6 oz, brushed clean and stems removed
- 2 tablespoons extra-virgin olive oil
- 4 whole grain burger buns, spilt
- 2 roasted red peppers or 4 thick slices tomato
- *********************************For the herb Vinaigrette:
- 4 TB olive oil
- 2 tablespoons extra-virgin olive oil
- 1 tablespoon red wine vinegar

- 1 tablespoon water
- 3/4 teaspoon Dijon mustard
- ½ teaspoon minced garlic
- sea salt and pepper to taste
- 1 teaspoon minced fresh thyme
- 1 teaspoon minced fresh rosemary
- 1 teaspoon minced fresh dill
- 5 oz torn mixed salad greens (about 4 cups loosely packed)
- ½ to 1 teaspoon tamari soy sauce

Direction

- Prepare a CHARCOAL OR GAS GRILL for direct-heat grilling over medium heat or preheat STOVE TOP grill pan or preheat OVEN to 400 F. Oil the grill rack. Lightly brush the mushroom caps with the olive oil.
- BY GRILL OR STOVETOP: Using tongs, place the mushrooms, cap side down, over the hottest part of the fire or directly over the heat elements and grill, turning once, until cooked through and tender when pierced with a knife, about 10 minutes. Transfer to a dish, cap side down. Toast buns, cut side down on grill 1-2 minutes.
- BY OVEN: Place the mushrooms, cap side down, on a baking sheet and roast for 10 minutes. Turn the mushrooms and continue to roast until they are cooked through and tender when pierced with a knife, about 10 minutes longer. Turn on the broiler (grill). Place the buns, cut side up, on a broiler pan and put in the broiler about 3 inches from the heat source. Broil (grill) until toasted, 1-2 minutes.
- To make the herb vinaigrette, in a small bowl, whisk together the vinegar, mustard, garlic, salt & pepper to taste, and 1 tablespoon water until blended. Stir in the thyme, rosemary, and dill. Whisk in the olive oil, measure out 2-3 teaspoons dressing into a separate bowl. Add ½ to 1 teaspoon tamari sauce and whisk well. Spoon ½ teaspoon of the reserved dressing with tamari over each of the mushrooms. Pour remaining vinaigrette over the salad greens and mix well.

- Layer the burger by placing the bottom half of each bun on a plate. Mound with salad greens and top with mushroom and roasted red pepper. Place top bun on burger and serve hot.

147. Grilled Seattle Salmon Burger Recipe

Serving: 4 | Prep: | Cook: 9mins | Ready in:

Ingredients

- 1 lb. salmon fillet (use tail or belly)
- 4 scallions (green parts only), cut into 1-inch pieces
- 4 garlic cloves, minced
- 2 Tbs. grated fresh ginger
- 2 Tbs. tamari
- 1 Tbs. toasted sesame oil
- 1/4 cup fine dry breadcrumbs
- 2 Tbs. sesame seeds
- Kosher salt
- Freshly ground black pepper
- Vegetable oil cooking spray
- 4 hamburger buns
- Lettuce leaves
- Peanut sauce or Asian sweet chili sauce

Direction

- Remove the skin from the salmon or have your fishmonger do it for you. Check the fillet over for pin bones and remove any you find with tweezers or needle-nose pliers. Cut the salmon into 2-inch chunks. Put the salmon, scallions, garlic, ginger, tamari, and sesame oil in the bowl of a food processor. Pulse until combined. This may take 5 to 6 pulses, but do not let the machine run. Pour this mixture into a medium bowl and add the breadcrumbs and sesame seeds. Use your hands to gently combine.
- Divide the salmon mixture into 4 equal portions and shape into patties about 3/4 inch thick. Remember to put a slight indentation

into the center of each patty. Season both sides of the burgers liberally with salt and pepper. Refrigerate for at least 1 hour. This will help the burgers hold together on the grill.

- Oil the grill racks well, and make sure that they are impeccably clean. Preheat your grill using all burners set on high and with the lid closed for 10 to 12 minutes.
- Remove the burgers from the refrigerator and spray both sides of each with the cooking spray. Place on the grill and cook for 5 minutes. Turn and cook for 4 minutes longer, so the burgers are just cooked through. Use a spatula to turn your burgers, but loosen them from the grill before you make the attempt. During the last minute or two, place the buns on the grill, cut side down, so they get warm and toasty. Remove all from the grill to a platter, and top with lettuce and either the peanut sauce or the sweet chili sauce.

148. Grilled Stilton Burgers Recipe

Serving: 4 | Prep: | Cook: 15mins | Ready in:

Ingredients

- 1-1/2 pounds ground beef
- 1/2 teaspoon salt
- 1 teaspoon freshly ground black pepper
- 2 ounces Stilton cheese cut into four 1/2" thick slices
- 4 crusty burger rolls split
- 4 tomato slices
- 4 crispy romaine lettuce leaves

Direction

- Preheat grill on high heat or preheat broiler for 5 minutes.
- Form ground beef into four burgers then sprinkle with salt and pepper.
- Cook burgers for 7 minutes without moving them or pressing down.

- Using a wide spatula then gently flip burgers over and press down only once.
- Cook 5 minutes longer.
- Add cheese to tops of burgers and grill or broil 2 minutes.
- Meanwhile grill or broil buns until warmed through.
- Place burgers on buns and top each with a slice of tomato and Romaine leaf.

149. Grilled Stuffed Turkey Burgers Recipe

Serving: 5 | Prep: | Cook: 25mins | Ready in:

Ingredients

- 2Tbs onion soup mix
- 1/2 tsp garlic powder
- 1/2 tsp worcestershire sauce
- 1/8 tsp salt
- dash pepper
- 1-1/4 lbs lean ground turkey
- 1/2 c finely chopped sweet red pepper
- 1/2 c shredded part-skim mozzarella cheese
- 5 whole wheat hamburger buns,split

Direction

- In small bowl, combine first 5 ingredients. Crumble turkey over mixture and mix well. Shape into 10 thin patties.
- Spoon red pepper and cheese into center of 5 patties; top with remaining patties and press edges firmly to seal.
- Grill burgers, covered, over med. heat or broil 4" from heat 5-7 mins. on each side. Serve on buns.

150. Grilled Super Duper Burger Recipe

Serving: 4 | Prep: | Cook: 20mins | Ready in:

Ingredients

- 1 lb 80/20 ground beef
- 2 oz Jimmy Dean hot sausage (DC Special Ingredient)
- 1/2 cup chopped onion
- 1 tbsp McCormick's italian seasoning
- 4 tbsp barbecue sauce
- 1/2 tsp sea salt
- 1/2 tsp fine ground black pepper
- potato Rolls
- leaf lettuce
- Sliced, Ripe tomatoes
- Sliced Raw onions
- American cheese
- pepper Jack cheese
- Mayonaise, ketchup, mustard

Direction

- Mix the sausage and onions into the ground beef, distributing evenly.
- Add Italian seasoning, barbeque sauce, salt and fresh ground pepper.
- Form the burgers.
- Place on a grill preheated to 375 degrees F. Grill on one side until you can see the juice begin to run at the surface. Flip over and grill on the other side, again until you can see some juice coming through the top.
- Grill the buns on remaining grill surface, using indirect heat.
- Serve burgers with lettuce, tomatoes, more raw onions, mayo/ketchup/mustard.
- Tips
- Don't overcook the burgers. It only takes a few minutes to get them to medium-rare / medium
- Then place on hamburger buns and eat until your heart contents

78

151. Grilled Taco Burgers Recipe

Serving: 4 | Prep: | Cook: 10mins | Ready in:

Ingredients

- 1 beaten egg
- 1/2 cup crushed corn chips
- 1/4 cup water
- 1/2 package taco seasoning mix
- 1 pound ground beef
- 4 hamburger buns toasted
- 1 large tomato sliced
- 1 cup shredded lettuce
- 1/2 cup shredded pepper jack cheese
- salsa

Direction

- In mixing bowl combine egg, corn chips, water and half the seasoning mix.
- Add meat and mix well then shape into 4 patties and cook over medium coals 6 minutes.
- Turn and cook 5 minutes longer then serve on buns with tomato, lettuce, cheese and salsa.

152. Grilled Turkey Burger With Roasted Red Pepper Mayonnaise Recipe

Serving: 6 | Prep: | Cook: 12mins | Ready in:

Ingredients

- 1 package ground turkey
- 2 finely chopped green onions
- 1/2 cup italian seasoned bread crumbs
- 1/2 cup chopped fresh spinach
- 1/2 teaspoon salt
- 1/2 teaspoon worcestershire sauce
- 6 kaiser rolls, split, toasted if desired

- _____
  _____
- roastED red pepper MAYONNAISE
- 1/3 cup light mayonnaise
- 2 tablespoons chopped roasted red pepper
- 1/2 teaspoon grated lemon peel
- 1/8 teaspoon salt

Direction

- In large bowl combine all turkey burger ingredients except Kaiser rolls. Mix well. Form into 6 (1/2 inch thick) patties.
- Heat boiler. Spray broiler pan with non-stick cooking spray. Broil burgers 4 to 6 inches away from heat, turning once, 4 to 6 minutes on each side or until center is no longer pink. Toast buns if desired.
- Meanwhile, in small bowl combine all mayonnaise ingredients; mix well. Refrigerate until serving time.
- Place each turkey burger inside roll; top with mayonnaise.
- **
- Grilled Turkey Burgers: Heat grill to medium heat. Carefully spray grill rack with non-stick cooking spray. Grill burgers, turning once, 4 to 6 minutes on each side or until center is no longer pink. Toast buns if desired.
- Serve With Suggestion: Sweet Potato Fries
- Make Ahead Tip: Make turkey burgers as directed; wrap individually in plastic wrap. Refrigerate up to 1 day. Make roasted red pepper mayonnaise, cover and refrigerate up to 2 days.

153. Gringo Burgers With Spicy Onions Recipe

Serving: 2 | Prep: | Cook: 15mins | Ready in:

Ingredients

- 1 tablespoon vegetable oil

- 1 large sweet onion, halved and thinly sliced
- 4 tablespoons TABASCO® brand Chipotle pepper sauce, divided
- 1 tablespoon worcestershire sauce
- 1 1/2 pounds lean ground beef
- 1/4 cup chopped cilantro
- 1/4 cup chopped green onion
- 1 teaspoon salt
- 4 slices monterey jack cheese
- 4 hamburger buns, toasted
- mixed baby greens

Direction

- Heat oil in a large skillet over medium-high heat; add onion and cook 5 minutes or until golden brown, stirring often.
- Stir in 1 tablespoon TABASCO® Chipotle Sauce and the Worcestershire sauce; mix well and remove from heat.
- Combine ground beef, cilantro, green onion, salt and the remaining 3 tablespoons TABASCO® Chipotle Sauce.
- Mix well and shape into 4 burgers.
- Grill over medium-high heat to desired doneness, about 3 minutes per side for medium-rare.
- Top each burger with a slice of cheese and grill just until melted.
- Place on buns and top with spicy onions and baby greens.
- Makes 4 servings

154.   Gs Veggie Burger Recipe

Serving: 4 | Prep: | Cook: 20mins | Ready in:

Ingredients

- 1 cup black beans, drained and rinsed
- 2 cups cooked lentils, drained and rinsed
- 1/4 medium red onion, diced
- 1 tsp grated fresh ginger
- 3 garlic cloves, minced
- 2 tbsp ground flaxseed

- 1 tsp smoked paprika
- 1/2 tsp cumin
- 2 tbsp minced fresh basil
- 3 tbsp whole wheat bread crumbs

Direction

- Mash beans and lentils with a fork until coarsely blended.
- Add onion, ginger, garlic, flaxseed, spices, basil and 1 tbsp. breadcrumbs. Mix well and divide into 4 even pieces.
- Coat each side of each patty with a dusting of breadcrumbs.
- Wrap patties individually in plastic wrap, refrigerate 4-6 hours or overnight.
- Preheat oven to 450F, lightly grease a baking sheet with spray oil.
- Bake patties 8-10 minutes per side, until crusty and hot throughout.

155.   Guys Killer Inside Out Burgers Recipe

Serving: 4 | Prep: | Cook: 18mins | Ready in:

Ingredients

- 1/4 pound bacon, chopped
- 1/2 cup minced red onions
- 3 tablespoons fresh uncooked chorizo, out of casing
- salt and freshly ground black pepper
- 2 pounds ground chuck, 80/20 mix
- 1/2 pound swiss cheese, thinly sliced, about 8 slices
- 4 kaiser rolls, split and toasted

Direction

- GUY did these on the stove top...would be just as awesome on the grill
- ***

- In a medium pan over medium to high heat, add bacon and onions, cook until the bacon is rendered but not crisp.
- Add the chorizo and cook until done.
- Remove the bacon mixture to a paper towel-lined plate to drain and cool.
- Make a cross with a large knife in the opened pack of ground beef, dividing into 4 equal portions (this will be the 4 burgers)
- Take 1/4, and divide into 2 equal portions
- Form a loose ball from one of these portions, and pat it out into a 4 inch round patty. Create a "lip edge" around the patty.
- Fill the center with a piece of cheese and 1/4 of the bacon mixture then another piece of cheese
- (Cheese should be torn to fit inside the "crater" of the patty)
- Form the 2nd half of the burger into the same type patty, with the lip edge, and place down over the stuffed side of the burger
- Pat around the outside edge to seal
- Repeat with remaining 3 burgers
- (Patties will be about 4 inches wide and 1 1/2 inches high).
- Heat a medium sauté pan over medium heat. Place all 4 patties in the pan and cook for 3 to 4 minutes on 1 side, then gently turn over and cook for another 3 to 4 minutes.
- Remove the pan from the heat, cover and pop it in a 250 degree F oven for 10 minutes.
- Remove from oven, place onto rolls and serve with Worcestershire Tomato Ketchup. (Posted separately)

---

156. Gyro Burger Recipe

Serving: 4 | Prep: | Cook: 10mins | Ready in:

Ingredients

- For the hamburger sauce:
- 8 Oz. plain yogurt.
- 1/3 cup chopped and seeded cucumber.
- 2 TBSP finely chopped white onion.

- 1 TBSP minced garlic.
- 1 tsp. sugar
- For the hamburger:
- 1 pound of ground chuck
- 1 1/2 tsp. dried oregano
- 1 tsp. garlic powder
- 1 tsp. onion powder
- 1 tsp. salt
- 1 tsp pepper
- 2 cups shredded lettuce
- 1 large tomato, sliced.
- 1 small onion, sliced.
- 4 slices of mozzarella cheese. (Or whatever cheese you like)
- 4 hamburger buns, toasted.

Direction

- To make the hamburger sauce:
- In a small bowl, mix together the yogurt, cucumber, chopped onion, minced garlic, and sugar. Store in refrigerator until needed.
- To make the Gyro Hamburger:
- Place the hamburger in a mixing bowl. Add the oregano, garlic powder, onion powder, salt, and pepper. Mix the ingredients together, and form into four 1/4 pound patties.
- Place hamburger patties on a grill, and grill over medium/high heat until no longer pink in the middle, about 160 degrees.
- At the last minute of cooking, top each patty with the cheese.
- Remove from heat, and place one patty on each hamburger bun bottom.
- Top each patty with a slice of onion, slice of tomato, shredded lettuce, and 1/4 of the prepared Gyro Sauce.
- Put top half on bun on hamburger, and enjoy.

---

157. Ha Cha Cha Burgers Recipe

Serving: 4 | Prep: | Cook: 10mins | Ready in:

Ingredients

- 1 pkg ground chicken
- 1 peach, peeled and diced
- 1 nectarine, diced
- 2 Tbs minced red onion
- 2 Tbs minced fresh cilantro
- 1 lime, juiced
- 1/4 tsp chopped pickled jalapeno pepper
- 2 tsp minced garlic
- 1 1/2 Tbs chili powder
- 1/2 cup plain bread crumbs
- .

Direction

- In a small bowl, blend peach, nectarine, onions, cilantro, lime juice and jalapenos; refrigerate. In a medium bowl, blend remaining ingredients and form mixture into four patties (patties will be wet). Place on a lightly oiled grill and cook over medium high direct heat for about 10 minutes, flipping halfway through cooking time.
- Burgers are done when a meat thermometer inserted into the sides reaches 165° or juices run clear and burgers bounce back to the touch.
- Serve with salsa, with or without a roll.

158.   Hawaiian Honey And Pineapple Burgers Recipe

Serving: 6 | Prep: | Cook: 10mins | Ready in:

Ingredients

- 1/2 cup honey
- 1/4 teaspoon ground cinnamon
- 1/4 teaspoon paprika
- 1/4 teaspoon curry powder
- 1/8 teaspoon ground ginger
- 1/8 teaspoon ground nutmeg
- 2 pounds ground beef
- 1/4 cup soy sauce

- 1 can (23 ounces) sliced pineapple, drained
- 8 hamburger buns, split and toasted
- lettuce leaves if desired

Direction

- In a bowl, combine the first six ingredients.
- Crumble beef over mixture; mix well. Shape into eight 3/4-inch-thick patties.
- Grill the burgers, uncovered, over medium-hot heat for 3 minutes on each side.
- Brush with soy sauce.
- Continue grilling for 4 to 6 minutes or until juices run clear, basting and turning several times.
- During the last 4 minutes, grill the pineapple slices until browned, turning once.
- Serve burgers and pineapple on buns with lettuce if desired.

159.   Hawaiian Teriyaki Burger Recipe

Serving: 4 | Prep: | Cook: 25mins | Ready in:

Ingredients

- PAM® For Grilling Spray
- 1 package (10 ounces) tri-color coleslaw mix
- 1/2 cup seasoned rice vinegar
- 1/4 cup pineapple juice
- 1-1/4 pounds lean ground beef
- 1/3 cup La Choy® teriyaki marinade and Sauce
- 4 large cloves garlic, finely chopped
- 8 slices pineapple, grilled until lightly browned
- 1 red bell pepper, seeded, grilled, sliced
- 4 large seeded hamburger buns
- 1/4 cup mayonnaise
- 4 leaves iceberg lettuce

Direction

- Spray grate of outdoor grill and utensils with PAM® for Grilling Spray. Preheat grill to medium heat.
- Toss coleslaw mix with rice vinegar and pineapple juice in small bowl. Refrigerate until ready to serve.
- Mix together beef, teriyaki sauce and garlic in large bowl. Shape into 4 equal size patties. Grill patties on one side until juices begin to appear on surface. Turn patties over. Cook about 4 minutes longer or to desire doneness. Grill pineapple slices and red bell pepper while grilling patties.
- Build burgers by topping heel of each bun with 1 tablespoon mayonnaise, lettuce leaf, burger, 2 slices pineapple, red pepper slices and crown of bun.
- Serve with prepared coleslaw.

160.   Herbed Turkey Burgers Recipe

Serving: 6 | Prep: | Cook: 10mins | Ready in:

Ingredients

- 1 lb ground turkey
- 3/4 orange pepper, diced small
- 1 small yellow onion, diced small
- 5-8 cloves garlic, minced (I used 8, 3 of which were small)
- 8-10 leaves sage
- 2 sprigs rosemary
- 4 sprigs thyme
- 1/2 cup shredded cheese (whatever you have on hand)
- 10 dashes hot sauce, optional (use more or less to suit your tastes)
- salt and freshly ground pepper, to taste

Direction

- Roughly chop all herbs.

- Combine all ingredients. Mix until just combined and mixture just holds together; longer will make the burgers tough.
- Form into 6 evenly sized patties.
- Grill over medium-high to medium heat for 5 minutes per side.
- Serve with assorted toppings (cheese, bacon, lettuce, tomato, onion, ketchup, relish, etc.).

161.   Homemade Burger Patty Recipe

Serving: 4 | Prep: | Cook: 27mins | Ready in:

Ingredients

- salt
- pepper
- paprika
- garlic (chopped)
- spring onions (chopped)
- Note:second time was onion (chooped) instead of spring onion. The flavor you can change to whatever flavour you like. Can add some brown sugar if you want it slightly sweet and if grilled it gives that nice caramelized looks. Can put in BBQ sauce (thick ones, not the watery type) or liquid smoke also
- binder used:
- 1 egg for 1lb meat
- about 2 tablespoon breadcrumb

Direction

- Method:
- 1. Mix all ingredients with hand and don't overwork it. Can use dough mixer also but don't overwork.
- 2. It's a quarter pounder i.e. 1lb of meat divided by 4
- 3. Flatten it and make a hole in the middle about 1/2 inch diameter, for best result flip it only once when the hole is almost closed
- 4. Grill the patty and when the hole is fully closed, the patty is done

- 5. Just before you take it off the grill, put slice cheese on the patty (used low fat cheddar cheese), just to let it melt a bit.
- Note: cheddar tastes so much better than other cheese when it's slightly melted
- 6. Served with salad, tomato, sliced onion and your favorite bun.

162. Homemade Burgers & Sweetcorn Relish Recipe

Serving: 0 | Prep: | Cook: 10mins | Ready in:

Ingredients

- 500g of Extra Lean beef mince
- 1 egg
- 1 Large red onion
- Lea and Perrins
- 6 slices of bread
- salt and pepper
- flour (Just Enough for dusting)
- For the sweetcorn relish (An optional side) :
- 2 x 15.oz Cans of sweetcorn (or 3 sweetcorn cobs with husks and strings removed)
- 1tbsp cornflour
- 1 small onion
- 1 large pepper
- 1 red chili
- 200g honey
- 300ml cider vinegar
- salt and pepper

Direction

- For the Burgers:
- 1.) Get a large mixing bowl and tip the mince upside down into it. (Do it upside down as they often have a paper sheet that must be removed from the underside)
- 2.) Break Up the slices of bread into breadcrumbs using a food processor. (Alternatively, I have before done it using my hands and a cheese grater in an emergency, and this worked surprisingly well giving a chunkier feel to the finished burgers, so if you don't have a food processor, you can still follow the recipe.)
- 3.) Add the breadcrumbs to the mixing bowl.
- 4.) Crack the egg into the bowl. (Make a small well for it with the breadcrumbs and it prevents it sliding all over.)
- 5.) Finely dice the onion and add this to the mixing bowl.
- 6.) Add a hefty splash of Lea and Perrins to give a strong flavor. At this point chili powder can be added to give spicy burgers as well as finely sliced red chili and pepper, or you can add cumin and fresh herbs for curry burgers which are also very popular with our family.
- 7.) Add Salt and Pepper to flavor, though it really doesn't need much.
- 8.) Have a plate covered with flour standing nearby to the mixing bowl.
- 9.) Plunge your hands into the mixture and make sure that everything is really well mixed together before forming patties out of the mixture and transferring them onto the floured plate to get a slight coating of flour all over.
- 10.) Cook the floured patties either by barbecue or grill until the juices run clear.
- For the Sweetcorn Relish:
- 1.) Add the sweetcorn to boiling water and cook. (Some canned sweetcorn is already cooked, so check this.)
- 2.) Drain the sweetcorn thoroughly and put to one side.
- 3.) Put peppers, vinegar, honey, onion and chili into a pan and bring to simmering point, boil for 15 minutes and then add sweetcorn.
- 4.) Dissolve the cornflour in 1tbsp of vinegar and add this to the pan, simmer for another 5 minutes.
- 5.) Leave to cool, or add to sterilized jars if you're planning to keep it bottled.

163. Honey Lager Burger Recipe

Serving: 4 | Prep: | Cook: 15mins |Ready in:

Ingredients

- 1 1/2 lbs. lean ground beef
- 3/4 cup honey lager (or any lager), divided
- 1/3 cup grated parmesan cheese
- 1 tbsp. worcestershire sauce
- 1/4 tsp. black pepper, or to taste
- 1/2-1 tsp. salt, or to taste
- 8 slices tomato
- 8 thin slices red onion
- sliced pickles(optional)
- 4 hamburger buns
- For the sauce:
- 3 tbsp. mayo
- 3 tbsp. ketchup
- 1/2 tsp. spicy brown mustard (or a mustard of your choice)
- 1 tbsp. honey

Direction

- For the sauce:
- In a small bowl combine 1 tbsp. honey lager, mayo, ketchup, mustard and honey. Mix well and reserve.
- Warm up the grill.
- Combine beef, 1/4 cup honey lager, Parmesan cheese, Worcestershire sauce, salt and pepper. Form mixture into 4 patties.
- Lightly oil the grill grate and cook burgers for 3 minutes over medium-high heat. Turn and brush burgers with some remaining lager. Grill 3 minutes, turn and brush with lager again. Repeat grilling and brushing until burgers are cooked to desired doneness.
- Grill red onions until lightly caramelized, or you can use them raw, if desired.
- Lightly grill the buns (optional).
- To assemble:
- Place 2 tomato slices, 2 onion slices, a couple of pickles and a burger on the bottom half of each bun. Spread with the sauce and cover with the bun top. Serve right away.

164. Hot N Blue Buffalo Burger Recipe

Serving: 4 | Prep: | Cook: 15mins |Ready in:

Ingredients

- BURGERS
- 2 lb. ground sirloin, 80-85% lean
- 1/2 cup Crumbled blue cheese
- 1 cup bread Crumbs
- 1 egg
- 1/2 cup chicken wing Sauce
- 1/2 tsp. salt
- 1/2 tsp. pepper
- 4 Soft kaiser rolls
- romaine lettuce
- SAUCE
- 1/4 cup mayonnaise
- 1/4 cup buffalo wing sauce
- **Optional, for hotter sauce
- 1 jalapeno pepper, finely chopped
- ¼ cup red pepper, finely chopped
- ¼ cup onion, finely chopped
- 1 T olive oil

Direction

- In a large mixing bowl, mix together ground beef and crumbled blue cheese until well blended.
- Add bread crumbs, egg, buffalo wing sauce, salt and pepper.
- Mix well.
- Divide mixture into 4 equal parts and shape into burgers.
- Grill over medium heat to desired doneness, turning only once. Do not mash with spatula
- MILD SAUCE

- While burgers are cooking, mix the sauce ingredients together in a small bowl and set aside until the burgers are done.
- HOTTER SAUCE
- Sauté onion and peppers in olive oil until tender.
- Cool and mix into mild sauce mixture

165. Hot Taco Burgers Sandwiches Recipe

Serving: 4 | Prep: | Cook: 60mins | Ready in:

Ingredients

- You will need
- ground beef Pattie
- Sheddred lettuce
- Diced rotel-Tomatoes
- Sliced onion
- Sheddred cheese
- hamburgers bun
- Hot taco seasoning package
- taco sauce

Direction

- Cook burgers in low heat of 1/2 cup of water with taco seasoning package
- With a lid to cover pan
- For one hour, turning burger after a half hour or until done
- Cut a small slit in burger before removing it to see if it done inside of it and not bloody and raw
- Let that flavor cook and soak in while it cook
- Get all ingredients in orders
- When burgers are cook to your taste place on bottom bun and add all on top of burgers
- Use taco sauce as topping, (mild if you prefer since hot seasoning is used?)
- Then add buns top and enjoy!!

166. Hunger Buster Burgers Recipe

Serving: 6 | Prep: | Cook: 25mins | Ready in:

Ingredients

- 600g-1kg premium beef mince
- 1/2 red onion, finely diced
- 1.5 ground weetbix
- 2tbsp grated parmesan
- pinch nutmeg
- pinch oregano
- 1 egg
- buns (to serve)
- lettuce
- beetroot
- Spicy mayo (or just make it yourself with mayo and sweet chilli sauce)

Direction

- Mix all the ingredients in a large bowl.
- Divide into 6-10 patties (depending on the amount of meat and burger size). Leave on a plate in the fridge for 1hr prior to cooking.
- Brush with a little oil and fry in a medium-hot pan. Turn every minute for about 10 minutes.
- Serve on a bun with lettuce, spicy mayo and a slice of beetroot.

167. In And Out Burgers Recipe

Serving: 1 | Prep: | Cook: 6mins | Ready in:

Ingredients

- 1 plain hamburger bun
- 1/3 pound ground beef
- Dash salt
- 1 tablespoon Kraft thousand island dressing
- 1 large tomato slice (or 2 small slices)
- 1 large lettuce leaf
- 4 slices American cheese (Singles)

- -or- 2 slices real American cheese
- 1 whole onion slice (sliced thin)

Direction

- 1. Preheat a frying pan over medium heat.
- 2. Lightly toast the both halves of the hamburger bun, face down in the pan. Set aside.
- 3. Separate the beef into two even portions, and form each half into a thin patty slightly larger than the bun.
- 4. Lightly salt each patty and cook for 2-3 minutes on the first side.
- 5. Flip the patties over and immediately place two slices of cheese on each one. Cook for 2-3 minutes.
- 6. Assemble the burger in the following stacking order from the bottom up:
- Bottom bun
- Dressing
- Tomato
- Lettuce
- Beef patty with cheese
- Onion slice
- Beef patty with cheese
- Top bun.

---

168.   Indian Burger Recipe

Serving: 6 | Prep: | Cook: 8mins | Ready in:

Ingredients

- 2 pounds all natural ground turkey, shaped into 6 burgers (for moister burgers, a mix of white & dark meat)
- 6 slices fresh pineapple, cored
- cucumber & Tomato chutney (recipe follows)
- mango Curry Sauce (recipe follows)
- Romaine, thinly sliced
- 2 Tbs. olive oil for brushing buns
- 6 Brioche or good quality hamburger buns
- Kosher or sea salt
- Freshly ground pepper
- 1/2 english cucumber, quartered lengthwise, seeded & thinly sliced
- 1/2 pint grape tomatoes, halved
- 1/2 small red onion, halved & thinly sliced
- 1 Tbs. fresh mint, finely chopped
- 1 jalapeno, seeded & finely chopped
- 1/2 cup fresh lime juice
- 1 Tbs. sugar
- 1/4 cup water
- 1/2 cup Mango Chutney- medium hot
- 1/2 cup Greek yogurt
- 1/2 cup mayonnaise
- 2 tsp. curry powder
- 1 Tbs. fresh cilantro leaves, finely chopped
- 1 tsp fresh ginger, finely minced
- 1 tsp fresh lemon juice

Direction

- To prepare chutney: In a small bowl, combine lime juice, sugar & water, stir well to combine. In another bowl, add cucumber, grape tomatoes, onion, mint, jalapeno & add lime juice mixture. Mix together & season with salt & pepper. Refrigerate 1 day.
- To prepare Mango Curry Sauce: Puree Mango Chutney in mini food processor. Put in mixing bowl, add yogurt, mayonnaise, curry, cilantro, ginger, lemon juice & combine. Season with salt & pepper & refrigerate.
- To prepare burgers: Prepare the grill to medium-hot heat & lightly oil grill. Spray vegetable or olive oil on pineapple & grill until lightly brown. Grill turkey burger to medium doneness (about 4 minutes per side) & season with salt & pepper.
- Brush inside of buns with olive oil & grill cut side down on cooler side of grill until golden brown. Put romaine on bottom of bun cover with turkey burger and top with pineapple, Cucumber-Tomato Chutney & Mango Curry Sauce.

169.   Inner Cheese Burger Recipe

Serving: 2 | Prep: | Cook: 15mins | Ready in:

Ingredients

- Burgers
- 1/2 pound ground sirloin
- Lawry's Seasoned Salt - to taste
- black pepper, freshly ground - to taste
- 1/4 cup water
- 1/4 cup Grolsch beer or similar
- 2 slices (about 2 oz.) extra sharp cheddar cheese (used Hoffman's)
- To Serve
- 2 Brioche buns
- spicy brown mustard
- 4 slices fresh tomato
- 4 pieces romaine lettuce
- Kosher dill pickles

Direction

- Burgers
- Put water in medium skillet and heat over medium.
- Season beef with Lawry's and black pepper. Separate into 4 equal portions and roll into balls. Flatten to between 1/4 - 1/2 inch thick. Fold cheese slices so stacked 2x2 inches. Place in center of one patty, top with another patty and gently press edges and if needed push edges back up to retain patty shape. Repeat.
- Place patties in skillet. Cover and cook about 2-3 minutes on each side, until water evaporates. When turning patties be careful not to press down or squeeze. Add beer after water has evaporated, cover and continue to cook 2-3 minutes on each side. Remove from heat.
- Note that some cheese will leak out and it's best not to over handle to meat as it compromises the juiciness.
- Serve with recommended fixings or your favorites.

170.   Inside Out Blue Burgers Recipe

Serving: 6 | Prep: | Cook: 15mins | Ready in:

Ingredients

- 2 Lbs. ground chuck I use 85/15
- 1/4 C. Chopped onion
- 3 T. Tabasco sauce
- 2 T. honey
- 1 T. garlic salt
- 1 t. crushed red pepper flakes
- 1 t. black pepper
- 6 Oz.. blue cheese cut into 6 pieces
- 1 Jar fire roasted red peppers
- 6 portabellas grilled.

Direction

- Combine chuck with first 7 ingredients in a large bowl mix well
- Form into six patties sealing the blue cheese in the middle
- Place on medium high grill for 8-10 minutes
- Put on a good hard roll and top with roasted peppers and portabellas
- Enjoy

171.   Iron Skillet Burgers Recipe

Serving: 4 | Prep: | Cook: 20mins | Ready in:

Ingredients

- 8 slices bacon
- 1/2 cup minced onion
- 2 pounds ground beef
- 2 tablespoons worcestershire sauce
- 2 teaspoons Dijon mustard
- 1 teaspoon prepared horseradish
- 1/4 teaspoon salt

- 1/4 teaspoon black pepper

Direction

- In a large iron skillet, fry bacon over medium heat until crispy. Drain bacon on paper towels reserving the drippings. Set aside.
- Put minced onion in the skillet and cook over medium heat until transparent. Drain onions on paper towel and set aside.
- Crumble the bacon into tiny pieces.
- In a large bowl, combine ground beef, Worcestershire sauce, mustard, horseradish, salt, pepper, onion and bacon mixing well. Form into 4 inch patties.
- Wipe out the skillet, heat to medium heat and add hamburger patties. Any ground beef has enough fat to make its own cooking oil. Cook for 4-5 minutes per side or until done to your liking.
- Serve them up with your favorite condiments.

172.   Italian Burger Recipe

Serving: 1 | Prep: | Cook: 10mins | Ready in:

Ingredients

- Approximately 1 pound ground beef
- 2 cloves garlic, minced
- 2 tablespoons butter, melted
- 1 1/2 teaspoons salt
- 1 teaspoon black pepper
- 1/2 teaspoon dried basil leaves (or 1 teaspoon fresh finely chopped basil)
- 1/4 teaspoon dried oregano
- Optional
- Mozzarella or Provolone

Direction

- Preheat barbecue grill to medium heat.
- Mix herbs, seasonings, and butter into the ground beef until it is evenly blended.

- Divide into four portions and form each portion into a firm patty.
- Cook over medium heat on the barbecue until cooked to appropriate temperature (160 degrees for medium).
- If desired, top with slices of cheese when the burgers are almost done cooking for cheeseburgers.
- Makes 4 good sized burgers. Serve on hamburger buns or on sliced Italian bread

173.   Jack O Lantern Burgers Recipe

Serving: 10 | Prep: | Cook: 15mins | Ready in:

Ingredients

- 1 envelope onion soup mix
- 1/4 cup ketchup
- 2 tablespoons brown sugar
- 2 teaspoons prepared horseradish (optional)
- 2 teaspoons chili powder
- 2-1/2 pounds ground beef
- 10 slices process American cheese
- 10 hamburger buns, split

Direction

- In a large bowl, combine soup mix, ketchup, brown sugar, horseradish and chili powder.
- Crumble beef over mixture; mix well.
- Shape into 10 patties.
- Grill, broil or pan-fry until the meat is no longer pink.
- Cut eyes, nose and mouth out of each cheese slice to create a jack-o'-lantern.
- Place cheese on burgers; cook until cheese is slightly melted, about 1 minute.
- Serve on buns.

174. Jalapeno Black Bean Burgers On Whole Wheat Buns Recipe

Serving: 8 | Prep: | Cook: 1hours |Ready in:

Ingredients

- Whole Wheat buns (sub half the flour in below recipe with whole wheat pastry flour):
- buns.html">Homemade Hamburgerhotdog buns
- black bean Patties:
- 3 tbsp olive or canola oil, divided
- 1 small onion, chopped
- 1 clove garlic, minced
- 1/2 jalapeno pepper, membranes and seeds removed, chopped
- 1 tsp ground cumin
- 1 tsp chili powder
- 1 (15 oz.) can organic black beans, drained and rinsed
- 1 1/4 cups cooked brown rice
- for breadcrumbs: 1/2 of one whole wheat bun, toasted
- fresh lime juice, to taste
- sea salt and freshly ground black pepper, to taste
- 1/4 cup chopped cilantro
- Toppings:
- organic monterey jack cheese, avocado, shaved red onion (rinsed), iceberg lettuce leaves, mayo

Direction

- For the patties: In the bowl of a food processor, pulse bread to form breadcrumbs. Pour into a bowl and set aside.
- Heat 1 tablespoon olive or canola oil in a large skillet set over medium heat. Add onion and sauté until soft. Add garlic, jalapeno, and spices. Sauté for additional 2 minutes.
- Scrape the mixture into the food processor. Add black beans, brown rice, lime juice, salt, and pepper. Pulse until the beans are chopped, but not pureed.

- Scrape the black bean mixture into a large bowl. Add some of the breadcrumbs and the chopped cilantro. Stir the mixture until combined. If the mixture is too moist to form patties, add more breadcrumbs.
- Divide the mixture into 8 equal portions and form into patties. Place the patties on a baking sheet lined with plastic wrap and cover with additional plastic wrap. Refrigerate for at least 1 hour.
- Heat 1 tablespoon canola oil in a large skillet (preferably not non-stick, so a good crust can form) set over medium heat. Add 4 patties and cook for 4 minutes per side. Repeat with 1 tablespoon oil and remaining 4 patties.
- Serve burgers on toasted buns with above suggested toppings.

175. Jalapeno Blue Cheese Burgers Recipe

Serving: 4 | Prep: | Cook: 16mins |Ready in:

Ingredients

- 2 pounds ground beef
- 6 jalapeno peppers, seeded and chopped
- 8 ounces crumbled blue cheese
- 2 tablespoons onion powder
- 2 tablespoons garlic powder
- 2 tablespoons soy sauce
- salt to taste
- 4 slices swiss cheese
- 4 hamburger buns, split

Direction

- 1. Preheat a grill for high heat
- 2. In a large bowl, combine the ground beef, jalapeno peppers, blue cheese, onion powder, garlic powder, soy sauce and salt to taste. Mix well using your hands. Pat lightly into 4 large fat patties.
- 3. Place patties on the grill, cook for about 8 minutes per side, or until well done. Place a

slice of cheese on top of each patty, and cover the grill until the cheese melts. Serve on buns with your favorite toppings.

Serving: 4 | Prep: | Cook: 8mins | Ready in:

Ingredients

- ½ C. vegetable oil
- ½ C. vegetable broth
- 1 large onion, chopped
- 2 green onions, chopped
- 2 habanero peppers, stemmed, seeded and minced
- 2 T fresh ginger, grated
- 1 T chopped fresh thyme
- 6 cloves garlic, minced
- ¼ C red wine vinegar
- 2 T brown sugar
- ¼ tsp. nutmeg
- ¼ tsp. cinnamon
- ¼ tsp. ground cloves
- 2 tsp. allspice
- 4 T fresh lime juice
- 4 portabella mushroom caps, stems removed
- 4 slices pepper-jack cheese
- 4 slices ripe beefsteak tomato
- 4 T chopped green chili peppers
- 4 whole-grain rolls, sliced and toasted

Direction

- Add all ingredients through lime juice to a blender.
- Puree until smooth.
- Arrange mushroom caps in a small, deep dish. Pour marinade over.
- Cover and refrigerate 4 – 6 hours, turning caps halfway through.
- Heat grill to medium-high. Remove caps from marinade and blot dry.

- Place caps (gill side down) on grill, cover and cook 4 minutes.
- Flip, top each with a slice of cheese and cook, covered, 4 minutes more.
- Place 1 slice tomato on the bottom half of each roll. Top with mushroom caps, then add 1 tbsp. chilies to the top of each. Top with remaining bun half.
- Serve with sweet potato fries and enjoy!

Serving: 4 | Prep: | Cook: 40mins | Ready in:

Ingredients

- Pickles:
- 1/2 cup rice vinegar
- 3 tbs sugar
- 1 1/2 tsp kosher salt
- 1 Thai green chile, halved lengthwise
- 1 1/2 tbs fresh lime juice
- 1 small seedless cucumber peeled and sliced crosswise 1/4-inch thick (1 cup)
- Russian Dressing:
- 1/2 cup ketchip
- 1/3 cup mayonnaise
- 2 1/2 tbs finely chopped cornichons (pickled gherkin cucumbers)
- 1 tbs finely chopped shallots
- 1 tbs red wine vinegar
- 1 tbs white miso paste
- 1 tsp Sriracha chile sauce (found in grocery store, thai chile sauce found in red bottle, green cap)
- salt
- Burgers:
- 2 lbs ground beef chuck formed into four 1 1/2-inch thick patties
- salt and freshly ground black pepper
- 4 kaiser rolls, toasted
- 4 large Boston lettuce leaves

- 4 slices of beefsteak tomato

Direction

- Make the Pickles: In a saucepan bring the vinegar, sugar, salt, and chili to a boil. Remove from the heat and let cool. Add the lime juice and pour then bring over the cucumber slices. Press the cucumber slices down into the liquid with a small plate and place a can on the plate; let stand at room temperature for 4 hours.
- Make the Russian dressing:
- In a bowl, combine the ketchup with the mayonnaise, cornichons, shallots, vinegar, miso and Sriracha and season with salt.
- Burgers:
- Light a grill, Season the patties with salt and black pepper and grill over high heat, turning once, until burgers are charred outside and medium-rare within, about 6 minutes.
- Spread the Russian dressing on the rolls and cover with the lettuce and tomatoes. Top with the burgers, and pickles; serve.
- Make ahead: the drained pickles can be refrigerated for up to 5 days. The dressing can be refrigerated for up to a week.

178. Jetts Souped Up Turkey Burgers Recipe

Serving: 4 | Prep: | Cook: 15mins | Ready in:

Ingredients

- 1 lb lean ground turkey
- 1 egg white
- 1 package Lipton onion mushroom soup mix (or whatever flavor you prefer)
- 2 teaspoons worcestershire sauce
- 1 teaspoon low sodium teriyaki sauce
- Cavenders salt-free seasoning to taste
- *liquid smoke if you'd like a smokey flavor*

Direction

- Line a baking pan with foil and spray with Pam non-stick spray. Preheat oven to 400 degrees F.
- Mix all ingredients together and make into patties.
- Place patties on baking pan and bake for about 15 to 20 minutes.
- You can eat these as a sandwich or a main meal with a salad or some fresh steamed broccoli. Feel free to add more chopped onions or mushrooms.

179. Jewels Award Winning Turkey Jasmine Burger Recipe

Serving: 4 | Prep: | Cook: 12mins | Ready in:

Ingredients

- cucumber salad:
- 1 cucumber, peeled and thinly sliced rounds
- 1/2 red onion, thinly sliced
- 1/4 cup rice vinegar
- 1/8 cup sugar
- 1 teaspoon salt
- Burger:
- 1 1/4 pounds ground turkey
- 1/3 cup steamed jasmine rice
- 1/4 cup panko
- 1/4 cup thinly sliced green onions
- 1 large egg
- 1/2 teaspoon sesame oil
- 1 tablespoon soy sauce
- 1 Thai chili or serrano chile, seeded and minced
- 1 teaspoon sugar
- salt and freshly ground black pepper
- 1 tablespoon peanut oil
- 4 sesame hamburger buns
- wasabi mayonnaise:
- 1/2 cup homemade mayonnaise or store-bought
- 1 teaspoon wasabi powder
- 1/2 teaspoon minced ginger

- 1 teaspoon finely chopped lemon peel

Direction

- Cucumber salad: Toss cucumbers, onions, rice vinegar, sugar, and salt in a medium sized bowl. Let it marinate at room temperature for 1 hour.
- Burger: Mix ground turkey, rice, panko, green onions, egg, sesame oil, soy sauce, Thai chili, and sugar very well. Make into 4 patties. Season with salt and pepper.
- Heat peanut oil in a large skillet over medium-high heat. Sauté burgers until cooked through, approximately 5 to 6 minutes per side (depending on how thick you make them).
- Wasabi mayonnaise: While burgers are cooking, toast buns, and mix mayonnaise, with wasabi powder, ginger, and lemon peel in a small bowl.
- Drain cucumber salad well.
- Smear 1 tablespoon wasabi mayonnaise on toasted bun halves, spread with a layer of drained cucumber salad, then top with burger and cover with bun top.

---

180.   Jewels Award Winning Turkey Jasmine Burger Recipe

Serving: 4 | Prep: | Cook: 12mins | Ready in:

Ingredients

- cucumber salad:
- 1 cucumber, peeled and thinly sliced rounds
- 1/2 red onion, thinly sliced
- 1/4 cup rice vinegar
- 1/8 cup sugar
- 1 teaspoon salt
- Burger:
- 1 1/4 pounds ground turkey
- 1/3 cup steamed jasmine rice
- 1/4 cup panko
- 1/4 cup thinly sliced green onions
- 1 large egg

- 1/2 teaspoon sesame oil
- 1 tablespoon soy sauce
- 1 Thai chili or serrano chile, seeded and minced
- 1 teaspoon sugar
- salt and freshly ground black pepper
- 1 tablespoon peanut oil
- 4 sesame hamburger buns
- wasabi mayonnaise:
- 1/2 cup homemade mayonnaise or store-bought
- 1 teaspoon wasabi powder
- 1/2 teaspoon minced ginger
- 1 teaspoon finely chopped lemon peel

Direction

- Cucumber salad: Toss cucumbers, onions, rice vinegar, sugar, and salt in a medium sized bowl. Let it marinate at room temperature for 1 hour.
- Burger: Mix ground turkey, rice, panko, green onions, egg, sesame oil, soy sauce, Thai chili, and sugar very well. Make into 4 patties. Season with salt and pepper.
- Heat peanut oil in a large skillet over medium-high heat. Sauté burgers until cooked through, approximately 5 to 6 minutes per side (depending on how thick you make them).
- Wasabi mayonnaise: While burgers are cooking, toast buns, and mix mayonnaise, with wasabi powder, ginger, and lemon peel in a small bowl.
- Drain cucumber salad well.
- Smear 1 tablespoon wasabi mayonnaise on toasted bun halves, spread with a layer of drained cucumber salad, then top with burger and cover with bun top.

---

181.   Kale Burgers Recipe

Serving: 4 | Prep: | Cook: 6mins | Ready in:

Ingredients

- 2 cups of kale leaves stems removed and sliced into thin ribbons two inches long and steamed for three minutes..
- 3 eggs or egg whites if you're watching cholesterol
- 1/4 cup shredded mozzarella or cheddar cheese
- 2 fresh red hot Cyanine peppers seeds removed and chopped fine
- 2 tsp garlic powder
- 1 teaspoon of sea salt
- A mix of Whole Wheat and panko bread crumbs
- olive oil for frying

Direction

- Combine all ingredients in med bowl; add enough breadcrumbs to make mixture easy to form into patties.
- Place on a preheated non-stick skillet over med-high heat with some olive oil
- Cook each side 4-6 min or until golden brown
- Serve on a plate with fresh garden tomatoes.
- Enjoy!

182.   Kickin Black Bean Burgers Recipe

Serving: 4 | Prep: | Cook: 15mins |Ready in:

Ingredients

- 1 15 oz. can of black beans
- 1 tbsp. oil
- 1 cup of corn (fresh or frozen)
- 1 1/2 tsp. garlic
- 1/2 cup chopped onion
- 1/4 tsp. cumin
- 2 tbsp. green chiles
- 2 tbsp. salsa (as mild or hot as you like!)
- 1/2 cup flour
- 1/2 cup dried breadcrumbs
- Non-stick cooking spray

Direction

- Drain and rinse black beans. Put in a bowl and set aside.
- Heat oil in large frying pan.
- Add onion, garlic, corn, chilies and cumin.
- Sauté 3-5 minutes over medium heat.
- Place sautéed items in a bowl with beans and let cool. Mash with a fork (not all ingredients will mash).
- Add salsa, flour and breadcrumbs.
- Blend ingredients with a rubber spatula.
- Form into 4 patties and place on wax paper. (Patties can be stored in Tupperware until ready to cook)
- Spray patties lightly on one side cooking that side first on medium heat, until browned. Spray the other side of the patty, flip and repeat.
- Dress as desired.
- *These are excellent if served with fresh avocado, tomato, lettuce and cheese.

183.   Kotlety (polish Meat Patties) Recipe

Serving: 8 | Prep: | Cook: 20mins |Ready in:

Ingredients

- 1 small onion, minced
- 1 egg, beaten
- 20 saltine crackers, finely crushed
- salt & pepper (lots!)
- 1 lb. ground beef (traditionally, a higher fat content, but I use 85% or 87%)
- 2 Tbsp margarine (or vegetable/olive oil)

Direction

- Mix together onions, egg and cracker crumbs in medium bowl. Let sit for about 5 minutes to soften up the crackers.
- Add ground beef and mix well, seasoning well with salt & pepper.

- Heat margarine or oil in large skillet over medium-high heat.
- Shape beef mixture into patties, about the size of a deck of cards. Cook for about 2 to 3 minutes at medium-high heat, then reduce heat to medium and cook 5 minutes; flip over and cook 5 more minutes.
- Serve any way you want - burger style or with gravy or sautéed onions.
- Notes: This was my husband's grandmother's recipe, although years ago there were more cracker crumbs than beef. They would serve leftovers in tomato sauce as meatballs. The margarine was a must, according to my father-in-law, but I have slowly weaned my husband over to olive oil (ssshhhh - he has no clue!) I like these for the history of them, but honestly I douse mine with steak sauce or mushroom gravy! ;) Still, it is total comfort food.

184. LIGHT CHILI BURGERS Recipe

Serving: 4 | Prep: | Cook: 10mins | Ready in:

Ingredients

- Ingredients:
- Non-stick cooking spray
- 2 cups cooked lean ground beef
- 2 tsp. chili powder
- ½ tsp. garlic powder
- ½ tsp. ground cumin
- 4 hamburger buns
- 1 medium tomato, diced
- 1 medium red onion, diced
- ½ cup trimmed watercress

Direction

- 1) Coat a non-stick skillet with non-stick cooking spray, place over medium heat until hot. Add beef and the next three ingredients, and sauté 4 minutes.

- 2) Divide meat mixture evenly among bottom halves of buns. Top each with tomato, onion, watercress and top halves of buns.

185. Lamb Burger With Cumin Yogurt Recipe

Serving: 6 | Prep: | Cook: 15mins | Ready in:

Ingredients

- 1 1/2 pounds ground lamb
- 3/4 tsp Mediterranean oregano leaves
- 1/2 tsp thyme leaves
- 1/4 tsp Ground cayenne red pepper
- 2 tsp fennel seed
- 1 tbsp parsley flakes
- 3/4 tsp paprika
- 1/4 tsp Coarse Grind black pepper
- 2 tsp coriander Seed
- 4 shallots, finely diced
- 1 tbsp olive oil
- 1 tsp salt
- cumin Yogurt:
- 1/4 tsp cumin seed
- 1/2 cup yogurt, plain
- 1 pinch Coarse Grind black pepper
- 1/8 tsp salt

Direction

- In a preheated, dry skillet, toast the fennel and coriander seeds over a medium heat for around 30 seconds, or until the seeds disperse an aroma. Remove from skillet then crush the seeds in small bowl, or with a mortar and pestle. In the same skillet, sauté the shallots in olive oil until they become translucent and just starting to release an aroma. Add in the oregano and thyme, then remove immediately from the heat and place aside.
- Mix together the lamb, remaining spices, and salt in a medium-sized bowl. Combine gently, then create 6 patties.

- In a preheated, dry skillet, toast the cumin seeds, over medium heat, for about 30 seconds (or until aromatic.) Remove them from the skillet, and crush as you did with the fennel and coriander seeds. Combine the yogurt with the toasted cumin, salt and pepper then place aside.
- Over a medium heat, grill the burgers to your desired doneness. Then, serve with grilled sourdough bread or hamburger buns and top with cumin yogurt.

186. Lamb Burgers With Cucumber Relish Recipe

Serving: 6 | Prep: | Cook: 12mins | Ready in:

Ingredients

- 2 pounds Lean minced/ground lamb
- 1 medium onion, finely chopped
- ½ a Romano/Pointed pepper, finely chopped *
- 1-tablespoon tomato paste
- (we now use Heinz tomato puree with Mexican spices and leave out the hot pepper sauce)
- ½-teaspoon hot pepper sauce
- 1 tablespoon, paprika
- 2 tablespoons, chopped fresh parsley
- 2 tablespoon, chopped fresh rosemary
- salt and freshly ground black pepper to taste
- 6 burger buns split and toasted to serve
- For The cucumber Relish
- 1 large cucumber, thinly sliced
- 1 small red onion, thinly sliced
- 3 tablespoons lime or lemon juice, fresh
- 2 tablespoons, olive oil
- 4 tablespoons, chopped fresh mint
- 2 spring onions/scallions, finely chopped

Direction

- To make the relish, mix together the ingredients in a large glass bowl, cover and chill for at least 2 hours or it is best chilled overnight.
- In a bowl mix the lamb, onion, pepper, and herbs, season with a little salt and pepper and mix thoroughly, preheat the grill.
- Divide the burger mix into 6 equal portions and shape into patties (we use the burger press available from Lakeland). Grill/broil allowing 5 minutes on each side for a medium burger and 8 minutes each side for a well-done burger.
- Toast the surfaces of the buns and serve the burgers on the buns with the cucumber relish. (I like fries with mine)
- * Romano pepper
- A long, narrow bright red fresh pepper, weighing around 100g, with a sweet-flavoured flesh and a tender skin
- Uses: Romano peppers are ideal for stuffing and roasting (this softens the flesh and concentrates the flavour). A variety of fillings can be used including cream cheese, butter bean, and chilli; cooked rice with mushrooms, ham and red onion or cooked chicken or turkey mixed with sweet corn, crumbled Cheshire cheese, and pesto. Serve the cooked peppers with a sauce such as tomato or cheese or a tangy salsa, and salad.
- To store: Keep refrigerated after purchase and use within 3 days.
- To prepare Wash before use. To prepare the peppers for stuffing, slice off a lid leaving the stalk intact and remove the seeds and core using a small sharp knife and a teaspoon. Spoon the stuffing into the cavity and press down firmly using a teaspoon. Lay on a greased baking sheet, season and drizzle with olive oil.
- To cook: Preheat the oven to 180C, gas mark 4. Roast the peppers for 30 minutes or until the flesh is tender.

187.   Lamb Burgers With Mediterranean Cucumber Sauce Recipe

Serving: 5 | Prep: | Cook: 10mins | Ready in:

Ingredients

- 1 pound ground lamb
- 1 pound ground round
- 2 eggs beaten
- 1/4 cup olive oil
- 1/2 cup finely chopped onion
- 2 teaspoons dried oregano leaves
- 2 teaspoons dried parsley flakes
- 1 teaspoon dried mint
- 1 teaspoon seasoned pepper
- 10 pieces pita bread
- Mediterranean cucumber Sauce:
- 1/2 cup light sour cream
- 1/2 cup plain yogurt
- 1 medium cucumber peeled seeded and finely chopped
- 1 clove minced garlic
- 1 tablespoon lemon juice
- 1/4 teaspoon freshly ground black pepper
- 1/4 teaspoon dried mint

Direction

- Thoroughly mix all ingredients together in a bowl.
- Mix ingredients together well in a mixing bowl.
- Form into 10 patties then cut each patty down center making half-moon shapes.
- Grill patties on a well-oiled grill.
- Baste each side of patties with olive oil while grilling and sprinkle with salt and pepper.
- Warm pita bread in an oven before serving.
- Place two of the half-moon patties on each piece of pita bread then top with cucumber sauce.
- Fold pita bread over.
- To make sauce thoroughly mix all ingredients together in a bowl then cover and refrigerate.

188.   Lamb Burgers With Seasonal Salad Recipe

Serving: 1 | Prep: | Cook: 50mins | Ready in:

Ingredients

- 1/2 lb (250g) minced lamb
- 1 large garlic clove (crushed or very finely chopped)
- 1 small red chilli pepper (deseeded and very finely chopped)
- 1/2 small red onion
- Tbsp of fresh mint (finely chopped)
- 1/2 small beaten free range organic egg
- salt and freshly ground black pepper
- A little plain flour for dusting
- sunflower oil for frying
- 6oz (150g) small new potatoes
- Handful of lamb's lettuce
- 3 closed cup mushrooms (quartered downwards through the stem)
- 6 radishes (halved)

Direction

- Put the potatoes, whole and unpeeled, on to boil in lightly salted water.
- Put all the burger ingredients in to a large bowl and mix thoroughly by hand.
- Split the mixture in two and form two round balls, subsequently and carefully flattening them in to burger shapes.
- Heat up a little sunflower oil in a non-stick pan.
- Dust the burgers with flour and fry gently for ten minutes each side, turning only once.
- When the potatoes are ready (they take about twenty-five minutes,) drain them well and allow them to cool a little while your burgers finish cooking.
- Just before the burgers are ready, half the potatoes and mix them with the other salad ingredients.
- Serve your meal.

189. Lamb Kofta Kabab Between In Khabsa Rice Burger With Tomato Parsley Salsa And Mutable Recipe

Serving: 0 | Prep: | Cook: 35mins | Ready in:

Ingredients

- For The lamb Kofta Kabab
- Minced lamb   : 100 gm
- onions, finely diced   : 15 gm
- garlic, minced   ; 02 gm
- Chopped fresh parsley   : 10 gm
- ground cinnamon   ; ½ gm
- ground allspice   : ½ gm
- salt   ; 01 gm
- white pepper   : 01 gm
- plain breadcrumbs   : 30 gm
- egg whites   : 01 no
- For The Khabsa rice Burger
- basmati rice   : 200gm
- carrots, peeled and finely diced   : 10 gm
- green pepper, seeded and finely diced   : 05 gm
- tomatoes, peeled and diced   : 100 gm
- Chopped onions   : 10 gm
- garlic cloves, minced   : 05 gm
- ground cumin   : 01 gm
- ground coriander   : 01 gm
- salt   : 05 gm
- black pepper   : 01 gm
- butter   : 50 gm
- toasted pine nuts   : 02 gm
- Ground green cardamoms   : 01 gm
- ground cinnamon   : 01 gm
- ground allspice   : 01 gm
- Ground dried limes   : 01 gm
- For The tomato parsley Salsa:
- tomatoes   : 100 gm
- parsley   : 10 gm
- balsamic vinegar   : 50 ml
- salt   : 01 gm
- black pepper   : 01 gm
- lemon juice   : 10 ml
- For The Mutable
- eggplants   : 100 gm
- tahini paste   : 50 gm
- lemon   : 10 Ml
- salt   ; 01 gm
- white pepper   : 01 gm
- virgin olive oil   : 10 ml
- garlic, minced   ; 02 gm
- yoghurt   : 50 gm

Direction

- For The Lamb Kofta Kebab Patty
- Combine all of the ingredients, Combine ground beef and seasoning blend in a bowl and mix gently but thoroughly to combine. Divide mixture into 4 even portions and pat each portion into a flattened patty. Preheat grill to medium high. Grill beef burgers about 3 to 4 minutes per side for medium rare. Alternatively, heat a broiler to 500 degrees F and position an oven rack about 6 inches from the broiler unit. Line a baking sheet with aluminum foil and position an ovenproof rack on top of the baking sheet. Place the burgers on the rack and broil until just cooked through, 6 to 7 minutes. Keep aside.
- For The Kabsa Rice Burger
- Place chopped onion and olive oil in a big pan on high heat. Stir till the onion color changes, add spices and stir. Add tomato juice and paste, green pepper, chilli powder, cinnamon stick, dried lemon, and lemon slice and stir them well till boil. Add the soaked rice into the boiling stock along with chopped coriander and cook covered over low heat or until liquid is absorbed. Place the butter pieces on the top of the rice. Cover the pan and cook the kabsa rice on low flame for about 20-30 minutes. Stir together rice, breadcrumbs Shape rice mixture into thick patties. Dredge in remaining breadcrumbs. Cook rice cakes, in 2 batches, in hot oil in a large non-stick skillet over medium-high heat 2 to 3 minutes on each side

or until golden brown and crispy. Drain on a paper towel-lined wire rack.
- For Tomato Parsley Salsa:
- Roughly chop tomatoes and parsley. Combine all salt and pepper and stir. Add lemon juice and dash of vinegar. Mix. Add more salt and pepper to taste.
- For The Mutable
- To make the Mutable: Preheat oven to 400 degrees. Cover cookie sheet with foil and pierce the eggplants with a fork to avoid explosion. Bake for 40-45 minutes. When eggplants are finished cooking take out of oven and cool until they can be handled. Peel eggplants, cut in half and remove seeds. Place in food processor and sprinkle with lemon juice. Add tahini, yogurt, garlic and salt and a drizzle of olive oil. Process until smooth. Drizzle with olive oil and garnish with parsley.
- Assembly
- Take Plate Arrange Kabsa Rice burger keep between Kofta kebab drizzle on top Salsa and accommodate Mutable, Onion salad and French fries.

190.   Lamb Mushroom Burgers Recipe

Serving: 3 | Prep: | Cook: 15mins | Ready in:

Ingredients

- 0.8 lb. ground lamb
- Approximately 8 oz. cremini mushrooms
- 2 tsp. worcestershire sauce, plus more to taste
- 1/4 cup red wine
- 1/4 cup water
- salt and pepper to taste
- cooking spray

Direction

- Coarsely chop about 1 cup of the mushrooms. Slice the rest and set aside.

- Mix the chopped mushrooms in a bowl with the lamb and 2 tsp. Worcestershire sauce. I find the best way to mix the stuff up is with your hands. Season with salt and pepper to taste.
- Shape the mixture into 3 fairly thick patties. Give the surfaces of the patties a liberal dusting with fresh-ground black pepper.
- Coat a non-stick skillet with cooking spray and heat it over medium high heat. Cook the patties until done (5 minutes per side for medium). Remove to a plate and keep warm.
- Add wine, water, and sliced mushrooms to the pan. Stir and cook until the liquid is reduced and the mushrooms are tender. Add salt, pepper, and additional Worcestershire sauce to taste. Serve burgers with mushrooms and sauce spooned over them.

191.   Lamb Burgers Recipe

Serving: 4 | Prep: | Cook: 10mins | Ready in:

Ingredients

- lamb miced 1lb
- onion x 1 finely diced
- garlic x 2 cloves minced
- green chillies x 2 finely chopped
- 2 tsp ground cumin
- 2 tsp paprika
- 1/2 tsp cinnamon
- salt & pepper

Direction

- Add all the ingredients together
- Season well
- Shape into patties
- Cook to your liking

192. Lemon Dill Chicken Burgers Recipe

Serving: 4 | Prep: | Cook: 15mins | Ready in:

Ingredients

- 1.5 - 2 lbs. ground chicken (or turkey), both white and dark meat to keep moist during grilling
- 1/2 c finely chopped yellow onion
- 2 T chopped fresh dill
- 1.5 T fresh squeezed lemon juice
- 1.5 t grated lemon zest
- Salt and fresh ground pepper
- vegetable oil for grill rack
- 4 slices havarti cheese
- 4 keiser or sourdough rolls, or other good hamburger buns
- butter - softened
- 1 ripe, red tomato, cut into 4 slices
- Red leaf or romaine lettuce

Direction

- Combine chicken, onion, dill, lemon juice and zest in large mixing bowl with hands
- Lightly sprinkle with salt and pepper and mix well
- Break into 4 equal balls and shape into patties
- Oil grill rack and arrange 4-5 inches from heat source
- Grill burgers on high until cooked through, internal temperature should be 165. About 5 minutes per side. Careful to turn only once, and avoid mashing!
- Top each burger with a slice of cheese and cook one minute longer - until cheese melts
- Spread butter on insides of bun and toast on the grill
- Serve with tomato and lettuce

193. Lemongrass Burgers With Beef Or Pork Recipe

Serving: 4 | Prep: | Cook: 10mins | Ready in:

Ingredients

- 1/2 pound ground beef or pork
- 2 tablespoons finely chopped fresh lemongrass
- 2 tablespoons finely chopped green onion
- 2 tablespoons finely chopped cilantro
- 1 tablespoon finely chopped garlic
- 1 tablespoon vegetable oil
- 1 tablespoon Vietnamese fish sauce
- 2 teaspoons soy sauce
- 1/2 teaspoon sugar
- 1/2 teaspoon salt
- 1/4 teaspoon black pepper
- DIPPING SAUCE:
- 1 tablespoon chopped garlic
- 2 tablespoons sugar
- 1 teaspoon crushed red pepper flakes
- 3 tablespoons fish sauce
- 3 tablespoons water
- 2 tablespoons fresh squeezed lime juice

Direction

- In a bowl, combine the ground beef with lemongrass, green onions, cilantro, garlic, oil, fish sauce, soy sauce, sugar, salt and pepper, and mix well. Refrigerate for at least 1 hour for flavors to combine.
- Build a hot charcoal fire. Divide mixture into four chunks and shape into patties. Cook on the hot grill until nicely browned and cooked to your liking, about 4-5 minutes per side. Serve in Bibb lettuce leaves with dipping sauce.
- Dipping Sauce:
- Combine all ingredients in a jar with a tight lid. Shake vigorously until sugar dissolves.

194. Lima Bean Patties Recipe

Serving: 8 | Prep: | Cook: 10mins | Ready in:

Ingredients

- 2 cups frozen lima beans
- 1/4 cup roughly chopped chives
- small handful of cilantro leaves
- small handful of parsley leaves
- 1/2 teaspoon ground cumin
- 2 garlic cloves, chopped
- salt and pepper, to taste
- pinch red pepper flakes
- 1 tablespoon flour
- some minced onion or shallot

Direction

- Cook lima beans in boiling water for about 5 minutes or steam until softened but not mushy.
- Drain and run under cold water to stop the cooking.
- In a food processor, combine all ingredients, except flour.
- Process to a finely chopped consistency.
- Adjust seasoning, if necessary.
- Transfer mixture to a bowl and stir in 1 tablespoon of flour.
- Form patties and sauté in an oiled skillet until browned on both sides.
- Place these in pita bread for falafels or wraps and add the fixins you like!

195. Loris Bodacious Big N Beefy Bluecheese Steak Burgers Recipe

Serving: 6 | Prep: | Cook: 24mins | Ready in:

Ingredients

- blue cheese FILLING
- 4 oz cream cheese, softened
- 4 oz crumbled blue cheese
- 1/2 c shredded colby Jack cheese
- juice froma lemon wedge
- 1 T Worcestershire
- Sprinkle fresh chives
- BURGERS
- 2 1/2 lbs ground sirloin
- 1 package beefy onion soup mix
- Generous shakes of seasoned salt and garlic pepper
- 1 T chopped roasted garlic (from jar is fine)
- 1/2 c grated parmesan cheese
- 4 T Worcestershire
- 2 t liquid smoke
- 1 egg
- 1/4 c breadcrumbs
- GARNISHES
- Romaine Letuce
- Thick cut ripe red tomatoes
- Good thick cut dill pickles
- Sliced red onion
- Great deli rolls, buttered and grilled

Direction

- Mix blue cheese filling with hands and form into disks about 3 inches in diameter, set in freezer
- Mix burger mixture together with hands and form into 6 patties, about 1/2 inch thick and 4-5 inches in diameter
- Place a cheese disk on top of each patty, and work the edges of the meat up over the disk until it is enclosed in the patty
- Heat grill while patties come to room temperature
- Grill over direct, medium heat, 10-12 minutes per side for a burger that is brown all the way through.
- ****NOTES*****
- Burger tips I learned on Food Network that have made a huge difference
- 1 Allow the meat to come to room temperature before grilling
- 2 Turn only once during the cooking process
- 3 Resist all urges to mash on the patties with the spatula while cooking

- 4 Let the patties be an uneven circle, those little crooks and crannies on the edges help it to cook evenly

196. Loris Mac Daddy Burgers N Secret Sauce Recipe

Serving: 6 | Prep: | Cook: 15mins | Ready in:

Ingredients

- MAC DADDY SECRET SAUCE (OR 1000 ISLAND DRESSING)
- 1 cup real mayonnaise - Dukes
- 1/3 cup Heinz 57
- 1/8 cup sweet pickle relish
- 1/8 cup Vlassic dill pickle relish
- 2 green onions, minced
- 1 hard boiled egg, chopped ** (I omit this for burgers, but use for salad dressing) **
- 1/2 teaspoon paprika
- 2 tablespoons chives, minced
- 2 teaspoons fresh parsley, minced
- salt and pepper to taste
- Tabasco sauce - to taste
- MACDADDY BURGERS
- 2 LB ground sirloin
- 2 T Worcestershire
- 2 T minced garlic
- Dash Tobasco
- Dash Heinz 57
- 1 beaten egg
- panko bread crumbs to texture
- Pinch kosher salt
- Couple turns ground black pepper
- GARNISHES
- Good, thick cut dill pickles, romaine lettuce, Big red tomato slices
- Sliced Havarrti or Smoked Cheddar, Thick-cut cooked bacon
- Sliced red onion
- Onion or kaiser rolls

Direction

- Sauce:
- Mix all ingredients, chill for about an hour
- Burgers:
- Mix all ingredients by hand in large mixing bowl.
- Form into 6 patties
- Grill over medium heat
- Turn only once
- Approximately 8-10 minutes per side, or to your liking
- DON'T MASH with the flipper, this dries out the burgers!!!
- Brush a little melted butter on the rolls and grill
- Top each burger with sauce and desired garnishes

197. Loris Rockin Barbq Blt N More Burgers Recipe

Serving: 8 | Prep: | Cook: 15mins | Ready in:

Ingredients

- BURGERS:
- 2 1/2 pounds ground chuck or sirloin, 15-20% fat for juicy burgers
- 1 beaten egg
- seasoned Salt
- garlic pepper
- Pinch cayenne pepper
- 1/4 t dried red pepper flakes, crushed
- 1/2 packet golden mushroom soup mix
- 1/2 c parmesan cheese
- 1/2 c grated colby jack cheese
- 1 T BBQ Sauce (posted - lori's almost homemade, or bubba's)
- 2 T worcestershire sauce
- 1/4 c BBQ Sauce, as above
- (Loris Almost Homemade Bbq Sauce)
- Bubbas Bbq Sauce)
- TOPPING:
- 1/2 pound thick cut, peppered bacon, cut into thirds

- 1/2 large red onion, cut in rings and halved
- 1/2 tub fresh mushrooms, wiped clean and sliced
- 1 c grated colby/jack or pepper jack cheese
- GARNISHES:
- Thick cut, good, dill pickles
- Ripe, Red tomato slices
- romaine lettuce leaves
- spicy brown mustard
- Mayo
- Kiaser or Onion rolls
- 2 T melted butter
- Cooler of beer

Direction

- BURGERS:
- Mix all ingredients, except 1/4 c BBQ, by hand in large mixing bowl
- Shape into 8 patties
- Grill to desired doneness, turning only once - do not mash with spatula!
- Baste burgers with 1/4 c BBQ Sauce last few minutes
- TOPPING:
- Cut bacon into thirds, fry till partially done
- Remove bacon from skillet
- Drain grease
- Return back on to skillet, add onions and mushrooms
- When bacon and veggies are done, add shredded cheese
- TO SERVE:
- Melt butter and brush on insides of rolls, then place on grill
- Place desired garnishes on bottom bun, top with burgers, and bacon topping, and top bun
- Serve on the deck with a cooler of beer handy!

198.	MINTED SALMON BURGERS Recipe

Serving: 4 | Prep: | Cook: 10mins | Ready in:

Ingredients

- Ingredients:
- 4 (10oz) baking potatoes, peeled and cubed
- 3 Tbs. water
- 1 medium leek, diced
- 2 (7 ½ oz) cans pink salmon, drained and flaked
- 2 ½ Tbs. minced fresh mint, divided
- 2 tsp. Prepared horseradish
- ½ tsp. Freshly ground pepper
- 1/3 cup dry breadcrumbs
- 2 Tbs. grated parmesan cheese
- Non-Stick cooking spray

Direction

- 1) Preheat oven to 375°.
- 2) Cook potatoes in boiling water 15 minutes or until tender. Drain well, and mash; set aside.
- 3) Combine 3 Tbs. water and leek in a non-stick skillet; cook over medium heat 4 minutes or until leek is soft and water evaporates, stirring constantly. Combine leek, potatoes, salmon, 1 ½ Tbs. mint, horseradish, and pepper; stir well. Shape mixture into 8 patties.
- 4) Combine remaining 1 Tbs. mint, breadcrumbs, and cheese; dredge salmon patties in mixture. Place patties on a baking sheet coated with cooking spray. Bake at 375° for 20 minutes, turning after 10 minutes.

199.	Made Rights Spicy Sweet Messiness Recipe

Serving: 5 | Prep: | Cook: 2hours | Ready in:

Ingredients

- 2 LB ground beef
- 1 sweet onion - Diced
- 3/4 Cup Hot banana peppers - Diced
- salt
- Pepper

- 1 Tablespoon sugar
- 2 cloves garlic Minced/pureed
- 3/4 -1 Cup Hot banana pepper juice
- 1/2 Cup beef stock
- 10 - 15 Thinly sliced provolone cheese

Direction

- Brown Beef with Onions. Drain return to skillet. Add diced banana peppers, Salt, Pepper, Garlic, and Sugar. Cook on high heat for about 3 min then reduce heat to medium-low add Banana pepper juice and beef stock. Cook covered partially for about 1 hr. or so stirring often and watching for the liquids to go away. Once liquid has cooked off serve on a bun or in a sub roll, cover with cheese while hot.
- Enjoy!

200.   Maid Rites Loose Hamburgers Recipe

Serving: 3 | Prep: | Cook: 15mins |Ready in:

Ingredients

- 1 1/2 pounds ground beef
- 1 small or medium onion, diced fine
- salt and pepper
- pickles
- mustard
- Miracle Whip
- ketcup
- slice cheeese
- hamburger buns

Direction

- Brown the beef and onion. Drain the excess fat.
- On a hamburger add the beef and your add ons.
- What I've been told that you could melt the cheese on the bun.

201.   Mar A Lago Turkey Burger Recipe

Serving: 8 | Prep: | Cook: 14mins |Ready in:

Ingredients

- * 1/4 cup scallions, thinly sliced
- * 1/2 cup celery, finely chopped
- * 3 granny smith apples, peeled and diced
- * 1/8 cup canola oil
- * 4 pounds ground turkey breast
- * 2 Tbsp. salt
- * 1 Tbsp. black pepper
- * 2 tsp. chipotle Tabasco™
- * 1 lemon, juice and grated zest
- * 1/2 bunch parsley, finely chopped
- * 1/4 cup Major Grey's chutney, pureed
- Mar-a-Lago pear chutney
- * 1 Anjou pear, peeled and diced
- * 1/2 tsp. cinnamon
- * 1 tsp. sea salt
- * 1 1/2 cups Major Grey's chutney
- * 1/4 cup dried currants or raisins
- Preheat oven to 350°.
- Toss the diced pears with the cinnamon and salt. Bake on a parchment-lined cookie sheet for 10 minutes.
- Cool and mix with the chutney and currants or raisins.

Direction

- Sauté the scallions, celery and apples in the canola oil until tender. Let cool.
- Place the ground turkey in a large mixing bowl. Add sautéed items and the remaining ingredients. Shape into eight 8-ounce burgers. Refrigerate for 2 hours.
- Season the turkey burgers with salt and pepper. Place on a preheated, lightly oiled grill. Grill each side for 7 minutes until meat is thoroughly cooked. Let sit for 5 minutes.

- Serve with a side of Mar-a-Lago Pear Chutney and your favorite toasted bread, pita or hamburger roll.

---

202. Masala Tofu Burger Recipe

Serving: 4 | Prep: | Cook: 30mins | Ready in:

Ingredients

- * 1 medium white onion- finely chopped
- * 1 red/orange/green bell pepper- finely diced
- * 1 cup frozen peas-carrots mix (thawed)
- * 3-4 small green chillies (not serrano)
- * 3/4 cup firm cubed tofu (I used Nasoya Brand)- drained well
- * 1 medium potato- boils, peeled, diced
- * 1-2 cloves garlic- minced
- * 1/2 tbsp black mustard seeds
- * 4-5 curry leaves
- * pinch hing (Asafoetida optional)
- * 1 tsp cumin powder
- * 1 tsp turmeric
- * 1 lemon
- * 1 tsp salt (or to taste)
- * 1/2 bunch cilantro- washed-finely chopped
- * 1/2-3/4 cup Indian breadcrumbs (recipe below)
- * 1/2 tbsp vegetable oil
- * PAM original flavor
- * 1 red/white onion- cut into thick slices
- * 1-2 beefsteak tomatoes- cut into thick slices
- * few sprigs of cilantro
- * 1/2 cup mint-cilantro chutney spread (recipe below)
- * 4 Portugese rolls (Or anything you like)- toasted
- (chutney & breadcrumbs recipe on my site: http://chefpriyanka.com)

Direction

- 1. In a large skillet over medium-high heat, add spray with a generous amount of PAM and add oil. Add mustard seeds and sauté for 30 seconds-till you hear popping noises. Add curry leaves- BE CAREFUL, they pop hot oil! Add onions and peppers- sweat for about 30 seconds. Add chopped garlic, chilies and turmeric. Sauté for about 5-7 minutes, until the onions and peppers are soft. Add peas and carrots mixture, cumin powder and salt. Sauté for about 7-10 minutes- you want all the veggies to be soft and cooked through. 2. Meanwhile in a small bowl, add the cubed tofu, a pinch of turmeric, cumin powder, coarse black pepper and some cayenne pepper (totally optional!). Mix and set aside to marinate for a bit.
- 3. Once the veggies are cooked, add the tofu- sauté until slightly brown and soft enough that it crumbles. Add juice form half a lemon and half of the chopped cilantro. Mix and add the diced boiled potato, and toss until everything is coated, soft and taste for salt/spices. Using a masher, mash the mixture until mushy and until the veggies are small. Set aside to cool. Once cooled, add a bit of the breadcrumbs and mix with your hands. Start forming into thick patties (mixture should make 4). If it's still giving you a hard time, add more breadcrumbs. Make 4 patties, place on a plate and wrap with plastic wrap until ready to use. 5. In a small skillet sprayed with PAM over medium-high heat, add one patty at a time. Cook for about 2 minutes on each side- until browned and crispy. At the same time, sauté the thick slices of onion, until charred and slightly soft. Spread a generous amount of the chutney spread on each side on the bread, place burger, onions tomato and cilantro leaves. Serve with a slice of lemon and reduced-fat chips on the side.

203. Mcdonald's Big Mac Recipe Recipe

Serving: 1 | Prep: | Cook: 30mins | Ready in:

Ingredients

- McDonald's Big Mac Sauce ingredients:
- 1/4 cup Miracle Whip
- 1/4 cup mayonnaise
- 2 tsp tbsp french salad dressing
- 1/2 tbsp sweet relish
- 2 tsp dill pickle relish
- 1 tsp white sugar
- 1 tsp dried, minced onion
- 1 tsp white vinegar
- 1 tsp ketchup
- 1/8 tsp table salt
- McDonald's Big-Mac Sandwich ingredients:
- 1 sesame seed bun
- 1 plain bun
- 2 beef patties (2 oz each flattened to bun size)
- 2 tbsp McDonald's Big Mac Sauce
- 2 tsp chopped onions
- 1 slice American cheese
- 2 pickle slices
- 1/4 cup shredded lettuce

Direction

- Mix all your sauce ingredients together and place it in the fridge for at least an hour to set all the flavours marinate together.
- Toast your sesame seed bun and the bottom of the plain bun. You don't need the top of the plain bun.
- On the bottom bun you want to add 1 tbsp. of McDonald's Big Mac sauce on it, a tsp. of chopped onions, a handful of chopped lettuce, a slice of American cheese and then one meat patty.
- Next add the exact same ingredients as the first bun to your second bottom bun, but instead of cheese add two pickles and a dash of ketchup, your second hamburger patty and the top of your sesame bun.

204. Meat Loaf Burgers Recipe

Serving: 6 | Prep: | Cook: 9mins | Ready in:

Ingredients

- 1 large onion, sliced
- 1 celery rib, chopped
- 2 lbs lean ground beef
- 1 1/2 teaspoons salt, divided
- 1/4 teaspoon pepper
- 2 cups tomato juice
- 4 garlic cloves, minced
- 1 tablespoon ketchup
- 1 bay leaf
- 1 teaspoon italian seasoning
- 6 hamburger buns, split

Direction

- Place onion and celery in a slower cooker.
- Combine beef, 1 teaspoon salt and pepper; shape into six patties.
- Place over onion mixture.
- Combine tomato juice, garlic, ketchup, bay leaf, Italian seasoning and remaining salt.
- Pour over the patties.
- Cover and cook on low for 7-9 hours or until meat is tender.
- Discard bay leaf.
- Separate patties with a spatula if necessary; serve on buns.
- Yield 6 servings.

205. Meaty Cheese Bella Burgers Recipe

Serving: 6 | Prep: | Cook: 30mins | Ready in:

Ingredients

- 6 large portobello caps(all I did was trim the stem down even with the inside(gills) of the mushroom. I didn't de-stem, and I'm glad I didn't. :-)
- 6 slices provolone or muenster cheese
- 1 clove garlic, minced
- 3T olive oil
- 1T smoked paprika
- fresh ground pepper
- 6 large round sandwich rolls
- sliced onion(I grilled mine a bit, and highly recommend that), fresh spinach, sliced tomato for serving
- Worcestershire Dijon-aise
- About 1 cup mayo
- About 2T Dijon
- About 1T worcestershire sauce
- About 2T fresh chopped chives
- several dashes hot sauce

Direction

- Combine all Worcestershire Dijon-aise ingredients and set aside.
- Combine the minced garlic, paprika, fresh ground pepper and olive oil in small bowl.
- Brush both sides of the mushrooms with the oil mixture.
- Grill over high heat for a couple of minutes each side.
- Add a piece of cheese to top of each and leave on the grill just till the cheese melts.
- Serve on lightly grilled buns with desired condiments and the Worcestershire Mayo.
- *if you want to add salt to the burgers, salt them AFTER you grill them. If you add salt to the marinade, you will lose a lot more liquid when the mushrooms start to cook. So, salt them after!

206. Mediterranean Burgers Recipe

Serving: 4 | Prep: | Cook: 20mins | Ready in:

Ingredients

- 2 pounds ground chuck
- 1/2 teaspoon salt
- 1/2 teaspoon freshly ground black pepper
- 1/4 shredded mozzarella cheese
- 3 tablespoons chopped green olives
- 2 tablespoons grated parmesan cheese
- 2 tablespoons capers
- 2 tablespoons pine nuts
- 2 tablespoons chopped fresh parsley

Direction

- Mix meat with salt and pepper and form into 8 patties.
- Combine remaining ingredients and divide between half the patties.
- Place remaining patties on top and press edges to seal.
- Grill over hot coals turning once halfway through cooking.

207. Memphis Mini Burgers Recipe

Serving: 12 | Prep: | Cook: 10mins | Ready in:

Ingredients

- 1 medium red onion, sliced
- 1 pound lean ground beef
- 1/2 teaspoon onion powder
- 1/4 teaspoon salt
- 1/4 teaspoon freshly ground black pepper
- 12 to 15 small potato rolls, split in 1/2
- mustard sauce, recipe follows
- mustard Sauce:
- 3 tablespoons mayonnaise
- 1 tablespoon Dijon mustard
- 1/2 teaspoon cayenne pepper
- salt and freshly ground black pepper

Direction

- Preheat a flat top grill pan to high heat.
- Add sliced onion to grill pan and cook until tender, about 10 minutes.
- In a medium bowl, mix ground beef, onion powder, salt and freshly ground pepper. Make burgers equal in size, about 2-inches across.
- Cook burgers on the flat top for 3 to 4 minutes on each side.
- Serve on split rolls with grilled onions and mustard sauce.

208. Mexican Beef Burgers Recipe

Serving: 4 | Prep: | Cook: 15mins | Ready in:

Ingredients

- 1/2 cup finely chopped green pepper
- 1/4 cup finely chopped green onion
- 2 small cloves garlic minced
- 1 teaspoon cumin
- 1 teaspoon oregano
- 1/2 teaspoon salt
- 1/2 teaspoon thyme
- 1/2 teaspoon paprika
- 1/4 teaspoon crushed red pepper
- 1 pound ground beef

Direction

- Mix together everything except beef then add beef and mix well.
- Make into patties and grill 15 minutes turning once.
- Serve with your favorite condiments on a toasted bun.

209. Mexican Burgers Recipe

Serving: 4 | Prep: | Cook: 10mins | Ready in:

Ingredients

- 1 egg
- 1/4 cup soft bread crumbs
- 1 1/2 tsp. garlic salt
- 1 tsp. chili powder
- 1 1/2 lbs. ground beef
- 1/3 cup sour cream
- 1/4 tsp. ground cumin
- Dash cayenne pepper
- 1 can (4 oz.) green chiles, seeded, cut in slivers
- 4 slices monterey jack cheese
- 4 onion rolls, split, toasted
- 4 tomato slices
- 4 lettuce leaves
- 4 thin slices red onion

Direction

- Beat egg in a mixing bowl; mix in bread crumbs, garlic salt, and chili powder. Add ground beef. Mix lightly to combine thoroughly. Shape into 4 hamburgers.
- Mix sour cream, cumin, and cayenne. Set aside.
- Grill hamburgers over low glowing coats until first sides are nicely browned; turn. Top each burger with about 1 Tbsp. of the sour cream mixture. Cover with green chilies and a slice of cheese. Continue barbecuing until hamburgers are done to your taste.
- Serve on onion rolls, topping each with a tomato slice, a lettuce leaf, and a slice of onion.

210. Middle Eastern Vegetable Grain Burgers Recipe

Serving: 6 | Prep: | Cook: 10mins | Ready in:

Ingredients

- 1/3 cup uncooked, dried lentils, sorted & rinsed
- 1/4 cup uncooked brown or basmati rice
- 1 T EVOO

- 1 lb. fresh mushrooms, sliced
- 1 medium onion, chopped
- 3/4 cup grated Parmesan
- 3/4 cup walnuts, chopped
- 1/4 cup fresh cilantro
- 2 lg. eggs
- 1/2 t black pepper
- 6 toasted sesame seed buns or toasted pita halves
- plain yogurt
- Sliced red onion
- Shredded lettuce
- Sliced tomatoes

Direction

- Place lentils in medium saucepan; cover with 1-inch water.
- Bring to boil; reduce heat to low & simmer, covered for 25-35 minutes until tender.
- Rinse; drain & set aside.
- MEANWHILE - cook rice according to package instructions; set aside.
- Heat oil in large skillet over medium heat. Add mushrooms & onion; cook & stir 20-25 minutes until mushrooms are brown.
- Combine mushroom mixture, cheese, walnuts, lentils, rice, cilantro, eggs & pepper in large bowl; mix well, cover & chill.
- Preheat broiler.
- Spray 15 X 10-inch jelly-roll pan with cooking spray.
- Shape lentil mixture into 6 1/2-inch thick patties. Arrange patties on prepared pan.
- Broil 4 inches from heat 3-4 minutes each side or until golden brown, turning once.
- Serve on buns/pitas with yogurt, red onion, lettuce tomatoes or whatever condiments you'd like.

211.   Mini Greek Burgers Recipe

Serving: 4 | Prep: | Cook: 30mins | Ready in:

Ingredients

- Sauce:
- 3/4c shredded,seeded,peeled cucumber
- 1/2c plain yogurt
- 2tsp lemon juice
- 2tsp snipped fresh dill
- 1 garlic clove,minced
- 1/4tsp salt
- 1/8tsp pepper
- Burgers:
- 3Tbs fine chopped onion
- 3Tbs minced fresh parsley
- 3/4tsp dried oregano
- 1/4tsp salt
- 1/4tsp pepper
- 1lb. ground turkey or lamb
- 4 pita breads(6"),halved and warmed
- 2 med. tomaotes,thin sliced

Direction

- In small bowl, combine first seven ingredients. Cover and refrigerate till serving.
- In a large bowl, combine onion, parsley, oregano, salt and pepper. Crumble turkey or lamb over mixture and mix well. Shape into sixteen 2" patties
- Coat grill rack with cooking spray before starting the grill. Grill burgers, covered over med. heat for 2 to 3 mins. on each side or till no longer pink. Serve in pita halves with tomatoes and reserved sauce.
- To make things easier, can use prepared Tzatziki sauce.

212.   Mini Salmon Burgers With Wasabi Sauce Recipe

Serving: 8 | Prep: | Cook: 6mins | Ready in:

Ingredients

- 1 pound boneless, skinless fresh salmon
- 1 / 4 cup dry bread crumbs

- 2 green onions, minced, divided
- 1/4 cup diced red pepper
- 1 teaspoon minced fresh ginger
- 1 teaspoon dill
- 1 / 8 teaspoon salt
- 1 / 4 teaspoon pepper
- 1 cup finely shredded iceberg lettuce
- 1 tablespoon minced cilantro
- tomato, sliced.
- 1 / 4 cup mayonnaise
- 1 teaspoon wasabi powder or paste (found in international food aisle)
- 8 whole-wheat dinner rolls or white (about 2 1 / 2 to 3 inches in diameter), split and lightly toasted . These are found in your bread aisle.

Direction

- Chill salmon well or place in freezer about 30 minutes or until very cold. Mince finely and place in mixing bowl. Add bread crumbs, 1 green onion, red pepper, dill, ginger, salt, pepper and egg white. Stir well. Shape into 8 patties, each 2 1 / 2 to 3 inches in diameter.
- Prepare the wasabi mayo by just blending the wasabi with the mayo and a few Tbsp. of green onion.
- Preheat grill or allow coals to burn down to white ash. Spray grill grate with non-stick spray coating. Grill patties over medium-high direct heat 2 to 3 minutes per side or until patties are lightly browned and set; do not overcook.
- Meanwhile, combine lettuce, cilantro and remaining green onion for your topping mix.
- Spread about 1 1/2 teaspoons mayonnaise mixture on each roll. Top with salmon patty and about 2 tablespoons lettuce mixture.
- Add tomato.
- Serve immediately

213.   Mojo Burgers Recipe

Serving: 6 | Prep: | Cook: 10mins | Ready in:

Ingredients

- 1 pound ground chuck
- 1/4 cup crumbled bleu cheese
- 1 heaping tablespoon regular coffee, ground extra fine
- 1 heaping tablespoon chili powder, or to taste
- 1 teaspoon brown or Dijon-style mustard
- 1/4 cup green onions, both green and white parts, chopped fine
- 1 small jalapeno pepper, seeds removed, sliced thinly
- 1/4 cup red pepper, chopped fine
- 1 tablespoon worcestershire sauce

Direction

- Directions:
- Put all the ingredients into a large mixing bowl and mix gently.
- Form into four large or six medium patties and cook.
- Any method will do: from frying in a hot skillet, broiling, or grilling outdoors.
- Serve with or without a bun, lettuce, onions and tomatoes as topping.

214.   Montreal Bacon N Cheddar Burgers Recipe

Serving: 6 | Prep: | Cook: 20mins | Ready in:

Ingredients

- 1/2 lb bacon
- 1 lb 85% lean ground beef
- 1 lb 93% lean ground beef
- 1/4 t liquid smoke
- 2 t montreal steak seasoning
- 2 t worcestershire
- 1 pkg beefy onion soup mix
- garlic pepper
- seasoned salt
- 1 c shredded cheddar (rough shred)
- 1 c shredded white cheddar (rough shred)

- 1 med onion
- 1 small tub sliced fresh mushrooms
- 1/2 red bell pepper (options)
- 2 T butter or margarine, softened
- Large Onion or kaiser rolls
- GARNISHES
- Large, ripe red tomato
- Real Mayo
- spicy mustard
- romaine lettuce leaves

Direction

- BURGERS
- Pre-heat grill to med heat
- Lightly oil grill rack, or spray with Pam
- Turn non-stick skillet on med-high heat
- Cut bacon into 1/2 - 1 inch pieces (This is easier if the bacon is frozen - sit on the counter about 10 minutes before you are ready to cut, and put in the pan frozen, it will fall into the cut pieces as it gets hot) and add to skillet; cook until crispy and drain on paper towel lined plate
- Shred cheese while bacon cooks
- Add ground beef, seasonings, bacon and cheese to large mixing bowl
- Mix together with hands until well blended
- *Shape into 6 large patties - the meat will draw up as it cooks, have them a little flatter than you want the finished burgers
- Turn heat down to low, and add burgers
- Cook about 8-10 minutes each side
- * BURGER NOTES *
- Don't try to even out all the crevices in the side of the burger, they help them to cook more evenly
- Turn only once
- Do NOT mash with the flipper - that makes for drier burgers
- The cheese will cause some flaming and smoking, keep a squirt bottle with water handy, and spray once or twice if needed
- WHILE BURGERS COOK
- Slice onions into thin rings and sauté with mushrooms in bacon drippings - or EVOO, etc.

- (Slice pepper into think rings if using, and sauté with onion and mushrooms)
- Drain on paper towel lined plate, if needed
- Butter the insides of the rolls and grill
- PUT IT TOGETHER
- Grill burgers to 160* internal temp
- Top with onion mixture and your fave garnishes
- *Flavored mayos would be good!*

---

215.   Mouth Watering Burgers Recipe

Serving: 8 | Prep: | Cook: 30mins | Ready in:

Ingredients

- 2 pounds hamburger meat
- 2 eggs
- 8 saltine crackers, finely crumbled
- 1/2 packet Liptons Beefy onion soup mix
- 2 tablespoons worchestershire sauce
- 2 cups shredded cheddar cheese

Direction

- Mix all the ingredients and form into patties and cook.
- In frying pan heat to med heat, turning every few minutes till desired doneness.
- Perfect for grilling on the "Q", or for the George Foreman.

---

216.   Mozzarella Beef Burgers Recipe

Serving: 4 | Prep: | Cook: 22mins | Ready in:

Ingredients

- 1 lb ground beef

- 1/2 cup low-moisture part-skim mozzarella cheese
- 1/2 cup fresh bread crumbs
- 1/4 cup original flavor barbecue sauce, divided
- 4 hamburger buns

Direction

- Preheat the grill to medium-high heat.
- Mix the meat, cheese, bread crumbs, and 2 tbsp. of the barbecue sauce. Shape into 4 patties.
- Place patties on the grill and then cover the grill with the lid.
- Grill 4 to 6 minutes on each side or until the burgers are cooked through (160 F).
- Brush with remaining 2 tbsp. of the barbecue sauce during the last 2 minutes of grilling time.
- Fill the buns with the burgers

217.　　Mozzarella Stuffed Turkey Burgers Recipe

Serving: 4 | Prep: | Cook: 10mins |Ready in:

Ingredients

- marinara sauce
- 2 teaspoons extra-virgin olive oil
- 1 small onion, finely chopped
- 4 cloves garlic, minced
- 2 cups chopped plum tomatoes, with juices
- 6 oil-packed sun-dried tomatoes, drained and finely chopped
- 1/2 teaspoon salt
- 1/2 teaspoon freshly ground pepper
- 2 tablespoons chopped fresh basil
- Burgers
- 1 pound 93%-lean ground turkey
- 1/4 cup finely chopped scallions
- 2 teaspoons minced garlic
- 2 teaspoons worcestershire sauce

- 1 teaspoon freshly grated lemon zest
- 1/2 teaspoon dried oregano
- 1/2 teaspoon freshly ground pepper
- 1/4 teaspoon salt
- 1/2 cup shredded part-skim mozzarella cheese, divided
- 2 tablespoons finely chopped fresh basil
- 2 teaspoons extra-virgin olive oil
- 4 4-inch-square slices foccacia bread (about 2 ounces
- each), toasted

Direction

- To prepare marinara: Heat 2 teaspoons oil in a medium saucepan over medium heat.
- Add onion and garlic, cover and cook, stirring frequently, until translucent, 5 to 7 minutes.
- Stir in fresh tomatoes and any juices, sun-dried tomatoes, 1/2 teaspoon salt and 1/2 teaspoon pepper.
- Bring to a simmer and cook, stirring occasionally, until the tomatoes have broken down, 8 to 10 minutes.
- Stir in basil and remove from the heat.
- Transfer to a food processor and pulse to form a coarse-textured sauce.
- Return to the pan and set aside.
- To prepare burgers: Place turkey, scallions, garlic, Worcestershire sauce, lemon zest, oregano, 1/2 teaspoon pepper and 1/4 teaspoon salt in a large bowl.
- Gently combine, without overmixing, until evenly incorporated.
- Form into 8 thin patties about 4-inches wide and 3/8 inch thick. Combine 1/4 cup cheese and basil and place an equal amount in the center of 4 patties.
- Cover with the remaining patties and crimp the edges closed.
- Heat 2 teaspoons oil in a large non-stick skillet over medium heat (see Grilling Variation).
- Add burgers and cook, turning once, until an instant-read thermometer inserted in the center registers 165 F, 8 to 10 minutes total.
- Warm the marinara on the stove.

- To assemble the burgers, spread 3 tablespoons of marinara on each toasted focaccia, top with a burger, about3 more tablespoons of marinara and 1 tablespoon of the remaining cheese.
- Grilling Variation: To grill the turkey burgers, preheat a grill to medium-high.
- Oil the grill rack
- Grill the patties, turning once, until an instant-read thermometer inserted in the center registers 165 F, 8 to 10 minutes total.

218. Mpiftekia Greek Burgers Recipe

Serving: 6 | Prep: | Cook: 45mins | Ready in:

Ingredients

- 1 kilo ground beef
- 2 eggs
- salt, pepper
- 250 gr. bread soaked in water
- 1 big onion grated
- 1 clove of garlic (optional)
- 2 - 4 pinches oregano
- ½ bunch of parsley finely chopped
- 1 table spoonful of olive oil
- 1 table spoonful of while dry wine
- 2 table spoonfuls of milk
- bread crumbs (if necessary)

Direction

- We put the bread in a bowl with water and when it has soaked we remove the crust and squeeze to remove water.
- Mince onion in the multi together with the milk. Add all other ingredients and refrigerate 3 or 4 hours, if possible.
- Form burgers into 2 cm. thick patties (if necessary add the bread crumbs) and can either grill them in the oven or for outdoors grill preheat in high heat, lightly oil grate, place burgers on grill. Cook for approximately 6 minutes, turning once)

- They are served hot with lemon juice and slices of onions mixed with parsley. For the children try the American style in a bun with ketchup and their favourite vegetables.

219. Munchable Mini Burgers With Flavorful Fruit Dips Recipe

Serving: 6 | Prep: | Cook: 8mins | Ready in:

Ingredients

- For Sweet tomato Dip:
- 1 can (8 ounces) crushed pineapple
- 1/4 cup ketchup
- For Tangy peach Dip:
- 1 can (15 ounces) peaches in juice, drained
- 2 teaspoons mustard, yellow or brown
- 2 teaspoons honey
- For apricot Mayo:
- 1 can (8 ounces) apricot halves, in light syrup
- 2 tablespoons mayonnaise, light or regular
- 1 teaspoon honey
- 1/8 teaspoon vanilla extract
- For the Burgers:
- 1 can (15 ounces) sweet potatoes (or yams) in syrup drained
- 1 tablespoon canned tomato paste
- 1 pound ground turkey or lean beef
- Spray vegetable oil
- 1 roll (7.5 ounces) refrigerated, lower-fat buttermilk biscuits, baked to package directions

Direction

- To make any dip or mayo: Purée the canned ingredients in a food processor, blender or immersion blender and mix in remaining ingredients; set aside.
- To make burgers: Mash sweet potatoes and tomato paste in mixing bowl with a fork. Mix in the ground turkey or beef until thoroughly

blended. Portion in 1/4-cup portions and form into 1/4- to 1/2-inch thick burgers, about 3-inches across.

- Heat a heavy skillet over medium-high heat and spray with oil. Cook burgers covered until no longer pink inside, about 4 minutes per side. The internal temperature of the patties should be 160°F.
- To serve: Split biscuits horizontally and make sandwiches with burgers. Serve dips or mayo for dipping.

220. My Bestest Garlicky Burgers Recipe

Serving: 6 | Prep: | Cook: 20mins | Ready in:

Ingredients

- 1-1/2 to 2 pounds lean ground beef (You can use any lean ground meat you like. Even a mixture of meats is good.)
- 4 - 5 garlic cloves, minced
- 1 Tablespoon extra virgin olive oil
- a good squirt of Heinz 57 Sauce or A1 Sauce
- 1/4 cup seasoned bread crumbs or if you don't have bread crumbs handy...shred 1 slice of bread
- 1-1/2 teaspoons onion powder
- 1 teaspoon salt
- 1 teaspoon black pepper
- 1 Tablespoon fresh or dried parsley
- 1/2 teaspoon fresh or dried basil leaves
- 6 whole wheat hamburger buns, split or if you have allergies you could use 2 slices of Spelt bread - even as a substitute for the bread crumbs.
- *Let mixture sit covered in the fridge for at least 1/2 hour so that all the ingredients get infused into the meat.

Direction

- Preheat your outdoor BBQ on high heat or preheat your skillet on the stovetop.

- Mix together all the above mentioned ingredients, except for the hamburger buns
- Divide the mixture into 5 or 6 balls (depending on the appetites), and flatten into patties.
- Cook patties for about 10 minutes on each side, or to your personal doneness.
- The internal temperature should be at least 160/170 degrees F (70 degrees C).
- Remove from BBQ or skillet and place on burger buns.
- Add your desired toppings and condiments. We like either Spanish or Red onions, sauerkraut (rinsed, drained and gently warmed in the frying pan), dill pickles, ketchup or salsa, relish and for those who like mustard any type will do. Lettuce instead of sauerkraut works well too ;-)
- Note: Always make certain the burgers have been cooked completely. Especially those cooked for young children or the elderly as they are more fragile. E. coli is a dreadful bacteria and has terrible and sometimes fatal consequences.

221. Nacho Burger Recipe

Serving: 4 | Prep: | Cook: 15mins | Ready in:

Ingredients

- 2 medium tomatoes diced
- 1/2 cup red onion diced
- 2 teaspoons fresh jalapeno pepper chopped
- 2 teaspoons fresh cilantro minced fine
- 1/4 teaspoon salt
- 2 small avocados
- 2 tablespoons sour cream
- 1/4 cup tomato diced
- 1/2 teaspoon jalapeno diced
- 1/4 teaspoon fresh cilantro chopped
- 1/4 teaspoon lemon juice
- 1/8 teaspoon salt
- 3 ounces ground beef
- 1 teaspoon all purpose flour

- 1/8 teaspoon salt
- 1/4 teaspoon freshly ground black pepper
- 16 ounce jar processed cheese
- 2 tablespoons milk
- 1/2 teaspoon chili powder
- 1/2 teaspoon cumin
- 1/2 teaspoon paprika
- 2 pounds ground beef
- 4 large sesame seed buns
- 2 cups iceberg lettuce shredded
- 2 tablespoons mayonnaise
- 1 green onion chopped
- 20 tortilla chips crumbled
- 3 fresh jalapenos sliced

Direction

- Combine tomatoes, onion, jalapeno, cilantro and salt together in a small bowl and mix well.
- Cover bowl then chill in the refrigerator.
- In a small bowl mash up most of the avocado leaving several chunks that are not mashed.
- Add sour cream, tomato, jalapeno, cilantro, lemon juice and salt and mix well.
- Cover bowl and chill in the refrigerator.
- In yet another small bowl mix together ground beef, flour, salt, black pepper and chili powder.
- Use your hands to work dry ingredients into ground beef.
- Brown beef in a small skillet over medium heat for 5 minutes.
- Use a spoon or spatula to crumble the beef as it cooks then cook until brown and set aside.
- Melt cheese with 2 tablespoons milk over low heat then add chili powder, cumin and paprika.
- Heat while stirring often until cheese is smooth and creamy.
- Cover saucepan and remove from heat.
- Preheat a griddle or large frying pan over medium heat.
- Lightly butter the face of each bun and brown buns face down on the heat.
- Separate ground beef into four portions.
- Roll each portion of meat into a ball then pat down into a circular patty.

- Cook hamburger patties for 10 minutes per side until done.
- Lightly salt and pepper each burger patty.
- Build the burger open faced in the following order.
- On bottom bun lettuce, beef patty, queso, tortilla chips and green onion.
- On top bun mayonnaise, pico de gallo, guacamole and jalapeno slices.
- Serve burger with extra queso and guacamole.

222. ONION RANCH BURGERS Recipe

Serving: 8 | Prep: | Cook: 10mins | Ready in:

Ingredients

- 2 lbs. ground beef
- 1 envelope onion soup mix
- 1-1 oz. pkg. ranch dressing mix
- 1 egg, lightly beaten
- 1 C. quick cooking oatmeal

Direction

- In a bowl mix the ground beef, onion soup mix, ranch dressing mix, egg, and oatmeal.
- Shape into patties.
- Cook as you usually do your hamburgers.

223. Once A Year Cholesterol Busting Burger Recipe

Serving: 3 | Prep: | Cook: 15mins | Ready in:

Ingredients

- 1 pound mixture of ground sirloin and ground chuck
- 4 tablespoons water

- seasonings (I use some garlic salt, pepper and a maybe a bit of steak seasoning)
- 1 large onion, sliced in rings
- 8 slices bacon, fried crisp
- real butter, and lots of it, for frying the onions (about 4 tablespoons)
- American or Velvetta cheese, any cheese that melts creamy (cheddar is a bit too "solid" for the topping – you want the cheese to "drip" off the burger a bit)
- 4 large eggs (why go small on this burger – you're splurging, remember??)
- 4 hamburger buns, cut sides spread with MORE real butter

Direction

- In a medium bowl, GENTLY combine meats with water and seasonings (yes, trust me, the water will give you an unbelievably moist burger), and shape into 3 patties.
- Melt butter in large skillet and fry onions until nicely browned and beginning to caramelize – you don't want a wimpy sauté for these…you want them FRIED.
- Remove onions from skillet and fry bacon in same skillet – no need to clean out first…the flavors blend well.
- Remove bacon from skillet and pour out MOST of the grease, but not all (leave about 1 tablespoon in the pan). Add a pat of butter (come on, you're splurging).
- Fry the burgers in the bacon drippings and butter. Place cheese slice on top of each burger just shortly before done (the cheese will finish melting as the cooked burgers "hold" while the eggs fry)
- While the burgers are frying in all that fat, butter the cut sides of the hamburger buns and toast them in a skillet or place under the broiler to get a nice crispy bun.
- While buns are toasting, finish frying the burgers and then set them aside. Add another pat of butter to that same skillet (we're getting a lot of use out of that one skillet).

- Now fry those eggs in that skillet (I break the yolks, because it's just too messy to eat the burger with the yolk running out).
- You are READY to assemble your masterpiece: bottom buttery toasted bun, cheese-topped burger, 1 fried egg, 2 slices of bacon, fried onions, a squirt of mustard (optional), and top it off with the remaining toasted top bun.
- You'll probably find this burger is easiest eaten with a knife and fork, but if you don't have company, pick it up and let it drip!

---

224.   Onion Burgers Recipe

Serving: 6 | Prep: | Cook: 10mins | Ready in:

Ingredients

- 1 1/2 lb. ground beef
- 1 pouch dry onion soup mix
- 3 Tbs. water

Direction

- Mix thoroughly beef, soup mix and water.
- Shape firmly into 6 patties, 1/2" thick each.
- Cook patties in skillet 10 min. or until done.

---

225.   Open Faced Pizza Burger Recipe

Serving: 4 | Prep: | Cook: 10mins | Ready in:

Ingredients

- Burgers
- 3/4 lb ground chuck
- 1 small white onion, fine dice
- 1 green bell pepper, small dice
- 1 cup chopped baby bellas
- 1/2 tsp fennel seed (optional)
- Pinch of cinnamon
- salt and pepper to taste

- Sauce
- 1 can crushed tomatoes
- 1 tbsp crushed red pepper flakes (optional)
- 1 tbsp minced garlic
- 1 tsp dried basil
- 1 tsp dried oregano
- 1/2 tsp sweet paprika
- Pinch of cinnamon
- Buns:
- 4 slices thick, hearty bread (I used sourdough..cause I like it.)
- 2-3 tbsp butter, margarine, whatever
- 1 tbsp chopped parsley
- garlic powder, to taste
- 4 oz shredded cheese of your choice

Direction

- Mix all burger ingredients until just combined. Divide into four even patties and allow them to rest a few minutes.
- In a medium saucepan, combine all sauce ingredients over medium heat. Bring to a gentle simmer and keep warm, stirring occasionally.
- Heat a heavy skillet large enough to hold all four patties over medium high heat. Plop the burgers in and let them cook, turning only once. When they are almost as done as you want them, remove patties and drain off grease. Add warm sauce to skillet and return burgers, nestling them down in the sauce. Let simmer a few more minutes until burgers reach desired level of doneness and keep warm.
- Meanwhile, get your broiler going. Combine butter, parsley, and garlic to taste and spread evenly over each slice of bread.
- Top bread with cheese and broil 3-4 minutes or until cheese is bubbly and edges are golden brown.
- Immediately top with burger patties and spoon lots and lots of delish sauce over them. Crack open a beer and enjoy.

226.   Oprah Turkey Burgers Recipe

Serving: 8 | Prep: | Cook: 10mins | Ready in:

Ingredients

- 1/4 cup thinly sliced green onion - chives (white and green parts)
- 1/2 cup finely diced celery
- 3 granny smith apples, peeled, cored and diced.
- 1/8 cup canola oil or peanut oil
- 4 Lbs. ground turkey
- 2 Tbsp salt
- 2 Tbsp black pepper
- 1 Tbsp chipotle Tabasco
- 1 whole lemon juice and a some grated zest
- 1/2 bunch parsley, finely chopped
- 1/4 cup Major Grey's chutney (buy and puree) - usually in the
- grocery store's section where mustards, bbq sauces, etc.

Direction

- Sauté the chives, celery and apples in oil until tender.
- Let cool Place the ground turkey in a large mixing bowl. Add the sautéed items and ALL remaining ingredients.
- Shape into eight 8-oz patties.
- Refrigerate at least 2 hours (or make burgers one night, cover with foil and cook the next night).
- Season the patties with salt and pepper.
- Place on preheated OILED grill (indoor or out) Grill each size about 7 minutes until meat thoroughly cooked. Let rest for 5 minutes.
- Serve with sides of cottage cheese, avocado, favorite toasted bread, pita, salsa, sliced red onions and/or ranch dressing.

227. Organic Grilled Portabella Mushroom Burger With Roasted Red Peppers And Goat Cheese Recipe

Serving: 2 | Prep: | Cook: 20mins | Ready in:

Ingredients

- 2 large organic portabella mushrooms
- 1 Small organic zucchini sliced into match sticks
- 2 Organic Whole Wheat buns
- One 4 oz. Package of Cypress Grove Chevre Goats milk cheese cut in half
- 4 Mediterranean Organic roasted red peppers
- 1 tablespoon of organic butter
- 2 Tablespoons of my Chipotle habanero BBQ Sauce
- sea salt

Direction

- First, remove the stems and clean the mushrooms with a damp towel.
- Spread the butter on each of the bun halves
- Next, Grill the organic whole-wheat buns and set aside.
- Oil the grill and place the mushrooms face down on it for 8 minutes.
- Turn over the mushrooms sprinkle with sea salt and grill for an additional 8 to 10 minutes until tender.
- Add some of my Chipotle Habanero BBQ sauce or your favorite BBQ sauce on the bottom bun.
- Place the mushroom gill side up on the bottom slice of the bun.
- Place the round of Goat cheese on top of the mushroom.
- Then place the roasted red pepper on top of the cheese round.
- Top with some sautéed zucchini match strips.
- Serving suggestions: Serve with spiced potatoes and a half sour pickle

228. Organic Hambugers Recipe

Serving: 0 | Prep: | Cook: 15mins | Ready in:

Ingredients

- 1 pound organic, grass fed beef
- 3 tablespoons low sodium worcestershire sauce
- 2 teaspoons low sodium steak seasoning
- 1/2 teaspoon sea salt

Direction

- Mix beef mixture with your hands until combined. Mix seasoning in thoroughly, but don't over mix.
- Form into either 3 or 4 burgers (depending on how big you want you burgers. Instead of completely flat, try forming a slight divot in the middle so that they don't plump up so much.
- On a grill pan set to medium heat, let burgers cook until juices pool in the middle. Or, grill on outdoor grill.
- Flip burgers and grill for another 3 to 5 minutes, depending on how you like them cooked.
- Let sit on a paper towel-line plate for a few minutes to drain some of the fat.

229. Pan Fried Salmon Burgers With Cabbage Slaw And Avocado Aioli Recipe

Serving: 6 | Prep: | Cook: 20mins | Ready in:

Ingredients

- 1 1/2 pounds skinless center-cut salmon fillet, finely chopped
- 1/2 cup mayonnaise

- 2 tablespoons Asian fish sauce
- 2 tablespoons sambal oelek (see Note) or hot sauce
- 2 garlic cloves, minced
- 1 medium shallot, minced
- 1 tablespoon minced fresh ginger
- 1/2 teaspoon finely grated lemon zest
- 1/2 cup plus 2 tablespoons chopped cilantro
- 1/2 cup plus 1 tablespoon chopped mint
- kosher salt and freshly ground pepper
- 1 1/2 cups Japanese panko or plain dry bread crumbs
- 2 tablespoons fresh lemon juice
- 2 tablespoons fresh lime juice
- 2 tablespoons unseasoned rice vinegar
- 1 teaspoon sugar
- 1/2 small green cabbage, shredded
- 1 small cucumber — peeled, halved lengthwise, seeded and julienned
- 1 small red onion, thinly sliced
- 1 small red bell pepper, thinly sliced
- 1/4 cup sesame seeds
- 1/4 cup vegetable oil
- avocado Aioli, for serving
- 6 onion rolls, split and toasted

Direction

- In a food processor, pulse the chopped salmon about 10 times, or until minced. Scrape the salmon into a bowl. Mix the mayonnaise with the fish sauce, sambal oelek, garlic, shallot, ginger, lemon zest, 2 tablespoons of the cilantro, 1 tablespoon of the mint, 1 teaspoon of salt and 1/2 teaspoon of pepper. Add the mixture to the salmon along with 1 cup of the panko. Fold the salmon mixture together with a rubber spatula. With lightly oiled hands, pat the mixture into 6 burgers. Cover with plastic wrap and refrigerate for 2 hours.
- Meanwhile, in a large bowl, combine the lemon and lime juice with the vinegar. Add the sugar; stir until dissolved. Add the cabbage, cucumber, onion, red pepper and the remaining 1/2 cup each of cilantro and mint and toss well.

- In a shallow bowl, mix the remaining 1/2 cup of panko with the sesame seeds. Pat the mixture onto the salmon burgers.
- In each of 2 large non-stick skillets, heat 2 tablespoons of the oil until shimmering. Add 3 salmon burgers to each skillet and cook over moderately high heat, turning once, until well browned but barely cooked in the center, about 7 minutes.
- Spread the Avocado Aioli on the rolls. Add the salmon burgers, top with the slaw, close the sandwiches and serve.
- MAKE AHEAD: The uncooked salmon burgers and the slaw can be refrigerated overnight.
- NOTES: Sambal is a condiment used in Indonesia, Malaysia, Singapore, the southern Philippines and Sri Lanka, as well as the Netherlands and in Suriname, made from a variety of peppers, although chili peppers are the most common. Sambal is used as a condiment or as a side dish, and is sometimes substituted for fresh chilies; it can be very hot for the uninitiated. It is available at exotic food markets or gourmet departments in supermarkets in numerous countries.

230. Parmesan Ranch Burgers Recipe

Serving: 8 | Prep: | Cook: 18mins | Ready in:

Ingredients

- 2. 5 lbs ground chuck or sirloin (15-20% fat - less will make for dry burgers)
- 1 package ranch dressing mix
- 1/4 c grated parmesan cheese
- 1 package beefy onion mushroom soup mix
- 1 egg, beaten
- 1 T minced garlic
- 3-4 T worcestershire
- 1 t liquid smoke, or 1 t charcoal grill taste dry rub

- 1 t seasoned salt
- 1 T garlic pepper
- 8 slices provolone cheese (or your fave)
- 1 white onion, sliced
- sliced fresh mushrooms

Direction

- Mix all ingredients - except provolone - well with hands, quickly (handling too much will make tougher burgers)
- Shape into 8 patties, large and about 1 inch thick
- Grill to desired doneness, turning once, AVOID mashing with the spatula!
- Add cheese slices
- Butter insides of rolls and place on grill.
- I sautéed onions and fresh mushrooms with olive oil, garlic, butter and Worcestershire for a topping.

231. Party Burgers Recipe

Serving: 4 | Prep: | Cook: 10mins | Ready in:

Ingredients

- 1½ pounds lean ground beef
- 4 slices of dark pumpernickle bread
- 8 large crisp lettuce leaves
- 2 tomatoes, cut into 8 slices
- Topping
- 1/3 cup mayonnaise
- 1/3 cup sour cream
- ¼ cup diced green onions
- 1 tablespoon dried parsley
- salt, pepper, garlic powder to your taste
- (if you like ranch dressing, omit seasonings and add 1 tablespoon of powdered ranch dressing mix instead)
- 1 cup shredded cheddar cheese

Direction

- For topping, mix together mayonnaise, sour cream, green onions and parsley; season to taste and set aside.
- Season ground beef with a little salt and pepper, or any seasonings you prefer.
- Form meat into 4 patties; grill or pan-fry until done.
- Place the cooked patties on a cookie sheet. Top each with the mayonnaise mixture, then with some shredded cheddar cheese.
- Broil just until cheese begins to melt and topping is hot.
- While broiling the patties, toast the bread slices; remove from toaster and butter one side.
- Place the toasted bread (buttered side up) on individual plates.
- Top each piece of toast with 2 crisp lettuce leaves and 2 slices of tomato.
- Place a broiled patty on each slice of tomato.
- Serve immediately (this is served open-face).

232. Paula Deens Tuna Burgers With Reenies Asian Onion Salsa Recipe

Serving: 4 | Prep: | Cook: 20mins | Ready in:

Ingredients

- tuna Burgers
- 2 (6-ounce) cans solid white tuna, drained
- 1/2 cup breadcrumbs
- 2 large eggs, lightly beaten
- 1/2 cup finely chopped onion
- 1/2 cup finely chopped celery
- 1 tablespoon chopped pimento, optional
- 1 tablespoon fresh lemon juice
- 1 1/2 teaspoons prepared horseradish
- 1 clove garlic, minced
- 1/4 teaspoon pepper
- 1 tablespoon olive oil
- Asian Style Onion salsa
- 1 tbls. sesame seeds

- 2 tbls lime juice, fresh
- 1 tbls. sesame oil
- 1 tbls. soy sauce
- 1 tsp. sugar
- 1/8 tsp. crushed red pepper flakes
- 1 cup sweet onion, finely chopped
- 1/4 cup green onions, thinly sliced
- 2 tbls. red bell pepper, finely chopped
- salt and pepper

Direction

- Tuna burgers
- Preheat the oven to 350 degrees F.
- In a large bowl, combine the tuna, bread crumbs, and egg, and stir lightly. Add the onion, celery, pimento (if using), lemon juice, horseradish, garlic, and pepper, and mix again. Form the mixture into 4 patties. Heat the oil in a non-stick skillet over medium heat and cook the patties, covered, until golden brown. Carefully flip the patties and cook the other side for 5 minutes. Finish baking in the oven until golden brown.
- Salsa
- Toast sesame seeds in skillet over medium low heat until golden brown
- Cool
- Add lime juice, sesame oil, soy sauce, sugar, red pepper flakes in a mixing bowl
- Add onion, green onion, red pepper, and sesame seeds and salt and pepper
- Toss to coat

233.   Pesto Burgers Recipe

Serving: 4 | Prep: | Cook: 15mins | Ready in:

Ingredients

- 1-1/2 lbs. lean ground beef
- .5 oz. pkg. dry pesto sauce mix
- 1/2 cup shredded mozzarella cheese
- 1 Tbsp. grated parmesan cheese
- 4 English muffins, split with a fork

- lettuce
- sliced tomatoes

Direction

- Prepare and heat grill. Combine ground beef and pesto sauce with 1 Tbsp. water and mix gently. Shape into 8 thin patties. Place 4 patties on platter and top each with 2 Tbsp. shredded mozzarella cheese and a bit of Parmesan cheese. Top with remaining patties and press edges to seal.
- Grill patties 4-6' from heat and cook 11-13 minutes until meat is no longer pink in center, or reaches 160 degrees on a meat thermometer (be sure you're not checking the cheese temperature in the center). Turn burgers only once, and very carefully. You can grill the English muffins until golden brown and toasted while burgers are cooking. Top with purchased pesto sauce, lettuce and tomato and serve on buns

234.   Philly Burgers Recipe

Serving: 4 | Prep: | Cook: 15mins | Ready in:

Ingredients

- 2 tablespoons worcestershire sauce, divided
- 4 teaspoons Dijon mustard, divided
- 1 (2.8 ounce) can French fried onions, divided
- 1 pound lean ground beef
- 1 (3 ounce) package cream cheese, softened
- 1 small can mushrooms, drained
- 1 teaspoon dried parsley flakes or 1 tablespoon fresh parsley, minced
- 4 hard or burger rolls

Direction

- In bowl, combine 1 tablespoon Worcestershire sauce, 3 teaspoons mustard and half the can of onions (I crush up this half a can). Add beef and mix well.
- Shape into 4 patties. Broil or grill as desired.

- Meanwhile, in small bowl, combine cream cheese, mushrooms, parsley, 1 tablespoon Worcestershire sauce and 1 teaspoon Dijon mustard.
- Spread over burgers. Top with remaining onions. Grill or broil 30 seconds or until onions are heated.
- Serve on rolls.

235. Pig Burger Recipe

Serving: 2 | Prep: | Cook: 20mins | Ready in:

Ingredients

- 1 lb hamburger (or more if needed for crowd)
- 1 lb pork sausage (or more, if needed)
- hot sauce (to taste)
- chopped onions (to taste)
- sage (to taste)
- seasoning salt (to taste)
- pepper (to taste)
- sauteed onions, for topping
- barbecue sauce, for topping

Direction

- Thoroughly mix together 60% ground beef, 40% ground sausage and form into 1/2 lb. patties. Grill until golden brown. Serve with sautéed onions. Serve with a generous amount of your favorite BBQ sauce on bun.

236. Pizza Burger Recipe

Serving: 4 | Prep: | Cook: 25mins | Ready in:

Ingredients

- 1 pound ground beef or a mixture of ground beef and italian sausage
- 4 teaspoons pizza or italian seasoning -- divided

- 1/2 teaspoon garlic powder
- 1/2 cup shredded mozzarella cheese
- 8 ounces tomato or pizza sauce
- 4 ounces sliced mushrooms -- drained
- 1/2 cup sliced onion
- 4 toasted hamburger buns

Direction

- Directions:
- Combine ground beef, 2 teaspoons pizza seasoning and garlic powder. Shape into eight thin patties.
- Top four of the patties with cheese. Cover with remaining patties; press edges to seal. Refrigerate until needed. Combine tomato sauce, mushrooms and remaining pizza seasoning in small saucepan; simmer for 10 minutes, stirring occasionally. In non-stick skillet, sauté onion until tender; set aside. Grill, broil, or pan fry burgers until no longer pink.
- Spread bottoms of buns with a little sauce, top with burgers, onion and remaining sauce. Replace tops.

237. Pizza Burgers Recipe

Serving: 2 | Prep: | Cook: 20mins | Ready in:

Ingredients

- 1/2 teaspoon minced garlic
- 1/2 teaspoon beef bouillon granules
- 1/2 teaspoon italian seasoning
- 1/4 teaspoon salt
- 1/2 pound ground beef
- 2 slices part-skim mozzarella cheese
- 2 hamburger buns, split
- 3 tablespoons pizza sauce, warmed
- 4 green pepper rings

Direction

- In a small bowl, combine the garlic, bouillon, Italian seasoning, and salt. Crumble beef over mixture; mix well. Shape into four thin patties. Place a slice of cheese on two patties; top with another patty and press edges to seal.
- Grill, covered, over medium-hot heat for 6-8 minutes on each side or until meat is no longer pink. Serve on buns with pizza sauce and green pepper rings.

238. Pork Prawn Burger Recipe

Serving: 4 | Prep: | Cook: 20mins | Ready in:

Ingredients

- 500g of pork (lean meat)
- 50g of prawn
- 1 pinch of pepper
- 1 pinch of salt
- 6 pieces of button mushrooms
- 1 teaspoon of dried fish flake
- 1 shallot
- 1 egg
- 2 teaspoon of corn flour
- 3 tablespoon of peanut oil for frying

Direction

- Blend all the ingredients except for corn flour, egg and oil till well mixed.
- Add in egg and flour and blend for another 20 seconds.
- Scoop one and half tablespoon and formed to a burger patty.
- Fry the burger patty on the pan till both side is golden brown.

239. Pork Burgers Dijon Recipe

Serving: 6 | Prep: | Cook: 20mins | Ready in:

Ingredients

- 2 egg whites
- 1 slice white bread cubed
- 1 pound lean ground pork
- 2 cups finely shredded cabbage
- 1/4 cup grated onion
- 1/2 teaspoon sugar
- 1/2 teaspoon ground black pepper
- 1/4 teaspoon ground coriander
- 1/8 teaspoon ground nutmeg
- vegetable cooking spray
- 8 ounces sliced fresh mushrooms
- 1 cup water
- 1 tablespoon Dijon mustard
- 1 teaspoon beef bouillon granules
- 2 tablespoons water
- 1 tablespoon plus 1 teaspoon cornstarch

Direction

- Combine egg whites and bread cubes in a large bowl then allow to stand 5 minutes.
- Add pork and next 6 ingredients then stir well and shape mixture into six patties.
- Coat a large non-stick skillet with cooking spray then place over medium heat until hot.
- Add pork patties and cook 7 minutes on each side then drain and pat dry with paper towels.
- Wipe drippings from skillet with paper towel.
- Coat skillet with cooking spray and place over medium high heat until hot.
- Add mushrooms and sauté until tender.
- Stir in water, mustard and bouillon granules stirring well.
- Return pork patties to skillet then cover, reduce heat and simmer 10 minutes.
- Transfer patties to a large serving platter.
- Combine 2 tablespoons water and cornstarch stirring well.
- Add to mushroom mixture and cook just until thickened stirring constantly.

- Spoon over patties and serve immediately.

240. Pork Burgers With Ranch Coleslaw Recipe

Serving: 4 | Prep: | Cook: 20mins | Ready in:

Ingredients

- 3 cups packaged coleslaw mix
- 1/2 cup prepared ranch salad dressing
- 1/4 teaspoon grated lemon peel
- 1 tablespoon butter
- 1/2 cup minced red onion
- 1-1/4 pounds ground pork
- 1/2 cup shredded zucchini
- 1/2 cup shredded swiss cheese
- 1/2 teaspoon salt
- 1/4 teaspoon freshly ground black pepper
- 4 kaiser rolls split

Direction

- Heat grill.
- In a medium bowl combine coleslaw mix, dressing and lemon peel.
- Cover and refrigerate 30 minutes.
- Melt butter in medium skillet over medium high heat then add onion and cook 5 minutes.
- Remove from heat and cool then cover a cookie sheet with plastic wrap.
- Lightly mix pork, onion, zucchini, cheese, salt and pepper in large bowl just until combined.
- Drop 4 equal mounds of pork mixture on prepared sheet.
- Cover with another piece of plastic wrap and gently press mounds into four 1/2" thick patties.
- Grill burgers over medium heat about 5 minutes per side or until browned.
- Meanwhile grill rolls cut sides down until toasted about 1 minute.
- Arrange burgers on bottoms of rolls then divide coleslaw among burgers and top with roll tops.

241. Portabella Bison Burgers Recipe

Serving: 4 | Prep: | Cook: 10mins | Ready in:

Ingredients

- 1 lb. ground bison
- 1 tsp. cumin
- 1/2 tsp. chipotle chili powder
- 1/2 tsp. dried thyme
- 1/2 tsp. dried oregano
- 3/4 cup chopped portabella (or cremini) mushrooms
- 1/4 finely chopped onion
- 1/2 cup shredded cheddar cheese
- salt and pepper to taste
- 4 Whole Wheat buns

Direction

- Preheat grill or pan over medium high heat.
- Combine ground bison, cumin, chipotle chili powder and herbs, blending to distribute seasonings thoroughly.
- Add mushrooms, onion and cheese and mix until combined. Season with salt and pepper.
- Divide mixture evenly into four sections and form into patties.
- Place burgers on grill and reduce heat slightly. If pan-frying these, you may want to add a little oil and/or butter to prevent patties from sticking) Grill 3 to 5 minutes, flip over and grill an additional 3 to 5 minutes.
- Serve on toasted whole wheat buns with your choice of garnishes - more sautéed mushrooms, caramelized onions, and some chipotle ranch dressing are my faves!

242. Portabella Mushroom Burger Recipe

Serving: 4 | Prep: | Cook: 10mins | Ready in:

Ingredients

- INGREDIENTS:
- onion roll hamburger buns, or try making your own buns from the recipe posted on Chefjeb page. You can find him in my friends list.
- mayonnaise
- portabella mushrooms, a bit larger than the buns since they will shrink, cleaned and stems removed
- olive oil
- balsamic vinegar
- Walla Walla or Vidalia sweet onions, sliced
- avocado, sliced
- tomato, sliced
- red bell pepper, sliced into ½" wide strips
- provolone cheese, sliced thin (this cheese is soft, if you can have it sliced at the store, do so)
- spinach leaf, stems removed
- Recommended substitutions: Keiser rolls, sourdough bread, Fresh French bread, focaccia bread, red onions, yellow onions, white onions, Tillamook Vintage Extra Sharp White Cheddar (http://tillamookcheese.com/), feta cheese, goat cheese, Grilled Onions, The Kitchen Sink. C'mon people, it's a burger, experiment, go for it! If you love cheese and haven't tired the Tillamook Vintage White Extra Sharp you are surely missing out! I highly recommend this cheese form the Oregon Coast.

Direction

- Drizzle the mushroom gills with balsamic vinegar and olive oil, guess about 1 tsp. or so to taste
- If broiling, broil them directly on oven grates in the middle of your oven or lower, not too close to the heat, with aluminum foil on another shelf underneath to catch drippings, medium heat, gills up, until edges start getting soft, about 3-5 minutes depending on heat. Flip and continue on other side 2-3 minutes, softening the mushroom but not making it limp. Adjust time to match heat and mushroom size.
- If grilling, grill them directly over low to medium heat, gills up, until edges start getting soft, about 3-5 minutes depending on heat. Flip and continue on other side 2-3 minutes, softening the mushroom but not making it limp. Adjust time to match heat and mushroom size.
- Top the mushrooms with cheese the last 30 seconds to 1minute of cooking depending heat, just enough to melt but not brown
- While cooking the mushrooms, prepare buns/bread by coating the inside with the mayo and lightly browning the mayo side in a non-stick pan or on a griddle like you would a grilled cheese sandwich, timing them to finish with the mushroom for warm buns.
- Assemble like you would any other burger, topping with the listed ingredients and serve immediately.
- Stand back and be amazed.

243. Portaobello Mushroom Burgers Recipe

Serving: 4 | Prep: | Cook: 25mins | Ready in:

Ingredients

- 4 portobello mushroom caps
- 1/4 c balsamic vinegar
- 2 Tbs olive oil
- 1 tsp dried basil
- 1 tsp dried oregano
- 1 Tbs minced garlic
- salt and pepper
- 4 (1 oz) slices provolone cheese

Direction

- Place mushroom caps, smooth side up in a shallow dish. In small bowl, whisk together vinegar, oil, basil, oregano, garlic, salt and pepper. Pour over the mushrooms. Let stand at room temperature for 15 mins or so, turning twice.
- Preheat grill to med-high heat
- Brush grate with oil. Place mushrooms on the grill, reserving marinade for basting. Grill 5 to 8 mins on each side or till tender. Brush with marinade frequently. Top with cheese during last 2 mins of grilling.

244.	Portobello Burgers With Roasted Pepper Paste And Smoked Mozzarella Recipe

Serving: 4 | Prep: | Cook: 12mins | Ready in:

Ingredients

- 2 tablespoons extra virgin olive oil (EVOO)
- 1/8 cup balsamic vinegar (3 splashes)
- 2 sprigs fresh rosemary (about 2 tablespoons), leaves stripped and chopped
- 1 lemon, juiced
- 4 large portobello mushroom caps
- 2 teaspoons grill seasoning, such as McCormick brand Montreal steak seasoning or 1 teaspoon combined coarse salt and pepper
- 1/2 pound fresh smoked mozzarella, sliced
- ....
- roasted pepper Paste:
- 1 jar roasted peppers (14 ounces), drained
- A drizzle of extra virgin olive oil (EVOO)
- A handful of flat leaf parsley leaves
- 1 large clove garlic, cracked away from skin
- salt and pepper
- ....
- 4 large crusty rolls, split

- ....
- Suggested toppings:
- Whole baby spinach leaves
- Thinly sliced red onions

Direction

- Combine first four ingredients in the bottom of a large sealable plastic bag. Add mushroom caps, seal bag and shake bag to coat caps, then let the mushrooms marinate for 15 minutes.
- Grill mushrooms on an indoor electric grill, starting with caps down, turning to caps up, 6 minutes on each side. You can also pan fry in large non-stick skillet for the same amount of time. As they cook, season caps on each side with grill seasoning or a little salt and pepper. Melt the smoked cheese over mushroom caps in the last minute of grill time.
- To make the pepper paste, combine the roasted peppers, EVOO, parsley, garlic, salt and pepper in food processor and pulse grind into a thick sauce.
- To serve, place the grilled mushroom caps topped with melted cheese on the bun bottoms. Top with spinach and onion. Spread bun tops with roasted pepper paste.

245.	Potato Burger Soupreme Recipe

Serving: 4 | Prep: | Cook: 20mins | Ready in:

Ingredients

- 1 lb lean ground beef
- 1/3 - 1/2 of a 20 oz. pkg hash brown potatoes (give these a rough chop)
- 1 pkt. onion-mushroom soup mix
- 1 egg, beaten
- worcestershire sauce (as much or as little as you like)
- salt
- pepper

- buns
- burger toppings of choice

Direction

- Combine first 5 ingredients and mix well
- Form into 4 equal patties, sprinkle both sides with salt and pepper
- Grill to perfection (or panfry) When using the grill, preheat and then reduce the heat and/or cook on a higher rack to avoid burning the potatoes, if pan frying, cook on a lower heat setting.
- Prepare remaining hash browns (crispy of course!) to serve on the side instead of fries

246. Pronto Pizza Burgers Recipe

Serving: 4 | Prep: | Cook: 20mins | Ready in:

Ingredients

- 1 pound lean ground beef
- 1/3 cup grated parmesan cheese
- 1 tablespoon chopped onion
- 1 tablespoon tomato paste
- 1 teaspoon dried oregano
- 1/2 teaspoon salt
- 4 English muffins, split
- 8 tomato slices
- 8 mozzarella cheese slices

Direction

- In a bowl, mix beef, Parmesan cheese, onion, tomato paste, oregano, salt and pepper just until combined.
- Toast the muffins in a broiler until lightly browned.
- Divide meat mixture among muffins.
- Broil 4 inches from the heat for 8 to 10 minutes or until meat is cooked.
- Top with tomatoes and cheese slices.
- Return to broiler until cheese is melted.

- If desired, sprinkle with Italian seasoning.
- Serve immediately.

247. Pueblo Burgers Recipe

Serving: 4 | Prep: | Cook: 15mins | Ready in:

Ingredients

- 1/2 cup chopped onion
- 1 Tablespoon butter or margarine
- 3/4 Ib. lean ground beef
- 2 cloves garlic, minced or pressed
- 1 Tablespoon chili powder
- 1/2 cup corn, fresh, canned or frozen
- 1/4 teaspoon each salt, dried sage leaves and black pepper
- -----Pueblo Bread-----
- 1 3/4 cups unbleached flour
- 1/4 cup cracked wheat
- 1 teaspoon baking powder
- 1/2 tsp. salt
- 1 tablespoon soft butter or margarine
- 3/4 cup warm water
- oil
- -----Toppings-----
- 2 medium tomatoes, seeded, diced
- 1 avocado, diced
- Chopped black olives
- Grated cheddar cheese
- sour cream, optional
- lettuce, optional

Direction

- Sauté onion in the butter until onion is soft. Add the beef and garlic, cooking until meat is browned. Drain excess fat. Stir in chili powder, corn, salt, sage and black pepper. Cover and keep warm.
- To prepare the bread, mix together flour, cracked wheat, baking powder and salt. Add butter and water to form a soft dough. Divide into 4 portions. Roll each into a round about

1/8 inch thick. Fry in hot oil until puffy and brown. Set on paper towel to drain.

- Sprinkle each fried bread with 1/4 of the meat mixture. Top with tomatoes and avocados. Add optional toppings, if desired.

248.   RRs Smoky Beer Burgers Recipe

Serving: 4 | Prep: | Cook: 15mins | Ready in:

Ingredients

- 2 pounds lean ground sirloin
- 1/3 pound smoked gouda cheese, diced into 1/4 to 1/2-inch cubes
- 1 medium onion or 1/2 large onion
- 2 teaspoons smoked sweet paprika, 2/3 palm full
- 1 teaspoon ground cumin, 1/3 palm full
- Grill seasoning (recommended: Montreal steak seasoning)
- coarse salt and freshly ground black pepper
- 2 cloves garlic, grated or finely chopped
- Generous handful finely chopped fresh flat-leaf parsley
- 1 tablespoon worcestershire sauce
- 1/2 (12-ounce) bottle beer
- extra-virgin olive oil, for drizzling
- 1/2 cup spicy brown mustard
- 1/4 to 1/3 cup sour cream
- 2 to 3 tablespoons chopped fresh dill or 1 teaspoon dried dill
- 4 crusty kaiser rolls, split and lightly toasted
- Green or red leaf lettuce, for topping
- Sliced sweet bread and butter pickles, for topping

Direction

- Preheat grill over medium-high heat.
- Place the meat in a bowl and add the cheese.
- Peel the onion and halve it, if using the medium onion.

- Grate about 3 to 4 tablespoons of onion directly over the meat into the bowl.
- Finely chop the remaining onion and reserve for topping.
- Add spices to meat: paprika, cumin and about 1 tablespoon of grill seasoning and/or some salt and pepper.
- Add garlic, parsley and Worcestershire and beer then form 4 large patties making them a little thinner at the center than at edges. Burgers plump when you cook them so this will prevent burger bulge.
- Drizzle a little olive oil over the burgers then grill about 4 minutes on each side for medium rare, 5 minutes on each side for medium and 6 to 7 minutes on each side for well done.
- Mix mustard and sour cream with dill.
- Serve patties on bun bottoms and top with lettuce, pickles, chopped raw onion.
- Slather bun tops with sauce and serve.

249.   Ranch Burgers Recipe

Serving: 8 | Prep: | Cook: 15mins | Ready in:

Ingredients

- * 2 pounds lean ground beef
- * 1 (1 ounce) package ranch dressing mix
- * 1 egg, lightly beaten
- * 3/4 cup crushed saltine crackers
- * 1 onion, chopped

Direction

- 1. Preheat the grill for high heat.
- 2. In a bowl, mix the ground beef, ranch dressing mix, egg, crushed crackers, and onion. Form into hamburger patties.
- 3. Lightly oil the grill grate. Place patties on the grill, and cook 5 minutes per side, or until well done.

250. Red Onion Maytag Blue Cheese Burger Recipe

Serving: 6 | Prep: | Cook: 15mins | Ready in:

Ingredients

- 2 pounds ground chuck
- 2 cloves garlic minced
- 1 teaspoon salt
- 1/2 teaspoon black pepper
- 4 ounces maytag blue cheese
- 1/3 cup coarsely chopped walnuts, toasted
- 2 medium red onions, sliced
- 6 sesame seed hamburger buns
- olive oil

Direction

- Combine beef, garlic, salt and pepper in a medium bowl. Shape meat mixture into 12 patties. Mash cheese and blend with walnuts in a small bowl. Divide cheese mixture equally and place on centers of 6 meat patties. Top with remaining meat patties then tightly pinch edges together to seal in filling. Oil hot grid to help prevent sticking. Grill patties and onions on a covered grill over medium coals for 12 minutes. Brush buns on one side with olive oil. Move cooked burgers to edge of grill to keep warm. Grill bread oil side down for 5 minutes. Serve burgers on toasted rolls.

251. Red River Burgers Recipe

Serving: 4 | Prep: | Cook: 14mins | Ready in:

Ingredients

- 1/2 cup chopped green onion or finely chopped white onion
- 2 tablespoons fine dry bread crumbs
- 2 red serrano peppers, seeded and finely chopped
- 3 canned chipotle peppers in adobo sauce, chopped
- 1/2 teaspoon salt
- 1 pound lean ground beef
- 4 whole wheat hamburger buns, split, or eight 1-inch-thick slices of bread
- roasted red pepper catsup, roasted garlic catsup, or other purchased flavored catsup (optional)
- 4 tomato slices (optional)
- Sliced red onion (optional)
- Red serrano peppers (optional)

Direction

- Combine green onion or white onion, bread crumbs, Serrano peppers, chipotle peppers, and salt in a large mixing bowl. Add beef; mix well.
- Shape meat mixture into four 3/4-inch-thick patties.
- For a charcoal grill, place patties on the grill rack directly over medium coals. Grill, uncovered, for 14 to 18 minutes.
- Grill or toast buns or bread.
- Serve burgers on toasted buns. If desired, with flavored catsup, tomato slices, red onion slices, and Serrano peppers.

252. Red Wine Brie Burgers Recipe

Serving: 8 | Prep: | Cook: 15mins | Ready in:

Ingredients

- 2 pounds ground sirloin
- 3 tablespoons red wine
- 1 teaspoon salt
- 1 teaspoon freshly ground black pepper
- 1/2 cup finely chopped red onions
- 1/2 cup brie cheese

Direction

- Mix sirloin with wine, salt, pepper and onions then form into 8 patties.
- Using a wooden spoon make a small pocket in center of each burger.
- Add 1 tablespoon brie and pinch meat around cheese to cover.
- Grill over medium high for 6 minutes per side.

253. Reuben Style Burgers Recipe

Serving: 4 | Prep: | Cook: 10mins | Ready in:

Ingredients

- 1 pound lean ground beef
- 3/4 tps. salt
- 1/2 tps. pepper
- 4 slices swiss cheese
- 4 hamburger buns
- 1 cup sauerkraut, drained
- 1/2 tps. caraway seeds
- 1/4 cup Thousand Island salad dressing
- 4 slices deli corn beef

Direction

- Heat gas grill on medium heat
- Combine ground beef, salt and pepper in medium bowl; mix lightly. Shape into 4 patties.
- Place patties onto grill. Grill turning once, until internal temp. reaches at least 160F. or until meat is no longer pink in center (10 to 12 minutes). Top each patty with 1 slice cheese during last minute of grilling. Place cut-sides of bun onto grill. Grill until toasted.
- Meanwhile, combine sauerkraut and caraway seeds in a small bowl.
- Spread 2 tsp. dressing onto each toasted bun half. Place burgers onto bottom bun half, top with 1 slice corn beef, 1/4 cup sauerkraut mixture and top bun half.

254. Rockin Guac Guacamole Burgers Recipe

Serving: 6 | Prep: | Cook: 12mins | Ready in:

Ingredients

- BURGERS:
- 2 pounds ground beef
- 2 tablespoons olive oil, extra virgin
- 3 green onions, white part only, minced
- 2 teaspoons ground cumin
- 2 teaspoons ground chili powder
- 2 teaspoons dried oregano
- 2 teaspoons fresh jalapenos, minced, seeds included (do not use canned)
- 2 teaspoons minced garlic
- 1 teaspoon sea salt
- 1/2 teaspoon freshly ground black pepper
- 6 slices pepper jack cheese
- 6 burger buns (use good quality buns. Onion, Keiser, Etc.) or better yet make your own from recipe posted on Chefjeb page. You can find him in my friends list.
- GUACAMOLE:
- See my Rockin Guac guacamole recipe post, make in advance and chill 30 minutes in the refrigerator.

Direction

- GUACAMOLE:
- Make guacamole per recipe. Chill 30 minutes.
- BURGERS:
- Mix all burger ingredients gently in a medium bowl.
- Form into six 3/4 inch thick patties
- ON THE GRILL:
- Cook over direct medium heat to an internal temp of 160F for medium. (4-5 minutes on a side) Top with cheese last 30 seconds to 1 minute, just enough to melt but not brown cheese.
- ON A GRIDDLE:

- Cook over medium heat to an internal temp of 160F for medium. (4-5 minutes on a side) Top with cheese last minute, just enough to melt cheese.
- Lightly toast buns on grill or griddle.
- Serve on hot on toasted buns topped with cool guacamole.

255. Rush St Burger Recipe

Serving: 6 | Prep: | Cook: 9mins | Ready in:

Ingredients

- 2 lbs. ground beef
- 1/4 c. chopped onion
- 3 tbsp. Tabasco sauce
- 2 tbsp. honey
- 1 tbsp. garlic salt
- 1 tsp. crushed red pepper flakes
- 1 tsp. black pepper
- 6 oz. colby/jack cheese (your choice blue cheese is good too)
- 6 hamburger buns-toasted
- roasted red peppers from jar (optional)
- 6 portabella mushrooms, grilled (optional)

Direction

- Pre-heat grill to medium-high
- Combine ground beef, onion, tabasco sauce, honey, garlic salt, red pepper flakes and pepper in large bowl.
- Divide into 6 portions
- Form into 6 patties AROUND pieces of cheese
- Grill 8-10 min. or until done
- Top with red peppers and mushrooms if using

256. SHRIMP BURGERS Recipe

Serving: 12 | Prep: | Cook: 20mins | Ready in:

Ingredients

- 2 cups fresh shrimp peeled. Wild caught makes best flavored.
- about a dozen sprigs parsley
- 1 medium onion chopped
- 1 medium green pepper chopped
- 2 stalks celery, chopped
- 10 green onion tops
- 2 eggs
- 3 slices of stale bread, soaked in water.
- 1/2 cup Italian flavored bread crumbs
- salt and pepper to taste
- 1 tablespoon garlic salt
- flour
- hamburger buns or Kieser rolls, toasted.
- lettuce, tomato or what ever you choose.
- oil

Direction

- Grind shrimp with Parsley, onion, green pepper, celery and green onion tops.
- Mix with eggs, soaked bread (squeeze out water), and bread crumbs. Add seasoning to taste.
- Shape into burgers. Roll in flour and fry in 1/2 inch of oil.
- Cook on medium heat until brown.
- Serve on rolls with your choice of toppings.

257. SOFT TACO BURGERS Recipe

Serving: 8 | Prep: | Cook: 20mins | Ready in:

Ingredients

- Ingredients:
- 1 can fat-free refried beans
- 1 can (4-oz) chopped green chilies, divided
- ¼ cup chopped onion
- ¼ tsp. salt
- 1 ½ pounds lean ground beef

- 1 cup (4-oz) shredded reduced-fat cheddar cheese
- 8 flour tortillas (6 inches), warmed
- 1 cup chopped lettuce
- 1 medium tomato, chopped
- ½ cup salsa

Direction

- In a bowl, combine the beans, 2 tablespoons green chillies, onion and salt. Crumble the beef over mixture and mix well. Shape into eight 5-inch patties. Top each patty with 2 tablespoons cheddar cheese; fold in half and press edges to seal, forming a half moon.
- If grilling the burgers, coat grill rack with non-stick cooking spray before starting the grill. Grill burgers, uncovered, over medium heat or broil 4 inches from the heat for 7-9 minutes on each side or until meat is no longer pink and a meat thermometer reads 160. Serve on tortillas with lettuce, tomato, salsa and remaining chilies. Yield: 8 servings.
- Nutritional Values: Serving size: 1 Sandwich calories 322, Fat: 12g, Cholesterol: 38mg, Sodium: 656mg, Carbohydrate: 26g, Fiber: 3g, Protein: 26g
- Diabetic Exchanges: 3 lean meat, 1 ½ starch, 1 vegetable, ½ fat
- Diabetic Friendly

258. Sage Turkey Burgers With Swiss Cheese And Honey Dijon Sauce Recipe

Serving: 4 | Prep: | Cook: 15mins | Ready in:

Ingredients

- For turkey patties:
- 1 thick slice pugliese bread (to make about 1 cup breadcrumbs)
- 4 fresh sage leaves
- 1 teaspoon fresh thyme leaves
- 1 teaspoons fresh parsely

- 1 clove garlic, crushed
- 1 lb. fresh ground turkey, thigh meat
- 1 cage free egg
- splash of heavy cream
- kosher salt and fresh ground black pepper, to taste
- olive oil
- ~~~~~~~~~~~~~~~~~~~~~~~~~~~~~~~~~~~~~~ ~~~~~~~~~~~~~~~~~~~~
- 4 slices swiss cheese, room temp (Dofino brand preferably)
- sliced red onion, rinsed
- organic baby lettuce
- 4 cracked wheat buns, sliced and toasted
- honey Dijon Sauce (mix 1/3 cup mayonnaise and 1 tablespoon each of honey and Dijon mustard)

Direction

- Remove crust from bread and break into chunks. Place bread, herbs and garlic in food processor. Pulse until bread is fine crumbs.
- Transfer bread crumbs to mixing bowl. Add the turkey and remaining ingredients. Mix to combine and shape into 4 patties. Refrigerate patties for at least an hour.
- Heat a large non-stick pan over med-high heat. Brush the patties with olive oil and place in pan. Pan sear on each side for 5 minutes. Add 1/4 cup water to the pan and cover with lid. Lower heat and allow patties to steam for 12-15 minutes. Remove lid and place cheese on patties the last minutes of cooking so it melts a little.
- To serve: Spread honey-Dijon sauce on both side of toasted buns. Place patties on bottom of bun, top with baby lettuce and red onions.

259. Sagittarius Burger Recipe

Serving: 4 | Prep: | Cook: 10mins | Ready in:

Ingredients

- 4 grilled hamburger patties
- 4 slices sharp cheddar cheese
- 2 grilled Portobello mushrooms chopped
- 4 tablespoons Dijon mustard
- 4 tablespoons mayonnaise
- tomato herb bread

Direction

- Slice bread in half lengthwise then cut into four equal portions.
- Lather bottom half of bread with Dijon mustard and mayonnaise combined.
- Top with a hamburger patty and a slice of cheddar cheese.
- Top with mushrooms then top bread.

---

260.   Salmon Burger Recipe

Serving: 2 | Prep: | Cook: 10mins | Ready in:

Ingredients

- 250 gr. salmon fillet
- 1 piece of fresh ginger, peeled and grated
- 250 gr. boiled potatoes
- 1 egg beaten
- 75 gr. all purpose flour
- 2 tbs soy sauce
- 2 scallions, finely chopped
- salt and pepper
- 2 tbs plain breadcrumbs

Direction

- Rinse the salmon under cold running water.
- Pat dry with a paper towel, skin, bone and chop.
- Dice the boiled potatoes.
- Put the scallions in a large bowl, add the salmon, potatoes, egg, salt and pepper, soy sauce, ginger and breadcrumbs and mix well with a fork. With your hands shape the mixture into medium sized balls, then with your palms flatten those forming burgers.

- In a plate, place the flour and dredge the burgers.
- Heat the oil in a frying pan until very hot.
- Add the burgers and cook for 5 mins, or until nicely browned on both sides.
- Drain on paper towels and serve hot.

---

261.   Salmon Burger Steak With Tomato Sauce Recipe

Serving: 3 | Prep: | Cook: 20mins | Ready in:

Ingredients

- 2 (6 oz) caned salmon
- 1 cup chopped onion
- 1/2 cup chopped shitake mushrooms
- 2 Tbsp parsley, diced
- 1 tsp mix of dried herbs (rosemary, paprika, chili pepper, lemon peel)
- a pinch of salt & pepper
- 1/2 cup bread crumbs, or fresh whole wheat bread crumbs
- 2 Tbsp grated parmesan cheese
- 1 egg, lightly beaten
- 1 Tbsp milk
- Spray oil or melted butter
- FOR THE SAUCE
- 14 oz canned diced tomato
- 1/4 onion, diced
- 1 Tbsp minced garlic
- 2 Tbsp olive oil
- 1 bay leaf
- 2 Tbsp hot sauce
- 1 Tbsp parsley, diced
- 1 tsp sugar
- a pinch of salt & pepper

Direction

- Preheat the oven at 370 degree.
- Drain and flake Salmon, sauté onions & shitake mushrooms lightly.

- Combine salmon, onion, shitake mushrooms, parsley, bread crumbs, milk, egg, Parmesan cheese, and seasonings; mix well.
- Spray with non-stick oil or melted butter inside of muffin pan
- Form into 6 large muffin pan (silicon pan). Bake 15 minutes or more.
- In the meantime, prepare the mushrooms and sauce.
- Slice the mushrooms and stir fry in the pan; season with salt & pepper; remove from the heat; set aside.
- Preheat the saucepan; add olive oil; heat the oil
- Add onions & garlic; sauté slightly.
- Add tomato, bay leaf; boil-stir often
- Add hot sauce, parsley, salt & pepper, sugar; mix well; simmer about 3 to 4 minutes.
- Remove from the heat. Set aside.
- Remove the salmon from the muffin pan gently.
- Put some sautéed mushrooms on the plate, then salmon steak & top with tomato sauce.

262. Salmon Burgers With Lemon And Capers Recipe

Serving: 10 | Prep: | Cook: 20mins | Ready in:

Ingredients

- 5 tablespoons olive oil
- 1 cup chopped shallots
- 1 cup dry white wine
- 1/2 cup fresh lemon juice
- 4 ounce jar capers drained and chopped
- 2 pounds chilled skinless salmon fillets cut into 1" pieces bones removed
- 3 cups fresh breadcrumbs made from French bread
- 2 large eggs beaten to blend
- 3 tablespoons chopped fresh dill
- 1-1/2 teaspoons salt
- 3/4 teaspoon freshly ground black pepper

- 10 hamburger buns split and toasted
- mayonnaise
- lettuce leaves
- tomato slices

Direction

- Heat 4 tablespoons oil in heavy medium skillet over medium heat.
- Add shallots and sauté until translucent about 4 minutes.
- Increase heat to medium high then add wine, lemon juice and drained capers.
- Cook until almost all liquid evaporates about 12 minutes.
- Transfer shallot mixture to large bowl then refrigerate 1 hour.
- Using on off turns coarsely grind salmon fillets in processor.
- Add salmon to shallot mixture then mix in breadcrumbs, eggs, dill, salt and pepper.
- Form salmon mixture into 10 patties dividing equally.
- Transfer to baking sheet then cover with plastic wrap and refrigerate.
- Heat 1 tablespoon olive oil in heavy large skillet over medium high heat.
- Working in batches add salmon patties to skillet and cook until patties are golden brown.
- Serve salmon burgers on toasted buns with mayonnaise, lettuce and tomato slices.

263. Salmon Burgers With Miso Sesame Sauce Recipe

Serving: 4 | Prep: | Cook: 8mins | Ready in:

Ingredients

- 1 1/4 lb skinless salmon fillet
- 1 tbsp garlic, minced
- 2 tbsp Dijon mustard
- handful of chopped cilantro
- 2 tbsp hoisin sauce

- 1 green onion, finely chopped
- 1 tsp cayenne
- 1 egg
- 1/2 cup panko breadcrumbs
- 1 tbsp toasted sesame seeds
- 1 tbsp miso
- 2 tbsp rice wine vinegar
- 1 tbsp honey
- 1 tbsp soy sauce

Direction

- Finely dice salmon fillet and mix together well in large bowl with next 8 ingredients.
- Form burger mixture into 4 equal sized burgers and place on plate covered with plastic wrap. Cover burgers with more plastic wrap and refrigerate for 1 hour.
- While burgers are chilling make sauce by whisking remaining ingredients. Chill.
- Heat BBQ, Frying/Griddle pan or Broiler to high, spray with cooking spray and cook 4 minutes a side until just a touch of rare inside.
- Top with sauce and enjoy. Excellent on a bun with lettuce, tomato, pickled ginger and a side of crispy French fries.

264.   Salmon Burgers With Spinach ,garlic, Cilantro And Ginger Recipe

Serving: 4 | Prep: | Cook: 35mins | Ready in:

Ingredients

- skinned salmon fillet, cut into very small pieces - 1 pound
- baby spinach, coarsely chopped (2 cups)
- spring onions 2, minced
- 1 tbs fresh ginger
- 1 tsp crushed garlic
- 1/4 tsp salt
- 1/4 tsp black pepper
- 1 large egg white

- 1 tbs oyster sauce
- olive oil as required for cooking on skillet
- 1/2 cup cilantro leaves, finely chopped
- 1/4 chilli flakes for those who like it a little spicy
- 1 tbs rice flour

Direction

- Marinate the salmon in oyster sauce, pepper, salt and chilli flakes for 15-20 minutes.
- Add the spinach, garlic, ginger and cilantro leaves in the food processor. Add it to the salmon and then add the egg and rice flour. Mix it well and make patties.
- Heat the oil in the pan and fry the patties until lightly crispy. Serve with onions and wasabi and/or tomato sauce.

265.   Salmon Burgers With Yogurt Cucumber Sauce Recipe

Serving: 4 | Prep: | Cook: 10mins | Ready in:

Ingredients

- 15-1/2 ounce can salmon drained and flaked
- 2 eggs beaten
- 1 cup bread crumbs divided
- 1/4 cup chopped green onions
- 2 tablespoons lemon juice
- 1/8 teaspoon freshly ground black pepper
- 1 cup vegetable oil
- yogurt cucumber Sauce:
- 1/2 cup plain yogurt
- 1/4 cup chopped pared cucumber
- 1 tablespoon fresh chopped ill
- 1/4 teaspoon salt
- 1/4 teaspoon freshly ground black pepper

Direction

- Combine salmon, eggs, 2/3 cup breadcrumbs, scallions, lemon juice and pepper.

- Mix until well blended then shape into 4 patties and coat with remaining breadcrumbs.
- Place patties on wax paper lined plate and chill 1 hour.
- In large skillet heat oil over medium heat.
- Add patties and cook 5 minutes on each side then drain on paper towels.
- Serve with yogurt cucumber sauce.
- To make sauce combine yogurt, cucumber, dill, salt and pepper.
- Cover and chill before using.

266. Salsa Burgers With Avocado Sauce Recipe

Serving: 6 | Prep: | Cook: 30mins | Ready in:

Ingredients

- For Burgers
- 2lbs lean ground beef, at least chuck
- 1 small can rotel style tomatoes
- 1t ground cumin
- 1t ground coriander
- 1 smoked paprika
- 1-2T sour cream
- couple T sliced green olives(optional)
- For avocado Sauce
- 1 ripe avocado, pitted and removed from skin
- juice from 1 lime
- 1/4 cup mayonnaise
- 2-3T sour cream
- several sprigs fresh cilantro
- kosher or sea salt and fresh ground pepper
- For Serving
- Slices monterey jack or pepper jack cheese(I used a smoked pepperjack)
- Raw or sauteed red onion rings(I like to cook mine a bit)
- fresh sliced tomato

Direction

- For Burgers

- Combine all burger ingredients and mix well by hand. Don't over mix and don't mix too roughly, but combine ingredients well.
- Grill over high flame (or broil) for a couple minutes, each side, until desired doneness. I suggest no more than a medium rare for burgers, but that's up to you :)
- For Avocado Sauce
- In blender or food processor, mix all ingredients until well blended and smooth. Chill until ready to use. You will probably have extra of this, but it's great as a dipping sauce, too!
- Serve burgers with the sauce and condiments of choice.

267. Salsa Turkey Burgers Recipe

Serving: 12 | Prep: | Cook: 15mins | Ready in:

Ingredients

- 3 lbs ground turkey breast
- 1 jalapeño chile, seeded, chopped
- 1 c Fontina cheese, shredded
- 3/4 tsp pepper
- 1 1/2 cups salsa
- 12 hamburger buns, split, toasted
- 12 pieces of romaine lettuce
- 12 slices tomato
- 12 slices of cucumbers

Direction

- Preheat bbq or grill.
- In a bowl, mix turkey, chilies, cheese, pepper and 1 1/2 cups salsa. Shape mixture into 12 patties about 3/4 inch thick.
- Grill paddies over medium heat 12 to 15 minutes, turning once. Paddies should be firm to touch.
- Serve burgers on buns with tomato slices, lettuces, cucumber and additional salsa.

268. Sausage Burgers Recipe

Serving: 8 | Prep: | Cook: 30mins | Ready in:

Ingredients

- 1 lb ground beef
- 1 lb pork sausage
- 2 tsp black pepper
- 2 tsp salt
- 1/2 T garlic powder
- 1/2 T onion powder
- 1 T Worstershire Sauce

Direction

- Combine all ingredients until well blended.
- Divide evenly into 8 balls.
- Form into solid patties, to desired thickness.
- Grill burgers until well done.
- Serve on toasted rolls or hamburger buns.
- Excellent served as is, but if you like, garnish with fresh sliced tomato, onion or any of your personal favorites and enjoy!

269. Savoury Mushroom And Bean Cake Recipe

Serving: 5 | Prep: | Cook: 1mins | Ready in:

Ingredients

- 2 oz dried porcini or 4 oz field mushrooms
- 1 lb. green beans (French)
- sea salt and freshly ground black pepper
- 2 slices crust-less white country-type bread
- 1/2 c. whole milk, plus 4 tbsp
- 5 tbsp olive oil
- 2 garlic cloves, peeled and very finely chopped
- 1 tbsp chopped fresh marjoram
- a handful of fresh flat-leaf parsley, chopped
- 4 large free-range eggs
- 1/2 c. ricotta cheese
- 4 tbsp mascarpone
- 1 oz parmesan cheese, freshly grated
- 2 oz dried white breadcrumbs, plus more for the tin

Direction

- Soak the porcini in cold water for 15 minutes. Dry them with kitchen paper and chop coarsely. If using field mushrooms just chop them finely without soaking.
- Top and tail the beans and wash them. Plunge into plenty of boiling salted water and cook them for just over 5 minutes. Drain and refresh under cold water and then drain again thoroughly. Now chop coarsely by hand. Put the bread in a bowl, add the milk and leave to soak.
- Preheat the oven to 180°C/Gas Mark 4. Heat half the olive oil, the garlic, marjoram and parsley in a frying pan. Add the soaked porcini (or field mushrooms) and beans and sauté gently for
- 2-3 minutes. Squeeze the excess milk out of the bread, and add the bread to the bean mixture, crumbling it through your fingers. Continue to fry for 5 minutes.
- Beat the eggs together lightly in a large bowl.
- Crumble in the ricotta, then add the mascarpone,
- Parmesan, dried breadcrumbs and some salt and pepper.
- Add the 4 tbsp. of milk.
- Now add the contents of the frying pan to the cheese bowl and mix thoroughly.
- Taste and check the seasoning.
- Grease a cake tin with a little of the remaining olive oil.
- Sprinkle with enough breadcrumbs to cover the surface.
- Spoon the bean mixture into the prepared tin and pour over the remaining olive oil in a thin stream.
- Bake for about 40 minutes.
- Allow to cool in the tin. Serve warm or cold.

270.   Scallipino Burgers Recipe

Serving: 6 | Prep: | Cook: 22mins | Ready in:

Ingredients

- 1 1/2 Lbs ground veal
- 1 cup soft bread crumbs
- 1 beaten egg
- 1/4 cup cookin oik
- i1 8 oz. can tomatoe sauce
- 1 3oz can mushrooms or 2/3 cups mushroom stems}
- 1/4 cup white wine
- 1Tablespoon finely snipped Parsely
- 1/4 Tsp oregano

Direction

- Combine veal, crumbs, eggs, 2 Tbs. Milk, 1/2 tsp. Salt and pepper. Shape into six patties. Coat lightly with 1/4 cup of flour. Brown in hot cooking oil in skillet. Drain fat. COMBINE: tomato sauce, undrained mushrooms, wine, parsley, oregano, and pour over meat. Cover. Simmer 20-25 minutes. Serve over Hot cooked noodles. Sprinkle with Parmesan cheese {6 servings}

271.   School Pizza Burgers Recipe

Serving: 6 | Prep: | Cook: 115mins | Ready in:

Ingredients

- 2 pounds lean ground beef
- 1 teaspoon oregano
- 1 Tablespoon diced onion
- 1 teaspoon ground pepper
- Combine and cook these ingredients until done.
- Drain any grease.

- ADD:
- 1 can spaghetti sauce
- 1 pound diced cheese (Velveeta, cheddar or whatever you like best)
- 1 small can tomato paste

Direction

- Do NOT add these (last 3 above) ingredients until the cooked mixture is COOL
- Add additional seasoning to TASTE!
- Put on open faced hamburger buns and bake at 350 for about 10 minutes and then turn on broiler for about 5 minutes.

272.   Seasoned Turkey Burgers Recipe

Serving: 6 | Prep: | Cook: 20mins | Ready in:

Ingredients

- 1-1/2 lbs ground turkey breast
- 1 (1oz) pkg dry onion soup mix
- 1/2 tsp ground blk. pepper
- 1/2 tsp garlic powder
- 1-1/2 Tbs soy sauce
- 1 egg,lightly beaten (optional)
- 6 hamburger buns,split

Direction

- In a large bowl, mix the turkey with the onion soup mix, pepper, garlic powder, soy sauce and egg. Refrigerate the mixture about 10 mins, then form into 6 patties.
- Preheat grill to med-high
- Lightly oil grill grate. Place the patties on the grill. Cook 20 mins, turning once, or till well done. The inside of the burgers will look whitish in color when cooked through. Serve on buns.

273.   Shrimp Burgers Recipe

Serving: 4 | Prep: | Cook: 5mins | Ready in:

Ingredients

- 1 1/2 pounds large shrimp, peeled
- 2 Tbsp chopped garlic (or less, but that is my preference)
- 2 tablespoons minced fresh ginger - I like the stuff that comes in the tube in the produce section
- 1 jalapeno pepper, seeded and minced
- 1/2 cup green onions chopped
- 1/4 - 1/2 cup Thai peanut sauce
- 1/4 cup dry whole wheat bread crumbs - you may need to add a little more

Direction

- Put shrimp in the food processor - if you do it in batches, it is easy. Pulse until you have a paste (yes, it looks weird!)
- Add the rest of the ingredients, playing w/ the peanut sauce and bread crumbs to make patties.
- Put these in the fridge for 20 minutes or longer - this will help them stay together on the grill.
- Fire up your grill.
- Spray the grill and cook for 3 1/2 to 4 minutes on each side or until done
- Serve this on a bun w/ some spicy slaw or eat this alone w/ a little extra peanut sauce.

274.   Sirloin Beef And Lamb Burgers With Feta And Cilantro Mint Sauce Recipe

Serving: 6 | Prep: | Cook: 10mins | Ready in:

Ingredients

- For the cilantro - mint Sauce
- 1/3 cup plain non-fat yogurt or Greek style yogurt
- 3 tablespoons chopped green onion
- 1/3 cup fresh mint leaves, lightly packed, coarsely chopped
- 3/4 cup cilantro leaves, lightly packed
- 1 1/2 tablespoon minced jalapeno
- 2 cloves garlic, minced
- salt, to taste
- For the Burgers:
- 3/4 pound lean ground sirloin
- 3/4 pound lean ground lamb
- 1 large clove garlic, minced
- 1/3 cup feta cheese, crumbled
- 1/4 cup kalamata olives, finely chopped
- 2 tablespoon extra virgin olive oil
- 1 teaspoon ground cumin
- 1 teaspoon dried mint leaves
- 1/2 teaspoon ground coriander
- 1/2 teaspoon salt
- 1/4 teaspoon pepper
- Additional ingredients:
- 6 hamburger buns, preferably whole grain
- 6 slices ripe tomatoes
- 6 slices red onion
- Red lettuce or spinach leaves

Direction

- Make the Cilantro-Mint Sauce: combine all the ingredients in the work bowl of a blender or food processor. Pulse until the vegetables are finely minced and all is well combined. Cover and refrigerate until ready to serve.
- Make the Burgers: combine all the ingredients in a large bowl. Using your hands mix to combine. Divide and form 6 patties.
- Preheat the grill to medium high. When the grill is ready, place the patties on; cover and cook, turning once, about 4 minutes per side, or to your desired degree of doneness. Remove and cover to keep warm.
- Place the bun halves on the grill and grill until lightly toasted.
- To Serve: Place a patty on each bun, top with Cilantro-Mint sauce, add tomato slice, onion, lettuce or spinach and serve.
- Per Serving: 536 Calories; 37g Fat (13g Sat, 15g Mono, 3g Poly); 26g Protein; 25g

Carbohydrate; 3g Dietary Fiber; 92mg Cholesterol; 870mg Sodium.

---

275. Skillet Charred Pepper Crusted Burger Recipe

Serving: 4 | Prep: | Cook: 12mins | Ready in:

Ingredients

- 8 slices baguette, toasted
- 1 pound ground sirloin
- 1 pound ground chuck
- fine sea salt and freshly ground pepper
- 1/4 cup olive oil
- 4 large shallots, thinly sliced
- 2 tablespoons green peppercorns packed in brine, drained and crushed with the side of a wide bladed knife
- 1/2 cup dry red wine, preferably Syrah or Zinfandel
- 4 Tablespoons unsalted butter, cut into pieces

Direction

- Push 2 baguette slices together in the center of each of 4 plates and set aside.
- Combine the sirloin and chuck in a bowl and knead together briefly by hand.
- Form the meat into 4 burger patties, making them tight but not overly crushed together.
- Season each burger with salt and pepper.
- Set a grill pan over medium high heat and let it get nice and hot.
- Pour in 2 tablespoons of the oil and heat it for 1 minute.
- Add the burgers to the pan and char the burgers on both sides, about 4 minutes per side for medium rare.
- Use a spatula to put 1 burger on the baguette slices and set aside.
- Pour the remaining 2 tablespoons oil into the pan, add the shallots and sauté until they begin to crisp, taking care not to burn them.
- Add the peppercorns and sauté for 1 minute.

- Pour in the wine, raise the heat to high, bring to a boil, and continue to boil until reduced by half, about 3 minutes.
- Remove the pan from the heat and swirl the butter into the sauce, 1 piece at a time.
- Then pour the sauce over each burger and serve.

---

276. Smokey Italian Onion Burger Recipe

Serving: 2 | Prep: | Cook: 15mins | Ready in:

Ingredients

- 1 ½ lbs. ground beef
- 1 yellow onion, chopped and divided
- 1 bunch green onions, diced and divided
- ½ red onion, sliced
- ¼ c. Italian seasoned bread crumbs
- ¼ tsp. liquid smoke, hickory flavor
- ½ c. red wine
- ½ tsp. italian seasoning

Direction

- Mix Liquid Smoke in the red wine. Place all other ingredients in bowl and mix well. Add wine mixture. Shape into 6 patties. Refrigerate for 1 hour, covered. Grill burgers till done to your satisfaction. Meanwhile, sauté ½ of the green onions with ½ the yellow onions in 3 tbsp. butter with 2 tbsp. red wine vinegar and 2 tsp. sugar added. Serve burgers in buns with sliced red onion, sliced tomato and caramelized onions.

---

277. Smoky Bacon Burgers Recipe

Serving: 4 | Prep: | Cook: 15mins | Ready in:

Ingredients

- 1 lb lean ground beef
- 1 egg
- 1/2 cup finely chopped onion
- 3/4 teaspoon salt
- 1/4 teaspoon black pepper
- 1/2 to 1 teaspoon liquid smoke flavoring
- 4 slices bacon
- 4 lettuce leaves
- 4 tomato slices
- 4 toasted hamburger buns

Direction

- Preheat broiler
- Combine beef, egg, onion, salt, black pepper and liquid smoke, blending well. Divide into quarters, shape each quarter into a thick patty. Wrap a strip of bacon around outside of each patty. Hold with a toothpick.
- Place burgers o oiled broiler rack. Broil 5 to 6 inches from source of heat for 5 to 8 minutes on each side or until meat is done to your liking.
- To serve, put lettuce and tomato on toasted hamburger buns. Top with cooked patties (removing toothpicks first). Enjoy

---

278. Smoky Surprise Burgers Recipe

Serving: 4 | Prep: | Cook: 20mins | Ready in:

Ingredients

- 1 3/4 lbs. extra lean ground beef
- 1 1/2 tsp. salt
- 1/4 tsp. ground black pepper
- 2 Tbsp. smoky tomato barbecue sauce
- 1 Tbsp. mayonnaise
- 1 Tbsp. dijon-style mustard
- 4 slices sharp cheddar cheese
- 4 slices swiss cheese

- 4 large sesame seed hamburger buns, split in half; toasted

Direction

- Mix beef, salt and pepper. Divide mixture into quarters, then divide each quarter in half (make 8 patties). Pat each portion out on a sheet of waxed paper to about 4-1/2 inches in diameter.
- Combine barbecue sauce, mayonnaise and mustard. Spread 4 of the patties with this mixture, dividing the mixture among them.
- Top each of the sauced patties with a slice of Cheddar cheese and a slice of Swiss cheese.
- Cover filled patties with remaining patties, pinching the edges to seal well; be sure to press out any air bubbles. Be careful to seal the cheese inside.
- Refrigerate or cook immediately. Place on an electric, gas, or charcoal grill, or on broiler pan. Broil about 6 inches from source of heat 6 to 8 minutes per side or until done to your liking. Place on hamburger buns. Serve immediately.

---

279. Sour Cream N Onion Burgers Recipe

Serving: 4 | Prep: | Cook: 16mins | Ready in:

Ingredients

- 2 T chopped onion, sauteed
- 2 lbs ground sirloin
- half packet onion soup mix
- 6 T worcestershire
- 4 T parmesan
- 1/4 c sour cream
- 2 t chives
- 1/4 - 1/2 c italian or panko bread crumbs
- salt and pepper

Direction

- Sauté 2 T chopped onion in butter or olive oil

- Drain on paper towel
- Mix together sour cream, chives, parmesan, Worcestershire, and soup mix
- Add onions to mixture
- Mix tighter well sirloin and sour cream mixture by hand
- Add in bread crumbs to consistency for burgers (till patties hold shape)
- Shape into 4 large patties and grill (or broil) about 8 minutes each side.
- Turn only once, and do not mash while cooking.

280.   Sourdough Melt Recipe

Serving: 6 | Prep: | Cook: 30mins |Ready in:

Ingredients

- 2lbs ground chuck or better
- 8 slices cheddar cheese
- 8 slices provolone cheese
- 1 large onion, sliced thin(or 2 medium ones :)
- 12 slices sourdough bread(a large "baguette" style would be nice, if it's a loaf, you might need to trim the slices a bit to fit the burger
- butter, softened
- kosher or sea salt and fresh ground pepper
- For Special Sauce
- 1/3 cup Thousand Island dressing
- 2T chili sauce
- 1/2-2t Sriracha sauce

Direction

- For Sauce
- Mix all ingredients together well and set aside
- For Sammich
- Form 6 1/3lb patties out of the ground beef
- Grill, broil or otherwise cook burgers to about medium, set aside
- Grill or sauté onions in butter until just beginning to turn golden, adding a bit of fresh ground pepper towards the end of cooking.(you can fully caramelize these, if

you'd like, but the sauce is rather sweet, and we didn't want the onions that sweet :),set aside
- Butter one side of each slice of the bread.
- Melt butter in a skillet or griddle over medium heat.
- Add a slice of bread, butter side down and immediately top with a piece of provolone, add a layer of the cooked onions, a beef patty, and finally a slice of cheddar cheese.
- On the "mate" piece of bread for each sammich, spread a generous amount of the sauce over the non-butter side and place it, sauce side down, onto the grilling sammich.
- Grill as you would a grilled cheese, turning once, until golden brown and cheeses are melty.
- Continue with remaining sammiches, making sure to keep the already cooked ones warm.
- Serve immediately :-)

281.   Southwest Stuffed Burgers Recipe

Serving: 6 | Prep: | Cook: 29mins |Ready in:

Ingredients

- 1-1/2 lb. extra-lean ground beef
- 1/4 cup KRAFT mayonnaise, divided
- 1 pkg. (1-1/4 oz.) TACO BELL® taco seasoning Mix
- 1/2 cup KRAFT Shredded colby & monterey jack cheese
- 1/4 cup TACO BELL® Thick 'N chunky salsa, divided
- 6 whole wheat hamburger buns
- 6 lettuce leaves
- 1 large tomato, cut into 6 slices

Direction

- HEAT greased grill to medium-high heat.
- MIX meat, 3 Tbsp. mayo and seasoning mix; shape into 12 thin patties.

- Combine cheese and 2 Tbsp. salsa; spoon onto 6 patties.
- Cover with remaining patties; pinch edges to seal.
- GRILL 7 min. on each side or until done (160°F).
- Meanwhile, combine remaining salsa and mayo.
- FILL buns with lettuce, tomatoes, burgers and salsa mixture.
- Grab a beer and Enjoy

---

282. Southwest Turkey Burgers Recipe

Serving: 6 | Prep: | Cook: 20mins |Ready in:

Ingredients

- Salsa:
- 1/4 cup corn
- 12 cherry tomatoes, seeded and chopped
- 1 tbsp. fresh lime juice
- 1 garlic clove, minced
- 1 tbsp. green onion, chopped
- 1 tsp. olive oil
- salt and pepper to taste
- Burgers:
- 1 1/2 lbs. lean ground turkey
- 2 cloves garlic, finely chopped
- 1 tbsp. fresh thyme, chopped
- 2 tbsp. fresh cilantro, chopped
- 1/2 small red bell pepper, seeded and finely chopped
- 1 small jalepeno pepper, seeded and finely chopped
- 2 tsp. ground cumin
- 1 to 2 tsp. louisiana hot sauce
- 2 tsp. seasoning blend (Such as McCormick Montreal steak seasoning)
- olive oil cooking spray
- 6 deli-style buns
- 1 small red onion, thinly sliced
- 1 small avocado, thinly sliced

Direction

- In a medium bowl, combine all salsa ingredients. Cover and place in the refrigerator until ready to use.
- In a large bowl, combine turkey, garlic, chopped red onion, thyme, cilantro, bell pepper, jalapeno pepper, cumin, hot sauce and seasoning blend; mix well.
- Divide mixture into 6 equal mounds and form into patties; spray patties with olive oil to coat.
- In a large skillet over medium-high heat, cook burgers for 6 to 8 minutes on each side or until cooked through.
- Place cooked burgers on buns and serve topped with salsa, sliced red onion and sliced avocado.

---

283. Southwestern Burger Wraps Recipe

Serving: 4 | Prep: | Cook: 20mins |Ready in:

Ingredients

- cooking spray, or oil, for coating broiler
- 12 oz 93%-lean ground beef
- 1 c. refried beans
- 1/2 c. fresh cilantro, chopped
- 1 tbs pickled jalapenos, diced
- 1 avocado, peeled and pitted
- 1/2 c. salsa
- 1/4 tsp garlic powder
- 1 tsp fresh lime juice
- 2 tbs fat free sour cream, OR yogurt
- 4 tortillas, whole-wheat (pre-warmed)
- 2 c. fresh spinach
- 1/2 c. cheese, shredded (any flavor you prefer)

Direction

- Position oven rack in upper third of oven and the preheat broiler. Coat a broiler pan with cooking spray.

- Gently combine ground beef, beans, cilantro and jalapenos in a medium bowl (do not overmix). Shape into four 5x2" oblong patties and place on the prepared pan.
- Broil the patties until an instant-read thermometer inserted into the center reads 165°F, about 14 to 18 minutes.
- In a bowl, chop (or mash) avocado. Mix in salsa, garlic powder, lime juice and sour cream or yogurt.
- Spread each pre-warmed tortilla with the avocado mixture, then place spinach on top followed by the cheese. Top each with a burger and roll into a wrap. Serve immediately.

---

284.   Southwestern Burgers Recipe

Serving: 4 | Prep: | Cook: 12mins | Ready in:

Ingredients

- Although we usually enjoy our burgers medium-rare, with extra ingredients added, tasters found that the burgers were too soft unless cooked through (basically, well-done).
- 1 1/2 pounds 85 percent lean ground chuck
- 1 cup shredded monterey jack cheese
- 1/4 cup minced fresh cilantro
- 4 teaspoons minced canned chipotle chiles in adobo
- 4 teaspoons yellow mustard
- 4 teaspoons taco seasoning (from packet)
- 1. Break beef into small pieces in medium bowl. Add cheese, cilantro, chiles, mustard, and taco seasoning. Using fork, toss until evenly distributed. Divide mixture into 4 equal portions and lightly pack into 1-inch-thick patties.
- 2. When coals are ready and grate is hot, dip wad of paper towels in vegetable oil and use tongs to rub oil over grate. Grill burgers over very hot fire, without pressing down on them,

until well seared on both sides and cooked through, 8 to 12 minutes. Transfer to plate, tent with foil, and let rest 5 minutes. Serve.

Direction

- We love burgers loaded with a lot of flavorful toppings, but a "Dagwood" style burger can be nearly impossible to eat. The toppings slide out from beneath the bun and end up covering everything but the burger itself. Is there way of putting the toppings inside the burger where they can't fall out? Here's what we discovered:
- Test Kitchen Discoveries
- Flavor the ground beef with shredded Monterey Jack cheese, chopped cilantro, chipotle chilies, and taco seasoning.
- To prevent the cheese-infused burger from tasting greasy, use relatively lean 85 percent lean ground beef.
- Combine the ground beef and flavorings gently; otherwise the burgers may be tough.
- Smoky-tasting chipotle chilies add both spiciness and a rich flavor to the burgers. These chilies, which are smoked jalapeños, come packed in a tomato-based adobo sauce. Small cans of chipotles are found in the Mexican foods aisle of most supermarkets.
- Because of the ingredients mixed into the meat, we found it best to cook the burgers to well-done. The cheese keeps them from being dry or tough.

---

285.   Southwestern Turkey Burgers Recipe

Serving: 4 | Prep: | Cook: 60mins | Ready in:

Ingredients

- Chipotle Ketchup:
- 1/2 c. ketchup
- 2 TBSP. chipotles in adobo, chopped
- 1 TBSP. honey

- 2 tsp. fresh lime juice
- Guacamole:
- 2 avocados, peeled, pitted, and chopped
- 2 TBSP. sour cream
- 1 TBSP. fresh lime juice
- salt
- turkey Burgers:
- 1 1/4 lb. ground turkey breast
- 1 TBSP. olive oil
- 1 tsp. kosher salt
- 1 tsp. dried oregano
- 1/2 tsp. ground black pepper
- 1/4 tsp. ground cumin
- 1/4 tsp. ground coriander
- 1 - 4.5 oz. can whole green chiles
- 1/2 c. monterey jack cheese, shredded
- 1/2 c. canned black beans, drained and rinsed
- 4 slices monterey jack cheese
- 4 hamburger buns, split and toasted
- 1/2 c. tomato, chopped
- 4 slices red onion, 1/4" thick
- Spicy tortilla chips, recipe follows

Direction

- Preheat grill to medium-high.
- Chipotle Ketchup: Whisk ketchup, chipotle chilies, honey, and 1 tablespoon lime juice. Set aside.
- Guacamole: Coarsely mash all ingredients together for the guacamole; cover with plastic wrap, pressing plastic wrap onto surface of guacamole (prevents browning), and chill.
- Turkey Burgers: Blend turkey, oil, and seasonings in a large bowl. Pulse chilies, shredded cheese, and beans in a food processor until coarsely chopped; add to turkey. Blend, shape into 4 patties, and then coat both sides of each patty with non-stick spray. Grill until cooked through, about 4 minutes per side; top burgers with cheese slices during the last minute of grilling.
- To assemble burgers, spread guacamole onto bottom of bun. Sprinkle with chopped tomato, top with a burger, chipotle ketchup, and onion slices; place bun top. Serve with Spicy Tortilla Chips

- Spicy Tortilla Chips: Preheat oven to 400 degrees F. Combine 1 tsp. kosher salt, 1 tsp. chili powder, 1/2 tsp. ground cumin, and 1/2 tsp. cayenne. Spread 6 oz. tortilla chips on baking sheet and sprinkle with seasoning mixture. Bake 5 minutes.

286.   Southwestern Burgers Recipe

Serving: 6 | Prep: | Cook: 10mins | Ready in:

Ingredients

- 1/2 cup mayonnaise
- 21/2 tbls. green chiles
- 2 lbs.ground beef
- 1 sm. onion
- 1 tsp. salt
- 1 tsp. pepper
- 2 tsp. taco seasoning or chili powder
- 6 slices pepper jack cheese
- 6 burger buns of your choice
- Toppings
- lettuce
- tomato
- red onion
- guacamole

Direction

- Mix together mayo and chilies.
- Cover and chill.
- Combine next 5 ingredients.
- Shape into 6 patties.
- Grill over medium- high heat 6-8 minutes until beef is no longer pink.
- Add cheese and let melt before removing from heat.
- Serve on bun with mayo and your choice of toppings.

287. Spam Burgers Recipe

Serving: 6 | Prep: | Cook: 10mins | Ready in:

Ingredients

- 1 can (12 oz) Spam® Luncheon Meat
- 1 Tbsp Miracle Whip salad dressing
- 6 lettuce leaves
- 6 hamburger buns, split
- 6 slices (3/4 oz each) American cheese
- 2 tomatoes, sliced
- 1 onion, sliced
- 12 thin slices dill pickle, optional

Direction

- Slice Spam into 6 slices.
- Using a large skillet sauté Spam until lightly browned, remove to paper towels.
- Spread Miracle Whip on both sides of each bun, layer remaining ingredients on the bun bottoms & cover with the tops.

288. Spiced Turkey Patties With Feta ~ Cucumber Mint Raita Recipe

Serving: 6 | Prep: | Cook: 30mins | Ready in:

Ingredients

- For burgers:
- 2 medium cloves garlic
- 1 1/2 teaspoon kosher salt
- 2 lbs. ground turkey (thigh meat)
- 1/4 cup chopped fresh mint
- 1/4 cup chopped fresh parsley
- 2 teaspoons smoked paprika
- 1 1/2 teaspoons ground cumin
- 1/2 teaspoons ground coriander
- 1/4 teaspoons cayenne
- 1/3 cup crumbled feta
- olive oil, to brush on burgers
- 6 butter/boston lettuce leaves, for wrapping
- ~
- cucumber-Mint Raita:
- 1/2 an english cucumber, peeled and seeded, finely chopped
- 1-2 tablespoons grated onion
- 1 cup plain, lowfat yogurt (greek/middle eastern style is best)
- a few tablespoons fresh mint, finely chopped
- ground cumin, to taste
- cayenne, to taste
- kosher salt, to taste

Direction

- Mix all ingredients for raita in a bowl and let chill.
- Press or chop the garlic finely and stir together with the salt. Gently break the ground turkey into pieces in a large bowl then mix the garlic paste, fresh herbs, paprika, cumin, coriander, cayenne, and feta into the ground turkey (it's easiest to use your hands for this). Shape the meat into 6-8 equal 1-inch-thick patties. Brush or rub the patties on each side with olive oil. Refrigerate, uncovered, for at least 20 minutes and up to 4 hours.
- While the burgers are chilling, prepare a charcoal or gas grill. Grill the burgers, covered with vents open, over direct medium heat until nicely marked and just cooked through (an instant-read thermometer inserted in a burger should read 165°F), about 4 to 6 minutes per side.
- Top burgers with Raita and serve wrapped in lettuce or your favorite flatbread.

289. Spicy Bean Burgers Recipe

Serving: 10 | Prep: | Cook: 12mins | Ready in:

Ingredients

- 2 15 oz cans pinto beans with jalapeno peppers rinsed and drained

- 1 15 oz can black beans rinsed and drained
- 1 cup quick cooking oats
- 4 green onions chopped
- 1 large egg beaten
- 1/2 cup ketchup
- 1 teaspoon garlic
- 1 teaspoon worchstershire sauce
- 1/2 teaspoon liquid smoke
- hamburger buns
- letuce and tomatoe for toppings
- oil for frying

Direction

- Mash beans in a large bowl
- Add next 7 ingredients and mix well
- Shape into 10 patties
- Heat oil in a skillet over medium high heat
- Fry patties 2 to 3 minutes on each side until browned
- Serve on warmed hamburger buns with your favorite condiments and toppings
- Salsa is terrific on top

---

290. Spicy Glazed Stuffed Burgers Recipe

Serving: 0 | Prep: | Cook: 2hours | Ready in:

Ingredients

- 3lbs ground beef(I used a mixture of regular ground beef and ground round)
- 1T steak seasoning of choice
- 1T worcestershire sauce
- dash of liquid smoke
- kosher or sea salt
- 6oz pepper jack cheese, cut into about 1/2 inch squares, but about 1/4inch thick
- For Spicy honey Glaze
- 2T hot pepper jelly
- 1/4 cup honey
- 2t worcestershire sauce
- juice from 1 lemon or 2 limes

Direction

- Combine beef, steak seasoning, Worcestershire sauce, liquid smoke and salt in large bowl, and mix well.
- Form into 12-16 equal sized patties(1/4lb patties, here, will give you 6, 1/2lb burgers, at serving, minus cooking weight, of course)
- Arrange a few slices of cheese on half of the patties, then top with a plain patty and press firmly together to seal the edges.
- Let burgers rest at least an hour in the fridge, then remove from fridge about 1/2 hour prior to grilling.
- For Spicy Honey Glaze
- Combine all ingredients in small glass bowl. Heat briefly in the microwave, if needed, to more easily incorporate. Glaze does not have to be hot, though, to apply...the citrus juice should keep it liquidy enough.
- To Prepare
- Grill burgers at a high heat, not flipping until the meat has charred and released... then flip them. After this first flip, brush with the glaze, and when that side chars and releases, lower grill temp, flip again, and glaze that side. Cook until your desired doneness(medium for us...pink, not red or bloody, just cooked through, with a lovely char on the outside), flipping one last time to make sure to heat both sides briefly, after glazing.
- Serve as desired with sliced tomato, lettuce, mustard, sweet onion, etc.

---

291. Spicy Black Bean Burgers Recipe

Serving: 2 | Prep: | Cook: 10mins | Ready in:

Ingredients

- 1 15 OZ can black beans,rinsed & drained
- 1/3 cup chopped red onion
- 1 jalapeno,seed & deribbed(white inner) minced

- 1/4 cup bread crumbs or cracker meal.(I prefer cracker meal)
- 2 Tblsp.chunky salsa
- 1 Tsp.ground cumin
- vegetable oil

Direction

- Mash beans in medium bowl with fork. Add onion, breadcrumbs, salsa, cumin, and jalapeno. Season with salt and pepper. Using moistened hands, shape bean mixture into 2 patties.
- Sauté in oil, (appx.2 tbsp. oil) for 4 minutes on each side.
- Serve warm.
- Can be made ahead and sautéed later, this give flavors a chance to meld.

292. Spinach Burgers Recipe

Serving: 4 | Prep: | Cook: 10mins | Ready in:

Ingredients

- 15 oz. can garbanzo beans,rinsed & drained
- 1 cup,packed chopped fresh spinach
- 2 scallions,sliced
- 1 clove garlic,crushed
- 1/4 cup flour
- 2 Tbs.tahini
- 1 Tbs.fresh lemon juice
- 1/8 tsp.cumin
- 2 tsp.olive oil
- 4 pita pockets
- 8 pepperoncini,drained & sliced
- 1 large tomatoes,chopped
- 1/2 cucumber,peeled & sliced

Direction

- In a food processor, combine garbanzos, spinach, scallions, garlic and flour. Pulse on and off several times to blend well. Add salt and pepper to taste, process briefly.

- Shape mixture into 4 patties about a 1/2 inch thick.
- In a small bowl, mix tahini with 2 tablespoons warm water (this will make tahini easier to mix) add lemon juice, cumin and salt to taste. Set aside.
- In a large non-stick skillet heat oil over medium-high heat. Add burgers and cook until browned, about 4 minutes each side, add more oil if necessary.
- Cut pitas in half. Cut burgers in half and place in pita bread. Spoon pepperoncini, tomatoes, cucumbers over burgers and drizzle with tahini sauce.

293. Spinach Artichoke Burgers (rachael Ray) Recipe

Serving: 4 | Prep: | Cook: | Ready in:

Ingredients

- 1 lb ground beef,chicken or turkey breast salt and freshly ground pepper Zest of 1 lemon
- A couple handfuls parmesan cheese, grated
- 1 garlic clove, finely chopped
- One (10 oz) package frozen chopped spinach, thawed and wrung dry in a kitchen towel
- 1 TBS fresh thyme (or 1 tsp dried thyme)
- extra-virgin olive oil (EVOO), for liberal drizzling
- Four 1/2" thick slices of ripe beefsteak tomato
- One (14 oz) can artichoke hearts in water, drained and thinly sliced
- 4 slices provolone cheese (or whatever cheese you like)

Direction

- Place the ground beef/chicken/turkey in a medium bowl and season with salt and pepper. Add the lemon zest, parmesan, finely chopped garlic, spinach, thyme and a drizzle of EVOO, about 2 tablespoons, and combine. Form into 4 patties and cook the burgers until firm and cooked through, about 6 minutes on each side. In the last 2 minutes of the burgers' cooking time, divide the sliced artichokes evenly among the burgers, then cover each with the sliced cheese. If cooking on the grill, drop the lid to melt the cheese. If cooking on the stovetop, tent your grill pan or skillet with aluminum foil. Place a tomato slice on top of each of the burgers and serve immediately.

---

294. Staceys Amazing Turkey Bacon And Ranch Burgers Recipe

Serving: 8 | Prep: | Cook: 15mins | Ready in:

Ingredients

- 2 pounds ground turkey
- 1 package ranch dressing mix
- 1 1/2 cups shredded cheddar cheese
- 6 slices cooked crumbled bacon

Direction

- Combine all ingredients in a large bowl.
- Form into 6 or 8 equal sized patties.
- Place on cookie sheet that has been lined with plastic wrap.
- Place cookie sheet in freezer for about 1/2 hour, to firm up patties. This will help hold them together while grilling,
- Grill over a medium flame for about 7 minutes per side, until no longer pink inside.
- Serve on buns with your favourite burger toppings.

---

295. Steak Burgers Two Ways Recipe

Serving: 0 | Prep: | Cook: 1hours | Ready in:

Ingredients

- For Chipotle Burgers
- 2lbs ground sirloin(or combine with venison, bison, elk, etc)
- 1T olive oil
- 1 can chipotle peppers in adobo, chopped(reserve about 2T adobo) {or to taste}
- 1/2t cumin
- 4oz monterey jack cheese, shredded
- salt and fresh ground pepper
- For 4 Star Burgers
- 2lbs ground sirloin(or combine with venison, bison, elk, etc)
- 1T softened butter(or olive oil)
- 2 cloves garlic, minced
- 2oz crumbed blue cheese(I use gorgonzola)
- 2T fresh chives, chopped
- dash of liquid smoke
- 2t worcestershire sauce
- salt and fresh ground pepper
- For Chipotle Mayo
- 1 cup mayonnaise
- 2T reserved adobo
- 1/2t fresh lime juice
- 1/2t cumin
- For Maitre D' Mayo
- 1 cup mayonnaise
- 2T softened butter
- 2T fresh parsley, chopped
- 1t fresh lemon juice

Direction

- For Burgers
- For each type of burger, mix all ingredients in large bowl until well combined.
- Shape into 1/3lb burgers
- Grill to desired doneness (preferably medium rare :)
- For Mayos
- For each type of mayo mix all ingredients until well combined.
- Chill until ready to use.
- Top burgers with any desired toppings, but I prefer, with these, to really taste the burgers,

and usually use nothing more than leaf lettuce (or spinach) and fresh sliced tomatoes!

296. Steakhouse Mushroom Burgers On Texas Toast With Creamed Spinach Sauce Recipe

Serving: 4 | Prep: | Cook: 14mins | Ready in:

Ingredients

- BURGERS
- 8 oz button mushrooms, sliced
- 2 T EVOO, divided
- 1 t minced garlic
- 1.5 lb ground sirloin, 85% lean
- 1/2 t each - kosher salt and fresh ground black pepper
- 4 slices Texas toast
- Parmesan for garnish
- CREAMED spinach SAUCE
- *Can be made a day ahead. After cooking the sauce, let it cool completely; cover and refrigerate, then reheat over medium low heat.
- 2 T unsalted butter
- 1/4 c minced onion
- 2 T all-purpose flour
- 1/2 c half and half
- 1/2 c chicken broth
- kosher salt, cayenne pepper and nutmeg to taste
- 4 c chopped fresh spinach
- 1 T grated parmesan
- 1/2 t fresh lemon juice

Direction

- BURGERS
- Preheat grill to medium high
- Sauté mushrooms in 1 T EVOO over medium high heat
- Cook until begin to brown, 3-4 minutes
- Stir in garlic and cook 1 minute
- Season with salt and pepper
- Remove pan from heat slightly cool mushrooms
- Combine ground sirloin with soy sauce, 1/2 t salt, 1/2 t pepper and mushroom mixture by hand in large mixing bowl
- Divide into 4 equal portions and shape into patties
- Grill uncovered on direct heat, turning only once, and not mashing with the spatula
- Cook to desired doneness, remove from grill and tent with foil
- Allow to rest
- Reduce grill heat to medium low
- Brush toast with remaining 1 T EVOO
- Place toast slices on grill and heat until lightly browned, 1-2 minutes per side
- Serve place each burger on open piece of toast and to with Creamed Spinach Sauce
- Garnish with parmesan and serve as open-faced sandwiches
- CREAMED SPINACH SAUCE
- Melt butter in a saucepan over medium low heat
- Add onion and cook until translucent, 3-4 minutes
- Stir flour into onion, cook 1 minute
- Whisk in half and half, broth, salt, cayenne, and nutmeg
- Bring sauce to a boil; reduce heat
- Simmer for 2 minutes
- Add spinach, stirring until wilted
- Mix in 1 T parmesan and lemon juice

297. Steakhouse Mushroom Burgers With Creamed Spinach Sauce Recipe

Serving: 4 | Prep: | Cook: | Ready in:

Ingredients

- Steakhouse mushroom Burgers:
- 8 oz mushrooms, chopped (any kind)
- 3 Tbs olive oil, divided

- 2 cloves garlic, minced
- 1 lb ground sirloin
- 1 Tbs soy sauce
- 2 tsp minced fresh thyme
- 2 tsp minced fresh parsley
- 1 Tbs Dijon mustard
- 1/2 tsp kosher salt
- 1/2 tsp black pepper
- 4 slices Texas toast bread (I made my own)
- garlic butter with parsley
- grated parmigiano-reggiano
- ~
- Creamed spinach Sauce:
- 2 Tbs unsalted butter
- 1 large shallot, minced
- 2 Tbs all-purpose flour
- 1/2 cup half-and-half, plus more as needed
- 1/2 cup roasted chicken stock
- kosher salt and black pepper
- pinch of freshly grated nutmeg
- 4 cups chopped fresh organic spinach
- 2 Tbs grated parmigiano-reggiano
- squeeze of fresh lemon juice

Direction

- Preheat the grill to medium-high.
- In a medium sauté pan, sauté the mushrooms in 1 tablespoon of olive oil over medium-high heat. Cook until the mushrooms begin to brown, 3-4 minutes. Stir in garlic and cook until fragrant, about 1 minute. Season with salt and pepper and remove from heat.
- In a large bowl, combine the sirloin with 1 tablespoon oil, soy sauce, salt, pepper, mustard, herbs, and mushroom mixture. Gently mix to combine using a fork or your hands. Divide the mixture into 4 equal portions, shaping each portion into a patty.
- Scrape the grate clean and brush with the remaining tablespoon of oil. Grill the burgers until cooked through, 3-4 minutes per side. Remove the burgers from the grill and cover to keep warm.
- To make the spinach sauce, melt the butter in a medium saucepan over medium-low heat. Add the shallot and cook until translucent, 3-4

minutes. Stir the flour into the onions and cook 1 minute.
- Whisk in the half-and-half, broth, salt, and nutmeg. Bring sauce to a simmer, then reduce heat and simmer for 2 minutes, until it begins to thicken.
- Add the spinach, stirring until wilted. Mix in the cheese and lemon juice, and add more half-and-half if the sauce has thickened too much. Season to taste with salt and pepper.
- In a skillet that has melted garlic butter, grill the bread on each side then sprinkle each side with cheese. Toast until cheese melts onto the bread and gets a little crunchy.
- Top each slice of grilled bread with a burger and spinach sauce. Serve immediately.

298.   Stuffed Burger Recipe

Serving: 4 | Prep: | Cook: 25mins | Ready in:

Ingredients

- 1 lb. ground beef
- 3 Tbsp. ranch dressing divided
- 4 slices (Maple) bacon, cooked, crumbled
- 4 Tbsp. of 4cheese shredded cheese
- 4 hamburger buns, split, lightly toasted
- 4 shiitake mushrooms, diced
- 4 lettuce leaves
- 4 Large tomato slices

Direction

- Cook and crumble 4 slices of bacon, dice up mushrooms, and set both aside.
- PREHEAT grill to medium heat.
- Mix meat and 2 Tbsp. of the ranch dressing. Shape into 8 thin patties.
- Mix remaining 1 Tbsp. dressing, bacon, and the mushrooms.
- Spoon about 1 Tbsp. of the bacon mixture onto center of each of 4 of the patties;
- Top with 1 Tb. of cheese and second patty.
- Pinch edges of patties together to seal.

- GRILL patties 7 to 10 min. on each side or until cooked through
- (160°F).
- Lightly toast the inside part of the buns on the grill for about 1 or two minutes.
- COVER bottom halves of buns with lettuce and burgers.
- Top with a tomato slice and the top half of the buns.
- Sink your teeth in.

299.   Stuffed Burgers Recipe

Serving: 6 | Prep: | Cook: 15mins | Ready in:

Ingredients

- 1 1/2 lbs ground beef or a beef, pork, turkey mix is great
- 1 1/2 cups soft breadcrumbs (2 slices) you can use quick cook oatmeal
- 1/2 cup onion (chopped, fine)
- 2 large eggs (beaten)
- 2 tablespoons sugar or stevia, but just a sprinkle
- 3 tablespoons soy sauce
- 1/4 cup water
- 1 small garlic clove (crushed)
- A dash ginger
- -STUFFING STUFF-
- sliced tomatoes
- cheese
- mushrooms
- onions
- bell peppers
- hot peppers
- bacon, precooked
- pepperoni

Direction

- Combine ground beef with remaining ingredients.
- Mix well.
- Shape into 12 patties.

- These will be thin-ish but remember you are going to put two together in the end.
- On six of the patties put your stuffing ingredients.
- Place another patty on top of the stuffing.
- Seal the edges together very well, you do not want them to split as you cook and lose the goodies.
- Broil 4 to 5 inches from heat for 10 minutes, turning once.
- These burgers can also be pan grilled, just be careful with the flips!!
- I now serve these on Oroweat Sandwich Thins. Not so much bread.
- Or just on a plate with a salad, no bread at all!!

300.   Stuffed Burgers Texan Style Recipe

Serving: 6 | Prep: | Cook: 20mins | Ready in:

Ingredients

- 2 pounds ground beef or ground turkey
- 6 frozen cheese filled poppers
- 1 cup mild or medium salsa
- 4 oz. Velvetta brand cheese
- 1 onion, chopped
- 1/2 cup chopped bell pepper
- 3 tablespoons butter
- 1 egg
- 1 tablespoon garlic powder
- 1 tablespoon creole spice
- 1/2 teaspoon cracked black pepper
- 6 hamburger buns, toasted lightly

Direction

- In skillet, sauté onions and bell pepper in butter until just tender.
- In a mixing bowl, mix together the ground beef, egg, and spices.
- Add onions and bell pepper and mix well.

- Divide ground beef mixture into six equal parts.
- Mold each part of ground beef around one popper.
- Cook on hot grill or on George Foreman type grill until cooked thoroughly.
- In a glass microwave safe dish, melt Velveeta cheese.
- Stir in salsa.
- Lightly toast buns on grill.
- Place one burger on each bun, top with cheese sauce and serve with additional burger dressings (tomatoes, lettuce, etc.)

301. Stuffed Turkey Burgers Recipe

Serving: 4 | Prep: | Cook: 10mins | Ready in:

Ingredients

- 1 1/4 pounds lean ground turkey breast
- 1/2 cup chopped roasted red peppers.
- 1/2 cup shredded part-skim mozzarella cheese
- 1/4 tsp. salt
- freshly ground black pepper to taste.

Direction

- Divide turkey into 4 equal sized rounds.
- Make 2 equal sized patties out of each round so you have 8 patties/total.
- Sprinkle 4 of the patties with 2 tablespoons red pepper and cheese
- Top with remaining patties, working the turkey around edges to seal the burgers closed.
- Season with salt and a few grinds of pepper.
- Grill or broil until cooked through completely, about 5 minutes on each side.

302. Super Salmon Burgers Recipe

Serving: 4 | Prep: | Cook: 10mins | Ready in:

Ingredients

- 1/2 cup plain nonfat yogurt
- 1 scallion chopped
- 1 teaspoon dried dill
- 15 ounce can salmon well drained and bones removed
- 4 egg whites
- 1/2 cup plain bread crumbs
- 2/3 cup chopped white onion
- 1/4 teaspoon freshly ground black pepper
- 4 whole wheat mini pita pockets
- 6 cups shredded romaine lettuce

Direction

- Place yogurt, scallion and dill in small bowl and stir to mix well.
- Cover and chill until ready to serve.
- Place salmon, egg whites, bread crumbs, onion and black pepper in medium bowl and mix well.
- Shape into 4 patties about 1" thick then coat a non-stick skillet with cooking spray.
- Preheat over medium high heat then add patties and cook 5 minutes on each side.
- Cut thin slice off top of each pita round and carefully open the round without separating halves.
- Place 1 burger in each pita and top with 1 tablespoon yogurt sauce and 1-1/2 cups lettuce.
- Serve immediately with extra sauce on the side.

303. Supreme Brandy Burgers Recipe

Serving: 2 | Prep: | Cook: 20mins | Ready in:

Ingredients

- 2 shallots (or scallions) finely chopped
- 4 tablespoons butter
- 1 pound ground lean chuck
- 1/4 pounds boiled ham, ground
- 4 tablespoons ice water
- 1 egg slightly beaten
- Pinck of thyme
- Freshly ground pepper
- flour
- 1 tablespoon oil
- 1/4 cup beef consomme'
- 1/4 cup Hiram Walker apricot Flavored brandy
- 2 more tablespoons butter

Direction

- Sauté the shallots. Drain.
- In a bowl add shallots and the next 7 ingredients.
- Wet hands and shape into patties; refrigerate for 1 hour.
- Dust patties with flour; sauté' until in oil until cooked and keep warm in oven.
- Add consommé, Apricot Brandy, and cook 5 minutes. Add butter and pour over patties. Sprinkle with parsley

---

304.   **Sweet Potato Black Bean Burgers**

Serving: 5 | Prep: | Cook: 12mins | Ready in:

Ingredients

- 1 large sweet potato
- 1 cooking spray
- 2 (15 ounce) cans black beans, rinsed and drained
- ½ cup quick cooking oats
- ¼ cup chopped onion
- 1 tablespoon Dijon mustard
- 1 teaspoon ground cumin
- ¼ teaspoon freshly grated ginger
- ¼ teaspoon salt
- 1 pinch ground cinnamon

Direction

- Preheat oven to 400 degrees F (200 degrees C). Poke a few holes into sweet potato with a fork; place on a greased baking sheet.
- Bake in the preheated oven until sweet potato can be easily pierced with a fork, 35 to 45 minutes. Remove from oven and cool until easily handled. Reduce heat to 350 degrees F (175 degrees C). Spray a baking sheet with cooking spray.
- Peel sweet potato and place into a large bowl. Add black beans and mash with a whisk or fork. Add oats, onions, Dijon mustard, cumin, ginger, salt, and cinnamon and mix until well combined. Shape mixture into 6 patties with wet hands and place onto prepared baking sheet.
- Bake in the preheated oven until cooked in the center and crisp on the outside, about 8 minutes on each side.
- Notes:
- Instead of freshly grated ginger, 1/4 teaspoon of ginger powder can be used.
- A food processor can be used in step 3 if desired.
- Both white and red onions work well for this recipe.
- Patties will keep fresh in the refrigerator for a few days or you can freeze them in a well-insulated container or freezer bag and reheat in the microwave or oven.
- Nutrition Facts
- 227.1 calories; protein 10.8g 22% DV; carbohydrates 44.7g 14% DV; fat 1g 2% DV; cholesterolmg; sodium 746.3mg 30% DV.

305. TACO CORN BURGER PIE Recipe

Serving: 4 | Prep: | Cook: 45mins | Ready in:

Ingredients

- 1 c. all-purpose flour
- 1/4 c. cornmeal
- 1/2 c. chopped onion
- 1/2 c. butter
- 1/4 c. water
- FILLING:
- 1 lb. ground beef
- 1 pkg. taco seasoning mix
- 3/4 c. water
- 12 oz. can whole kernel corn
- 1 c. shredded lettuce
- 2 oz. shredded cheese
- 1 med. tomato, chopped

Direction

- Heat oven to 375 degrees. Mix flour, cornmeal, and onion; add butter, water and stir until dough holds together. Press in bottom and sides of large pie plate, ungreased. Bake for 20 to 25 minutes or until light brown. In large skillet brown beef, drain. Stir in taco seasoning mix, add 3/4 cup water and simmer 20 minutes until liquid is reduced. Stir in corn and cook until thoroughly heated. Spread in baked crust. Top with lettuce, cheese and tomatoes.

306. TURKEY BURGERS Texas Style Recipe

Serving: 4 | Prep: | Cook: 25mins | Ready in:

Ingredients

- Ingredients:
- 1 Lb. ground turkey breast
- 1 cup whole wheat bread crumbs

- 1 egg white
- ½ tsp. Dried sage leaves
- ½ tsp. dried marjoram leaves
- ¼ tsp. salt
- ¼ tsp. ground black pepper
- 1 tsp. vegetable oil
- 4 Whole Grain Sandwich rolls, split in half
- ¼ cup Cowpoke barbecue sauce (Recipe follows) Or Prepared barbecue sauce
- Cowpoke Ingredients:
- 1 tsp. vegetable oil
- ¾ cup chopped green onion
- 3 cloves garlic, finely chopped
- 1 can (14 ½ oz) crushed tomatoes
- ½ cup ketchup
- ¼ cup water
- ¼ cup orange juice
- 2 Tbs. cider vinegar
- 2 tsp. chili sauce
- Dash worcestershire sauce

Direction

- Burgers method:
- 1) Combine turkey, bread crumbs, egg white, sage, marjoram, salt and pepper in large bowl until well blended. Shape into 4 patties.
- 2) Heat oil in a large non-stick skillet over medium-high heat until hot. Add patties. Cook 10 minutes or until patties are no longer pink in centers, Turning once.
- 3) Place one patty on bottom half of each roll. Spoon 1 Tbs. of Cowpoke Barbecue Sauce over top of each burger. Place tops of rolls over burgers. Serve with lettuce and tomato and garnish with carrot slices, if desired.
- Calories per burger: 319
- Cowpoke Barbecue Sauce Method:
- Heat oil in large non-stick saucepan over medium heat until hot. Add onions and garlic. Cook and stir 5 minutes or until onions are tender. Stir in remaining ingredients. Reduce heat to medium-low.
- Cook 15 minutes, stirring occasionally. Makes 2 cups.
- Calories per serving: 310 serving size 1 Tbs.

307.   Taco Burgers Recipe

Serving: 4 | Prep: | Cook: 8mins | Ready in:

Ingredients

- 1.5 pounds ground round
- 1 egg
- 1 can diced green chilles
- 2 T salsa
- 2 T taco seasoning
- 2 T finely chopped onion
- 1/4 c crushed tortilla chips
- 1 clove garlic, finely chopped
- 1 t chili powder
- 1 t cumin
- 4 large hamburger buns
- 1 c grated mexican cheese
- 1 c shredded lettuce
- 1 c chopped tomatoes
- guacamole
- taco sauce
- sour cream
- sliced ripe olives

Direction

- In a large bowl, combine all ingredients from meat to cumin, and mix together with hands until just combined.
- Gently shape meat into 4 burgers about 3/4 inch thick and 4.5 inches across.
- Grill about 6-8 minutes per side for medium well. (4 minutes for med rare, 5 medium).
- RESIST all urges to smash burgers while cooking, as this lets the juices cook out. ALSO - turn only once while cooking
- Serve immediately with garnishes

308.   Tangy Turkey Burgers Recipe

Serving: 6 | Prep: | Cook: 10mins | Ready in:

Ingredients

- 1 ½ lb. ground turkey
- 3 Tbs. Minced green onion
- 1tsp. Reduced-sodium soy sauce
- 1tsp. Minced fresh ginger or ½ tsp. ground ginger
- 2 tsp. dijon-style mustard
- ¼ tsp. black pepper
- 6 whole-grain hamburger buns, lightly toasted
- Green-leaf lettuce and scallion (green onion) brushes for garnish

Direction

- 1 Preheat the broiler. Line a broiler pan with foil
- 2 In a large bowl, combine the turkey, green onion, soy sauce, ginger, mustard and pepper. Mix well. Shape mixture into 6 patties.
- 3 Place patties on rack in prepared pan. Broil 2 inches from the heat until patties are cooked through, about 5 minutes per side
- 4 Place the buns on serving plates; place lettuce on buns and top with burgers. Garnish with scallion brushes and serve.
- Variation:
- The typical burger condiments — ketchup, yellow mustard, relish, and pickles-- are high in sodium. For a change of pace, try topping burgers with healthy alternatives such as tomato, red and green bell pepper, and a little homemade salsa. Also make wise bread choices — English muffins and whole-wheat pita pockets are low-fat options.
- Per serving: Calories 288, carbohydrates 22g, protein 24g, sodium 432mg, fat 11g, cholesterol 83mg.

309.   Tater Burgers Recipe

Serving: 4 | Prep: | Cook: 15mins | Ready in:

Ingredients

- 1 lb. ground beef
- 2 Tbs. beef broth
- 1 C. shredded hash brown potatoes
- 1/4 C, chopped onion

Direction

- Mix all together shape into patties.
- Cook in skillet on low heat so the hash browns will have time to cook.

---

310. Texas Hold Ums Mini Chipotle Beef Burgers With Warm Fire Roasted Garlic Ketchup Recipe

Serving: 6 | Prep: | Cook: 6mins | Ready in:

Ingredients

- 2 pounds ground sirloin
- 1 medium onion, peeled and cut in 1/2
- 2 tablespoons worcestershire sauce
- 2 chipotles in adobo and 2 tablespoons of adobo sauce
- 2 tablespoons grill seasoning, a couple of palm fulls, (recommended: Montreal steak seasoning by McCormick)
- 1 tablespoon extra-virgin olive oil, plus some for drizzling
- 3 cloves garlic, finely chopped
- 3 tablespoons brown sugar
- 1/4 cup vinegar
- 1 (15-ounce) can crushed fire roasted tomatoes, about 2 cups
- salt and pepper
- 12 slices, 1/2-inch thick, brick-cut smoked Cheddar or sharp Cheddar, (recommended: Cabot), optional
- 12 small round rolls, split
- (Many markets sell mini Keiser rolls or use dinner rolls in any flavor you like)

Direction

- Preheat grill pan to high.
- Place the meat in a bowl. Cut the onion in half. Grate half the onion into the meat using the small grate on a box grater.
- Chop and reserve the other half onion. Add Worcestershire, chipotles and sauce and grill seasoning to burgers.
- Drizzle a little extra-virgin olive oil over the bowl and mix meat. Score the meat into 4 sections. Make 3 mini-burgers, each 3 inches wide, 1-inch thick, from each half-pound of meat.
- Heat a small sauce pot over medium heat. Add extra-virgin olive oil and garlic.
- Cook garlic 2 to 3 minutes then add sugar and vinegar, cook 2 minutes more and stir in tomatoes.
- Season sauce with salt and pepper and allow it to reduce 5 to 6 minutes more.
- Grill meat 2 to 3 minutes on each side and top with cheese, if you like.
- Place burgers on buns and top with raw chopped onions and warm fire roasted ketchup and serve.

---

311. Thai Burgers With Gingered Mushroom Recipe

Serving: 4 | Prep: | Cook: 20mins | Ready in:

Ingredients

- 2 pounds ground sirloin
- 1/4 cup finely chopped fresh cilantro
- 2 tablespoons finely chopped fresh mint
- 1 tablespoon fresh lime juice
- 1 tablespoon finely chopped jalapeno pepper
- 1 tablespoon finely chopped garlic
- 1 teaspoon grated lime zest
- 1 teaspoon grated ginger
- 1/2 teaspoon salt
- 1/2 teaspoon freshly ground black pepper
- Mushrooms:
- 3 tablespoons butter

- 2 tablespoons peanut oil
- 2 teaspoons grated fresh ginger
- 8 ounces fresh shitake mushrooms stems removed and sliced
- 1/2 teaspoon salt
- 1/2 teaspoon freshly ground black pepper

Direction

- Combine all burger ingredients in large bowl and mix gently but thoroughly.
- Form into 4 patties and grill directly over hot coals 5 minutes per side.
- Heat butter and peanut oil in a skillet over moderate heat and sauté ginger for 30 seconds.
- Add mushrooms and sauté 5 minutes then season with salt and pepper.
- Serve burgers on toasted buns topped with mushrooms.

312. Thai Chicken Burgers Recipe

Serving: 4 | Prep: | Cook: 10mins | Ready in:

Ingredients

- 1 Lb. ground chicken
- 1 Cup Fresh cilantro
- 1 Cup roasted and salted peanuts (Crushed)
- 1/4 Cup oyster sauce
- 2 Tbs. ground ginger
- 2 cloves of garlic (minced)
- 1/2 Cup coconut milk
- 2 Tbs. Vietnamese Spicy garlic Sauce (Rooster Label)
- 1 Tbs. brown sugar
- 1 Cup cooked rice
- 2 Tbs. Salt
- 2 Tbs. pepper

Direction

- Mix together all ingredients and allow to sit in the fridge for 10 - 20 minutes.

- Form the mixture into patties.
- Fry them in a skillet on medium heat for about 5 minutes for each side, or to desired doneness.
- Slop them up with peanut sauce and eat them.

313. Thai Chicken Burgers With Spicy Peanut Slaw Recipe

Serving: 4 | Prep: | Cook: 30mins | Ready in:

Ingredients

- BURGERS:
- 1 1/2 lb ground chicken
- 1/2 cup panko or whole wheat bread crumbs
- 1 tbsp lime juice
- 1 tbsp chopped cilantro
- 2 tsp. fresh ginger, grated
- salt & pepper
- 1 tsp hot sauce (like Sriracha)
- 1 clove garlic, minced
- 1/2 cup chopped red bell pepper
- 4 whole wheat buns
- COLE SLAW:
- 1 bag coleslaw mix (or 4 or 5 cups grated cabbage/carrot)
- 1 cucumber, peeled seeded and coarsely grated
- 1 tbsp cilantro, chopped
- 1/4 cup natural peanut butter
- 1/4 cup rice vinegar
- 2 tbsp lime juice
- 1 clove garlic, chopped
- 1 tbsp fresh ginger, minced
- 1 tbsp hot sauce (or to taste)
- 1 tbsp honey
- 1 tsp toasted sesame oil
- 1/4 cup peanut oil
- Dash sot sauce
- salt & pepper
- 1/4 cup coconut milk (optional)
- 1/2 cup peanuts, chopped
- cilantro for garnish

Direction

- For Cole Slaw:
- Combine everything except coleslaw mix, cucumbers, peanuts and cilantro for garnish in a blender. Blend until smooth (you can drizzle oil in while processing if you like - I forgot to and it still worked fine!)
- Pour over slaw and cucumbers and toss to coat. (You can refrigerate if making ahead)
- Garnish with additional cilantro and peanuts before serving.
- For Burgers:
- Combine everything together and shape into patties.
- Preheat oiled grill or pan over medium-high heat; place burgers on grill and reduce heat to medium. Cook about 3-4 minutes each side, or until done.
- Place burgers on buns. If desired, top with some of the spicy peanut slaw as a garnish.

---

314.   Thai Style Chicken Burgers Recipe

Serving: 4 | Prep: | Cook: 10mins | Ready in:

Ingredients

- 1 pound ground chicken
- 2 1/2 tablespoons lime zest
- 1 tablespoon lime juice
- 1 teaspoon fresh chili, minced
- 3 cloves garlic, minced
- 1/8 teaspoon sesame oil
- 1 egg
- 2 tablespoons coriander, chopped
- 1 shallot, minced
- 1/2 teaspoon soy sauce
- 2 teaspoons ginger, minced
- 1 teaspoon scallion, sliced
- 3/4 cup panko bread crumbs
- 1 teaspoon fish sauce
- 4 buns, toasted

- lettuce
- tomato
- papaya Ketchup (recipe posted)

Direction

- Make burgers: combine all ingredient in a large bowl until well combined.
- Add more or less panko breadcrumbs as needed to make the mix pliable and soft, but not falling apart.
- Shape into 4 patties and refrigerate for 1 hour to let the flavours meld and the burgers keep their shape.
- Grill on preheated grill until the internal temperature hits 180°F.
- Serve on buns with lettuce, tomato and pineapple ketchup.

---

315.   The 5000 Calorie Deep Fried Burger Recipe

Serving: 1 | Prep: | Cook: 10mins | Ready in:

Ingredients

- 14 oz burger patty made with ground beef tenderloin
- 3 beer battered onion rings
- 4 pieces of thick cut bacon
- 3 slices of cheddar cheese
- 1 homemade milk bun
- 2 cups beer batter
- 5-8 wooden skewers to hold it all together

Direction

- Don't eat anything for about 1 day prior
- Grill off hamburger to rare
- Fry onion rings and bacon
- Layer slice of cheddar, bacon, slice of cheddar, onion rings, slice of cheddar on top of burger and briefly place in 500 degree oven to melt together.

- Place your heart healthy burger stack inside your homemade milk bun, press together, and skewer with your wooden skewers.
- Dust well with flour and dip in bear batter, spooning the batter into all crevices.
- Drop burger into deep fry basket. If you made your burger right, it will be too tall for the oil to actually cover completely. Carefully ladle hot oil from the fryer over the top of the burger to compensate.
- Cook until golden brown.
- Remove from fryer, let rest for about 2-3 minutes, and cut in half with a serrated knife.
- Serve with lettuce, tomato, onion and horseradish Remoulade.
- After eating, call your cardiologist, tell him what you've done, and sit in amusement as he has a heart attack for you over the phone.
- Disclaimer: Following this recipe and consuming the finished product may be hazardous to your health. Eating The Deep Fried Hamburger may cause acne, soar stomach, huge butt syndrome, or sudden and unexpected cardiac arrest. Eating the whole thing in one sitting will make you a true American Hero.

---

316.   The Bucket Shop Beef Burgers Recipe

Serving: 0 | Prep: | Cook: 45mins | Ready in:

Ingredients

- 3 pounds ground beef
- 1 to 2 large onions, chopped
- 2 cups water
- 1 pound brick chili
- 1 tablespoon salt
- 1/2 tablespoon black pepper
- yellow mustard, to your liking (optional)
- ketchup to your liking
- 2 packages hot dog buns

Direction

- Cook ground beef and onion in water. Drain and add the remaining ingredients but the hot dog buns. Cook thoroughly. Serve on an open hot dog bun. Could serve on hamburger buns.

---

317.   The Perfect Hamburger

Serving: 4 | Prep: | Cook: 20mins | Ready in:

Ingredients

- 1 large egg, lightly beaten
- SEASONINGS:
- 2 tablespoons chili sauce
- 1 teaspoon dried minced onion
- 1 teaspoon prepared horseradish
- 1 teaspoon Worcestershire sauce
- 1/2 teaspoon salt
- Dash pepper
- BURGER:
- 1 pound lean ground beef (90% lean)
- 4 hamburger buns, split
- TOPPINGS:
- Sliced tomato, onion, pickles and condiments, optional

Direction

- In a large bowl, combine egg and seasonings. Crumble beef over mixture and mix well. Shape into four 3/4-in.-thick patties.
- Grill, covered, on a greased grill rack over medium heat or broil 4 in. from the heat for 5-7 minutes on each side or until a thermometer reads 160° and juices run clear. Serve on buns, with toppings as desired.
- Nutrition Facts
- 1 burger: 321 calories, 12g fat (4g saturated fat), 109mg cholesterol, 758mg sodium, 24g carbohydrate (5g sugars, 1g fiber), 27g protein.

318. The Ultimate Burger Recipe

Serving: 4 | Prep: | Cook: 25mins |Ready in:

Ingredients

- 1 1/2 pounds chuck roast, ground
- 1/4 cup mushroom, chopped
- 1/4 cup sweet onion, chopped
- 4 Ounces cheese, shredded
- 2 Tablespoons A-1® steak sauce
- 2 Tablespoons Worchestishire Sauce
- salt, to taste
- pepper, to taste

Direction

- Blend all ingredients by hand. Shape into 6 oz. balls. Shape into patties about 4-1/2 inches in diameter by 3/4 inch thick.
- Press the center of the patty down to about 1/2 inch to make a depression in the middle.
- Cook on medium hot fire to sear the surface quickly. If you have a high rack move burgers to it to bake out the interior. If not use indirect heat at one end of the grill.
- Serve immediately with favorite condiments!

319. The Uncle Louie Burger Recipe

Serving: 4 | Prep: | Cook: 10mins |Ready in:

Ingredients

- 1/4 cup plus 2 tablespoons ketchup
- 1/4 cup mayonnaise
- 1/4 cup finely chopped bread-and-butter pickles
- 2 teaspoons distilled white vinegar
- 1/2 teaspoon dry mustard
- 1/4 teaspoon cayenne pepper
- 1/4 teaspoon Old Bay Seasoning
- kosher salt and freshly ground black pepper

- 2 pounds ground chuck
- 4 hamburger buns, preferably brioche, split and toasted
- butter lettuce, sliced tomato, sliced cheddar cheese, crisp bacon
- and sliced avocado, for serving

Direction

- Directions
- In a medium bowl, mix the ketchup with the mayonnaise, pickles, vinegar, dry mustard, cayenne and Old Bay; season with salt and pepper.
- Refrigerate until ready to serve.
- Light a grill or preheat a grill pan.
- In a large bowl, season the chuck with 2 teaspoons of kosher salt and 1/2 teaspoon of pepper.
- Gently mix the seasonings into the meat and shape into four 3/4-inch-thick patties.
- Grill the hamburgers over moderately high heat for about 4 minutes per side for medium-rare.
- Set the burgers on the buns, top with the ketchup sauce, lettuce, tomato, cheese, bacon and avocado and serve.

320. This N That Burgers Recipe

Serving: 8 | Prep: | Cook: 16mins |Ready in:

Ingredients

- 1 oz sliced mushrooms, chopped
- 1/2 white onion, chopped
- 1 T margarine
- 1 T EVOO
- 3 lbs ground sirloin, 85% lean
- 2 oz jarred roasted red peppers, chopped
- 1/4 c parmesan cheese
- 1/2 c shredded mozzerella
- 2 T chopped garlic
- seasoned Salt

- garlic Pepper
- Dash red pepper flakes
- 3 T Dry ranch dressing
- 4-5 T worcestershire
- 2 t liquid smoke
- **
- Sliced tomatoes
- Good dill pickles
- Sliced cheese (I had cheddar, he had pepper jack)
- romaine lettuce
- Onion Sandwich rolls
- spicy mustard
- Dukes Real Mayo

Direction

- Sauté onions and mushrooms in margarine and EVOO (can add garlic here if you want)
- Mix all ingredients from meat down to tomatoes by hand - including drained, sautéed veggies
- Shape into 8 patties about 1/2 inch thick (they will draw up a little as they cook, and be thicker)
- Grill to desired doneness, about 8 - 10 minutes each side for light brown throughout burger - Turn only once, and don't mash with the flipper!!
- Add cheese to allow it to melt
- Let burger rest about 8 minutes
- Build burger on bun with desired condiments
- ** If I'd had the tail end of some bacon, I would have added it!
- *** Next time, I will throw in an egg, some seasoned bread crumbs, shape it into a loaf, and microwave it 20 minutes for a meatloaf!

321. Thyme Pepper Burgers Recipe

Serving: 4 | Prep: | Cook: 20mins | Ready in:

Ingredients

- 1 egg beaten
- 2 tablespoons milk
- 3/4 cup soft bread crumbs
- 3/4 teaspoon salt
- 1/2 teaspoon ground nutmeg
- 1 pound ground beef
- 1/2 cup chopped onion
- 1 cup beef broth
- 1 tablespoon all-purpose flour
- 1-1/2 teaspoons worcestershire sauce
- 3/4 teaspoon dried thyme
- 1 medium green bell pepper cut into strips

Direction

- In large bowl mix egg, milk, bread crumbs, salt and nutmeg.
- Add ground beef and mix by hand until well blended then shape into 4 patties.
- Place a skillet over medium heat.
- Add patties and brown for 4 minutes on each side then remove from skillet.
- Add onion to skillet and cook until tender but not browned then drain off excess fat.
- Whisk together beef broth and flour.
- Pour into skillet and stir in Worcestershire sauce and thyme.
- Cook over medium heat stirring until thickened.
- Return patties to skillet and add green peppers.
- Cover and simmer until burgers are cooked through about 5 minutes.

322. Tomato Cheddar Packed Turkey Burgers Recipe

Serving: 4 | Prep: | Cook: 30mins | Ready in:

Ingredients

- 4 tbs olive oil
- 1 large onion, fine chopped

- 1 cup grape tomatoes, halved; or 1 large ripe tomato, diced
- salt and fresh ground black pepper
- 2 large garlic cloves, fine chopped
- 1 lb ground turkey
- 1/4 cup dry white or red wine
- 2 - 3 oz. extra sharp cheddar cheese, cut into 1/4 to 1/2-inch cubes
- 4 large hamburger buns

Direction

- Heat 2 tbsp. oil in non-stick skillet over high heat. Add onions, and tomatoes with generous sprinkles of salt and pepper. Sauté over high heat; stirring frequently, until the onions begin to brown, about 3 minutes. Add the garlic and sauté for 1 minute. Remove from heat. Scoop half the onion mixture into a large bowl and the rest into a small one. Rinse skillet and dry it.
- Add to a large bowl the turkey, 1/4 tsp. salt. 1/8 tsp. pepper, and the wine. Blend well, and shape into 4 balls. Make a deep whole in each with thumb and insert 1/4 of the cheese into each hole. Pinch hole closed, and flatten balls to 3/4 -1-inch thick patties. Patties should be soft and sticky.
- Heat remaining 2 tbsp. olive oil in same skillet over medium-high heat. Sear burgers for 30 seconds on each side. Turn carefully.
- Lower heat to medium-low and cook for 5 min. per side. Serve on buns with reserved onions.

---

323.   Tomato Basil Hamburgers With Mushrooms Recipe

Serving: 4 | Prep: | Cook: 15mins | Ready in:

Ingredients

- 1 lb lean hamburger
- ¼ cup diced basil

- ¼ cup diced onion
- 2 large mushrooms, diced
- 1 clove garlic, minced
- ½ large Roma tomato, diced (¼ cup)
- 1/8 tsp. minced rosemary (about 3 needles)
- ½ tsp salt
- 1/8 tsp red pepper flakes (several shakes)
- 3 grinds of black pepper

Direction

- Place all ingredients in a bowl and mix well.
- Form 4 patties.
- Grill on medium-high until desired doneness.

---

324.   Tortilla Burgers Recipe

Serving: 4 | Prep: | Cook: 15mins | Ready in:

Ingredients

- 1tsp. ground cumin
- 1/2tsp dried oregano
- 1/2tsp red peper flakes
- 1/4tsp seasoned salt
- 1lb. ground pork
- 4 flour or corn tortillas(6") warmed
- salsa,sour cream,shredded cheddar cheese

Direction

- In bowl, combine first 4 ingredients. Crumble pork over seasonings and mix well. Shape into 4 oval patties.
- Grill, covered, over med. heat for 6 to 7 mins. on each side or till no longer pink.
- Serve on tortillas with salsa, sour cream and cheese.
- Good with guacamole also.

325. Trailside Cafe Burgers Recipe

Serving: 8 | Prep: | Cook: 60mins | Ready in:

Ingredients

- 5 pounds lean ground beef
- salt and pepper
- 5 large onions, minced
- 5 to 10 cups chicken broth
- Slices of American cheese
- potato chips
- pickle spears

Direction

- Start this before you need to serve about 3 hours. The longer it cooks on low the better it seems to be.
- Cook the meat and onions up in a large pan or roaster. It should be really crumbly. Drain the grease off.
- Place back into the pan or roaster.
- Add chicken broth, salt, and pepper.
- Slow/Low cook this for a couple of hours.
- Take a scoop of this and place it on the bottom half of a bun. Use a slotted scoop so it is not to wet on the bun.
- Cover with a piece of American cheese.
- Put top of bun on sandwich.
- Microwave this sandwich for 12 seconds.
- Serve with a pickle and chips.
- Enjoy!

326. Tricked Out Burgers Recipe

Serving: 610 | Prep: | Cook: 15mins | Ready in:

Ingredients

- 2 pounds ground venison (you could use turkey burger or beef)
- 1 carrot, grated

- 1 Gold potato, shredded
- 1 medium onion, shredded
- 1 sweet potato, medium in size, shredded
- 1 egg
- 3 TBSP Minced garlic
- 5-6 Good shakes of Wochestire Sauce
- Mrs. Dash, italian seasoning, and salt and pepper, to taste (I like spice, so the top of my burger looks green from all of the spices until I mix it up.)
- Highly recommended - red pepper (like cayenne) - give it a little zip.

Direction

- Shred the vegetables
- Mix the shredded vegetables together.
- Mix the shredded vegetables with the burger
- Add the egg
- Mix well
- Add the Worcestershire Sauce and the seasonings and mix well
- Make the burger patties
- Grill until desired level of doneness
- Serve with toasted bun, sliced cheese, and everyone's favorite condiments. I paired the burgers with brown rice, a salad, and a berry smoothie.
- This recipe made about 15 burgers, many of which I froze for future use.

327. Tropic Thunder Jerk Burgers Recipe

Serving: 6 | Prep: | Cook: 1hours15mins | Ready in:

Ingredients

- Marinade:
- 1/2 cup chopped cilantro
- 1/2 cup chopped parsley
- 3 tbsp chopped fresh mint
- 3 tbsp chopped fresh thyme
- 1/2 cup chopped scallions

- 1 seeded, minced habanero pepper
- 5 cloves minced garlic
- 2 tsp grated fresh ginger
- 1 tbsp ground allspice
- 1 tsp cloves
- 1/4 tsp cinnamon
- 2 tbsp olive oil
- 1/4 cup red wine vinegar
- 2 tbsp zinfandel wine
- 1 tbsp Jamaican rum
- 1/4 cup tamari
- 1 tbsp water
- 2 tbsp demerara sugar
- 3 tbsp lime juice
- ---
- Burgers:
- 1 lb extra-lean ground beef
- 1 lb ground turkey breast meat
- 2 tsp smoked sea salt
- 1/2 cup prepared Jerk marinade (above)
- 3 tbsp diced or crushed pineapple, well drained

Direction

- To make the marinade, combine all the ingredients in a blender and puree.
- In a large bowl, combine beef, turkey, salt, 1/2 cup marinade and diced pineapple.
- Mix gently (your hands are the best tool for this) and form into 6 patties, avoiding compacting the meat as much as possible. Place on a platter, cover with plastic wrap and refrigerate 1 hour.
- Preheat grill to medium-high and brush grate with oil.
- Place the patties on the rack and brush with marinade.
- Cover and cook 6 minutes, then turn and brush other side with marinade.
- Re-cover and cook 5-6 minutes longer, until cooked through.
- Serve on your choice of crusty bread or rolls.

328. Tuna And Salmon Burgers Recipe

Serving: 6 | Prep: | Cook: 10mins | Ready in:

Ingredients

- 1 pound fresh tuna fillet
- 1/2 pound fresh salmon fillet
- 1/4 cup snipped fresh cilantro
- 2 tablespoons fresh lime juice
- 2 cloves garlic, minced
- 2 tablespoons olive oil
- 1 tablespoon purchased pickled ginger, finely chopped
- 1 tablespoon chili sauce
- 1 to 2 teaspoons wasabi paste
- 1/4 teaspoon sea salt
- 1/4 teaspoon freshly ground pepper
- 6 soft flatbreads or split rolls
- yellow tomatoe slices (optional)

Direction

- Finely chop the tuna and salmon. In a large mixing bowl combine tuna and salmon with cilantro, lime juice, garlic, 4 teaspoons of the olive oil, the ginger, chili sauce, wasabi, salt, and pepper.
- Shape into 6 patties about 3/4 inch thick.
- Place burger patties on the lightly oiled rack of the grill directly over medium heat. Grill for 10 to 12 minutes, turning burgers once halfway through grilling.
- Brush the flatbread with remaining olive oil. Toast on grill rack for 1 to 2 minutes or until golden brown.
- Serve burgers folded in flatbread or burger bread, topped with green cabbage slaw and, if desired, yellow tomato slices.

329. Tuna Burger Recipe

Serving: 2 | Prep: | Cook: 10mins | Ready in:

Ingredients

- 1 can Star Kist tuna, drain and squeeze off liquid
- 1 egg, slightly beaten
- 8 saltine crackers, crushed fine
- 2 scallion tops, chopped fine
- 1-2 T Hellman's/Best Food mayonaise, add as needed to bind ingredients
- dash white pepper
- oil for frying
- 2 slices tomato
- lettuce
- hamburger bun, seeded

Direction

- Mix the 1st six ingredients and mix well.
- Add oil to pan and heat on medium high.
- Make mixture into 2 patties for burgers or 4 patties for breakfast and place in pan.
- Brown until golden on the 1st side (approximately 4-5 minutes).
- Turn patties and brown the 2nd side (approximately 3-5 minutes).
- Place burger on bun with lettuce and a slice of tomato.

330.   Turkey Burgers Recipe

Serving: 5 | Prep: | Cook: 20mins |Ready in:

Ingredients

- 1-2 Tbls. olive oil
- 1/2 onion chopped
- 1/2 green bell pepper chopped
- 2-3 cloves garlic
- 1/2 diced jalapeno
- 1 1/4 lbs. Fresh ground turkey
- 1 Tbls. lemon pepper seasoning
- 1 Tbls. chicken rub seasoning (I use Emerald's chicken Rub) any BBQ rub will do the job
- 2 pinches of kosher salt
- 3 Tbls. chopped cilantro

- 1 egg
- 2 cups fresh bread crumbs (I make my own but dried bread crumbs are fine but you will not need as much)

Direction

- Sautee Onions, Bell pepper and garlic in Olive Oil for a few min. until soft adding the jalapenos for the last couple of min. let cool
- Mix Turkey, onion and pepper mix and all other ingredients with hands until well blended
- Form into 5 patties
- Put in freezer for 15-20 min until firm turning once grill over med to high heat for 6-8 min. per side until done
- Enjoy with your favorite fixins'

331.   Turkey Burgers With Spinach Amp Cheddar Recipe

Serving: 4 | Prep: | Cook: 10mins |Ready in:

Ingredients

- Drizzle of olive oil
- ½ pound ground turkey
- ½ cup chopped frozen spinach, liquid squeezed out
- ¼ cup shredded cheddar cheese
- salt and pepper
- 1 tsp. garlic powder
- 2 onion rolls
- 2 tbsp. mayonnaise
- 1 tsp. spicy mustard
- lettuce and tomato

Direction

- Heat olive oil in medium skillet over medium/high heat.
- In a medium bowl combine ground turkey, spinach, salt, pepper and garlic powder, mix well.

- Add cheddar cheese to mixture, mix gently.
- Sauté burgers until cooked through.
- In a small bowl combine and mayonnaise and mustard, spread on rolls. Layer burgers, lettuce and tomato on rolls.

332. Turkey Burgers With Sweet And Sour Pepper Relish Recipe

Serving: 6 | Prep: | Cook: 15mins | Ready in:

Ingredients

- 1 small yellow onion, cut crosswise into 1/2-inch-thick slices
- extra virgin olive oil
- 3 red/yellow bell peppers
- 1-1/2 tablespoons cider vinegar
- 2 tablespoons honey
- 1/2 teaspoon kosher salt
- 1/4 teaspoon freshly ground black pepper
- 1/8 teaspoon ground cayenne pepper
- 2 pounds ground turkey (93% lean)
- 1/4 cup plain bread crumbs
- 1-1/2 teaspoons kosher salt
- 1 teaspoon dried sage
- 1/2 teaspoon freshly ground black pepper
- 1/4 teaspoon ground nutmeg
- 1/4 teaspoon ground ginger
- 2 to 4 tablespoons milk
- 6 hamburger buns or other round rolls
- 1/3 cup stone ground mustard

Direction

- These directions are for an all grill preparation - most steps do not need to be completed on the grill.
- Brush or spray both sides of the onion slices with oil. Grill the onions and peppers over direct medium heat until the onions are tender and the peppers are blackened and blistered all over, turning occasionally. The onions will

take 8 to 12 minutes and the peppers will take 12 to 15 minutes. Cut the onions into 1/4-inch pieces. Divide the onions, reserving half for the relish and half for the burgers. Place the peppers in a bowl and cover with plastic wrap. Let stand for 10 minutes and then peel away the charred skins. Cut each pepper into 1/4-inch pieces.

- In a small saucepan over medium heat, combine the vinegar and honey with 2 tablespoons of water. Stir until the honey dissolves and then simmer for 3 minutes. Add the salt, pepper, and cayenne. In a medium bowl combine the peppers and half of the reserved onions, and pour the warm vinegar mixture over the vegetables. Mix well.
- In a large bowl, gently mix the reserved onions and all the burger ingredients except the milk. Add as much of the milk as the mixture will absorb. Form into 6 burgers, each about 4 inches in diameter and 1 inch thick. Brush the burgers with oil and grill over direct medium heat until fully cooked but still juicy, about 15 minutes, turning once.
- Grill the buns, cut sides down, over direct medium heat until toasted, about 1 minute. Spread mustard inside each bun, add a burger, and top with the relish. Serve warm.

333. Turkey Club Burgers With Bacon And Swiss Cheese Recipe

Serving: 6 | Prep: | Cook: 15mins | Ready in:

Ingredients

- 1.5 lbs ground turkey
- 3/4 c Italian bread crumbs (or more if needed for texture)
- 1 pkg dry Italian dressing mix
- 2 T celery flakes
- 2 T white wine Worcestershire, or Lea and Perrins chicken marinade

- Dash red pepper flakes (more if you like)
- 1/2 c grated parmesan
- white pepper
- 8-10 slices thick cut peppered bacon (or turkey bacon)
- 6 slices swiss cheese
- 6 sandwich buns (your fave)
- 3 T melted butter or margarine
- romaine lettuce
- Sliced tomato
- Thin sliced red onion
- Mayo
- spicy mustard

Direction

- Combine by hand in large mixing bowl: Turkey, bread crumbs, dry Italian dressing mix, celery flakes, Worcestershire, red pepper flakes, parmesan, and white pepper
- Mix together and form into 6 large patties
- Place in hot skillet, or on grill pan (or grill) brown each side, then turn skillet on low and cover, cook about 12 more minutes
- While patties are cooking, fry bacon and drain (I use the foreman grill for easier clean-up); then break slices in half
- Melt butter and brush on insides of buns and place under broiler for a couple of minutes (or on grill pan, etc.)
- When patties are done, top with slice of Swiss cheese and cover allowing cheese to melt
- Spread bun with mayo and mustard, top each burger with lettuce, tomato and onion as desired

334.   Turkey Meatloaf Burgers Recipe

Serving: 8 | Prep: | Cook: 25mins | Ready in:

Ingredients

- 2 pounds ground turkey
- 1 1/3 cup seasoned bread crumbs

- 2 eggs
- 1 small onion, grated & liquid drained
- 2 tsp chili powder
- 1 tsp paprika
- 1 tsp kosher salt
- 3 tbsp apple sauce
- 2 tbsp olive oil
- (optional: lettuce greens, tomatoe, etc condiments)

Direction

- In a large bowl, combine turkey, bread crumbs, eggs, onion, chili powder, paprika, salt, and apples sauce together. Mixing thoroughly. Divide mixture in to 8 portions. Shape each portion into a hamburger patty shape.
- Pre-heat oven to 375. Meanwhile, in a large 10 to 12-inch skillet, place olive oil in pan and heat to med-high heat. Place patties into pan. Cooking for 3-5 minutes on each side, and remove to a paper towel lined plate to drain excess grease off.
- When all patties have grease drained, place in an 11x8-inch pan to finish off cooking process in the oven. About 10 minutes.
- Serve on a hamburger roll, with veggies and condiments. With a side of chips or raw crispy veggies.

335.   Turkey Satay Burgers Recipe

Serving: 6 | Prep: | Cook: 10mins | Ready in:

Ingredients

- 8 Tbs peanut butter
- 2 lbs ground turkey
- 6 scallions minced
- 4 tbs minced cilantro
- 6 Tbs plain dry bread crumbs
- 1/2 tbs lemon zest
- 2 Tbs lemon juice

- 2 Tbs minced pickled jalapeno peppers
- 1/2 tsp black pepper
- 1/4 tsp kosher salt
- 1/2 tsp 5 spice powder
- 2 Tbs vegetable oil

Direction

- Place peanut butter over a bowl and set that over a pot of boiling water.
- Stir to barely liquefy peanut butter
- Remove from heat and add the ground turkey and mix very well
- Add and stir in remaining ingredients to blend lightly and do not overmix which would make burgers tough
- Form into 6 or 8 patties
- Heat oil in a non-stick pan and cook each side about 5 minutes on each side or cooked through
- Serve as is or in buns with lettuce, sliced onions etc.

336.   Turtle Burgers Recipe

Serving: 4 | Prep: | Cook: | Ready in:

Ingredients

- Turtle Burgers
- Ingredients
- 1 lb. lean ground beef
- 12 all-beef wieners, each divided in-half (total of 24 halves)
- 4 slice sharp cheddar cheese
- 1 lb. bacon
- aluminum foil
- 4 hamburger buns
- condiments for burgers

Direction

- Directions
- Pre-heat oven to 400 degrees.

- Make four good-sized hamburger patties, nice and round and thick. Top w/ single slice of sharp cheddar cheese (this is optional, if you don't want cheese).
- Wrap each beef patties in bacon strips, making a basket weave as you go. Cover entire patties.
- Next, take the hot dog halves and make turtles' legs, head and tail. Cut the one for the tail at a diagonal on the end, so the tail looks "pointed". In the legs, put a few tiny 'slits' in the ends, so they will look like feet w/ claws after they bake.
- Line a baking sheet (with sides on it!) with foil, and place a baking rack over the foil. Arrange your "turtles" on the baking rack.
- Cook for 30 - 40 min., in your pre-heated oven. A little crispy, not too crunchy ... just the way a turtle ought to be, right?

337.   Twisted Turkey Burgers Recipe

Serving: 4 | Prep: | Cook: 15mins | Ready in:

Ingredients

- 1 pound ground turkey meat
- 2 egg whites
- 1/4 tsp. cumin
- 1/4 tsp. chili powder
- 1/2 tsp. fresh ground black pepper
- 1/2 tsp. ground cilantro
- 1/4 tsp. liquid smoke
- 1/2 tsp. worsteshire sauce
- 1/2 vidalia onion, finely chopped
- 1/4 cup black olives, finely chopped
- 2 cloves garlic, roasted and minced
- 1 tbsp. ketchup

Direction

- Peel and finely chop onion and garlic. Lightly grease skillet with olive oil and sauté onion and garlic until tender. Remove from heat.

- Combine all remaining ingredients with the ground turkey, mixing well.
- Form 4 patties and allow to sit for five minutes.
- Grill patties for 7 to 10 minutes, or until burger is well done.
- Serve with standard condiments, and Swiss cheese, if available.

Serving: 20 | Prep: | Cook: 15mins | Ready in:

Ingredients

- 5 Pounds ground pork
- 1 Packet Dry Ranch seasoning
- 10 Slices turkey, cut in half
- 20 Pieces Better bacon - see my recipe at http://www.cookingwithcaitlin.com
- 4 Large tomatoes
- 1 head romaine lettuce
- 20 Soft buns

Direction

- Cook your bacon (see my Better Bacon recipe) and set aside.
- Toss ground pork with the Dry Ranch seasoning and form 20 4oz burgers (about the size of a palm).
- Cook your burgers on the grill for 7 minutes on the first side and 4-5 minutes on the second side (you do not want the meat to be pink).
- While your burgers are cooking, slice your tomatoes into 1/4 inch thick slices and tear your lettuce into burger/bun-sized pieces.
- To assemble: Add your burger to the bottom of your bun. Add 1 piece of turkey loosely folded in half, followed by 1 piece of bacon torn in half, 1 tear of lettuce and 1 slice of tomato. Add the top of your bun, serve and enjoy!

Serving: 4 | Prep: | Cook: 10mins | Ready in:

Ingredients

- 1/3 cup teriyaki sauce
- 1 tablespoon minced ginger
- 2 teaspoons minced garlic
- 1 tablespoon honey
- 1 tablespoon Dijon mustard
- ½ teaspoon champagne or rice wine vinegar
- 1 ½ pounds yellow-fin tuna (don't spring for beauty here, end cuts are perfect!)
- 1 ½ tablespoons minced garlic
- 2 tablespoons Dijon mustard
- ¼ teaspoon cayenne pepper
- 1 teaspoon kosher salt
- ½ teaspoon freshly ground black pepper
- 4 whole-wheat hamburger buns, toasted (or warmed pitas, yum!)
- ¼ cup pickled sushi ginger, divided in 4

Direction

- Preheat broiler, and lightly spray a baking sheet with PAM.
- Combine all the teriyaki sauce through vinegar in a saucepan and bring to a boil. Lower the heat and simmer 8-9 minutes.
- Strain and reserve. (Can be prepared up to two days ahead and stored, covered, in the refrigerator.
- Grind or finely dice the tuna to the texture of hamburger meat. (Do not use a food processor, which will shred the tuna rather than chop it).
- Combine tuna with garlic, mustard, cayenne, salt and pepper. Mix thoroughly.
- Divide the tuna into four equal amounts.
- Using your hands, roll each part into a smooth ball and flatten slightly.
- Broil until browned and medium rare, about 2-3 minutes per side.
- Spread each with a tablespoon of warm glaze.

- Garnish the burgers with 1 tbsp. of pickled ginger.

340. Veal Burgers Recipe

Serving: 4 | Prep: | Cook: 12mins | Ready in:

Ingredients

- 1 slice bread, torn into small pieces
- 2 tablespoons milk
- 1 tablespoon worcestershire sauce
- 1 egg
- 2 fresh basil leaves, chopped
- 1 teaspoon minced fresh rosemary
- 1 teaspoon fresh ground pepper
- 1 pound ground veal

Direction

- Place torn bread into a bowl and sprinkle with milk and Worcestershire sauce.
- Mix in egg until combined.
- Season with basil, rosemary, and pepper.
- Mix in veal until evenly mixed.
- Shape veal mixture into four patties. Make a small indent in the middle of each patty. This helps keep your patties flat after grilling.
- Preheat a grill for medium heat.
- Grill veal burgers to desired degree of doneness, about 5 minutes per side for medium. Place a slice of cheese on each burger, and allow to melt for about 1 minute before serving on grilled buns.

341. Vegans Giving Skillet Burgers Recipe

Serving: 6 | Prep: | Cook: 3hours | Ready in:

Ingredients

- 1/2 tbsp olive oil
- 1 small white onion, minced
- 2 stalks celery, minced
- 4 cloves garlic, minced
- 12 oz low-fat extra firm tofu, drained well
- 1 tbsp low-sodium soy sauce
- 2 tbsp pumpkin puree (not pie filling!)
- 2 tbsp nutritional yeast flakes
- 1 tbsp poultry seasoning
- 1/2 tsp sea salt
- 1 tsp black pepper
- pinch nutmeg (optional)
- 1/3 cup dried cranberries, minced finely
- 1/4 cup mashed potato flakes
- 1/4 cup vital wheat gluten flour
- 1/4 cup whole wheat breadcrumbs

Direction

- Heat the oil in a large non-stick pan over medium heat until it shimmers, then add onion and celery.
- Cook, stirring often, 5 minutes.
- Add the garlic (with a small splash of water if needed) and cook just until fragrant, about 1-2 minutes. Remove from heat.
- In a large bowl, crumble the tofu with your hands into roughly "ground meat" texture.
- Stir in the soy sauce and pumpkin puree, then add the sautéed mixture, nutritional yeast, poultry seasoning, salt, pepper and nutmeg and mix until it's all combined.
- Add cranberries, potato flakes, gluten flour and breadcrumbs and fold through well.
- Divide mixture into 6 pieces, flattening slightly, and place on a foil or parchment-lined baking sheet. Cover with plastic and refrigerate 1 hour.
- Preheat the oven to 350F and bring a clean large non-stick pan to medium-high heat.
- Spray the pan with non-stick spray and add the patties, 3 at a time.
- Cook for 2 minutes each side, then place back on the lined sheet. Repeat for remaining patties.
- Place the sheet in the oven and bake for 15 minutes.
- Make ahead:

- Form the patties, place on lined sheets and freeze, covered, until solid.
- Transfer to a freezer bag or container, sandwiching between layers of parchment.
- To re-heat, place on a lined sheet and bake at 350F for 45-50 minutes, until hot.
- If extra crispness is desired, broil on HI 1 minute per side.

342. Vegetarian Hearty Burger Recipe

Serving: 4 | Prep: | Cook: 12mins | Ready in:

Ingredients

- 1/2 cup plus 1 tbl egg whites (about 5 eggs)
- 3/4 cups shredded low fat mozzarella cheese
- 1/2 cup minced dried onion
- 1 tbl light soy sauce
- 1 cup rolled oats
- 4 1/2 tbls finely chopped walnuts
- 1 tsp garlic powder
- 1/2 tsp sage

Direction

- Mix egg whites, cheese, onion and soy in bowl
- Stir in oats, walnuts, garlic powder and sage
- Mix well
- Makes 4 (1/2 inch thick) patties by pressing between pieces of wax paper
- Spray a skillet with non-stick spray
- Grill burgers over medium heat for 6 minutes on each side or until golden brown

343. Veggie Burgers Recipe

Serving: 8 | Prep: | Cook: 20mins | Ready in:

Ingredients

- 2 teaspoons olive oil
- 1 small onion grated
- 2 cloves crushed garlic
- 2 carrots shredded
- 1 small summer squash shredded
- 1 small zucchini shredded
- 1-1/2 cups rolled oats
- 1/4 cup shredded cheddar cheese
- 1 egg beaten
- 1 tablespoon soy sauce
- 1-1/2 cups all purpose flour

Direction

- Heat olive oil in a skillet over low heat and cook the onion and garlic for about 5 minutes.
- Mix in the carrots squash and zucchini.
- Continue to cook and stir for 2 minutes.
- Remove pan from heat and mix in oats cheese and egg.
- Stir in soy sauce then transfer mixture to a bowl and refrigerate 1 hour.
- Preheat grill for high heat.
- Place flour on a large plate.
- Form vegetable mixture into eight patties.
- Drop each patty into the flour lightly coating both sides.
- Oil the grill grate and grill patties 5 minutes on each side.

344. Wasabi Salmon Burgers Recipe

Serving: 4 | Prep: | Cook: 6mins | Ready in:

Ingredients

- 1/2 cup soft tofu (about 4 ounces)
- 1 (7-ounce) can red sockeye salmon, drained, skin and bones discarded
- 1 (6-ounce) can skinless, boneless pink salmon in water, drained
- 1/4 cup chopped fresh chives
- 2 teaspoons Dijon mustard

- 1/2 teaspoon wasabi paste
- 1/8 teaspoon freshly ground black pepper
- 1 large egg white
- 1/2 cup panko (Japanese breadcrumbs)
- 1 teaspoon canola oil
- 4 curly leaf lettuce leaves
- 4 hamburger buns with sesame seeds
- 4 (1/4-inch-thick) slices tomato
- 4 (1/4-inch-thick) slices sweet or red onion
- 1/2 cup prepared pesto

Direction

- Place tofu on a plate covered in several layers of heavy-duty paper towels. Cover with additional paper towels and cover with another plate. Weigh down the plate with a can; let stand 5 minutes.
- Place tofu in a large bowl. Add salmon to bowl; mash with a fork to crumble. Add chives, mustard, wasabi paste, pepper and egg white; mix well. Divide mixture into 4 equal portions, shaping each into a 1/2-inch-thick patty. Place panko in a shallow dish; dredge patties in panko.
- Heat oil in a large non-stick skillet over medium-high heat. Add patties to pan; cook 3 minutes on each side or until golden brown. Place 1 lettuce leaf on each of the bottom halves of buns; top each serving with 1 tomato slice, 1 patty, and 1 onion slice. Spread 2 tablespoons pesto over each serving; top with top halves of buns.

345. Way Down South Jalapeno Burgers Recipe

Serving: 6 | Prep: | Cook: 15mins | Ready in:

Ingredients

- 3 pounds lean ground beef
- 4 sliced pickled jalapeño peppers
- 1/2 package dried onion soup mix
- 1/2 tablespoon seasoned salt

- 1/2 tablespoon steak seasoning
- 1/4 cup worcestershire sauce
- 6 slices of your favorite cheese

Direction

- Add all seasonings (including jalapenos) to ground beef in a bowl and combine well.
- Form into 6 patties.
- Broil or grill until desired level of doneness is achieved.
- Place cheese on burgers when done.

346. White Castle Burgers Recipe

Serving: 6 | Prep: | Cook: 15mins | Ready in:

Ingredients

- 1 lb lean ground beef
- 1 egg
- 2 tablespoons dried minced onion, soaked in a little water
- 2 tablespoons milk
- 1 teaspoon worcestershire sauce
- 1/2 cup bread crumbs
- 1 teaspoon salt
- 1/4 teaspoon pepper
- 2 packages dinner rolls from the bread aisle (the recipe will make about 1 1/2 dozen)
- American cheese slices, folded to make 4 pieces per slice
- hamburger dill slices

Direction

- Pour the excess water off the onion
- Mix ground beef, egg, onion, milk, Worcestershire sauce, bread crumbs, salt, and pepper.
- Split dinner rolls in half
- Spread the mixture fairly thin on each half of roll

- Place meat side down into a skillet over medium heat, filling the entire skillet. (You'll have 2 skillets or 2 batches)
- Cook about 3-4 minutes uncovered, 3-4 minutes covered.
- Remove the cooked rolls from the skillet, placing them on a plate with the meat side up. Using the bottom half, place a piece of cheese on the meat and then the pickle. Add ketchup or mustard here, if you want either or both. Now place both sides back together. Follow this procedure with the remaining rolls.

347.   White Castle Slider Klone Recipe

Serving: 8 | Prep: | Cook: 20mins | Ready in:

Ingredients

- 1 lb. ground chuck
- 2/3 cup beef broth
- 1 1/4 cups dried chopped onions (about 3 1/3 oz.) *
- 2 1/2 cups hot water (or more if needed)
- 20 small dinner rolls (I made homemade slider buns; recipe posted)
- Cheese and condiments (optional); pickle choice is important for authenticity

Direction

- 1. Line a 10-by-14-inch rimmed baking sheet with plastic wrap. Mix beef and beef stock in a large bowl. Transfer mixture to lined baking sheet, and use a spatula to flatten. Place second sheet of plastic wrap over meat, and use rolling pin or hands to further flatten meat so it covers entire surface of pan.
- 2. Remove top layer of plastic wrap, and use spatula to score flattened beef into 2.5-inch squares. Reapply wrap, and place pan in freezer until meat is frozen solid.
- 3. Place dried onion in a small bowl, and add the hot water; let stand at least 10 minutes.

Meanwhile, take frozen beef from freezer, and remove from plastic wrap. Re-score it with a sharp knife, and gently break patties apart.

- 4. Heat a large skillet (cast iron works best) or grill pan over medium-high heat. Add 1/4 of onion-and-water mixture to skillet. When water begins to steam (which should happen almost instantly), place 5 patties on top of onions . Cook, flipping once, to desired doneness. (Cooking time will depend on whether your patties are still frozen solid or have thawed a bit.) After flipping, place a bun top on each patty.
- 5. Remove patties and buns, with a helping of onion, from skillet. Add bun bottoms, and any cheese or condiments as desired.
- 6. Repeat with remaining ingredients.

348.   Wild Mushroom Cheddar Burgers Recipe

Serving: 4 | Prep: | Cook: 20mins | Ready in:

Ingredients

- 2 tbs. olive oil
- 1 tbs. unsalted butter
- 12 oz (about 1 1/2 cups) assorted mushrooms Chopped
- 1 small shallot, finly diced
- kosher salt and freshly ground pepper
- 1 tbs. chopped fresh thyme leaves
- 2 tbs. chopped fresh flat leaf parsley leaves
- 1 1/2 lbs. ground chuck(80 percent lean) or ground turkey (90 percent lean)
- 1 1/2 tbs. canola oil
- 4 slices sharp cheddar cheese
- 4 hamburger buns, split; toasted, if desired
- Chipotle ketchup (recepi below)

Direction

- Heat olive oil and butter in large sauté pan over high heat until almost smoking. Add mushrooms and cook, stirring occasionally, until soft, about 5 minutes. Add shallot, season with salt and pepper, and cook until mushrooms are golden brown, about 5 minutes. Stir in thyme and parsley and transfer to bowl.

- Divide meat into 4 equal portions (about 6oz. each). Form each portion loosely into 3/4- inch burger and make deep depression in center with your thumb. Season both side of each burger with salt and pepper.
- brush burgers with canola oil, and grill on high, turning once (for beef, 7 minutes for medium rare or 10 minutes for well; for turkey cook through about 10 minutes) Top each with a slice of cheese, and use a basting cover to melt cheese during last minute of cooking.
- Place burgers on bun bottoms and top each with chipotle ketchup, if using and a large spoonful of mushrooms. Cover with bun tops and serve.
- Chipotle Ketchup
- Makes 1 cup
- 1 cup of ketchup
- 2 to 3 tbs. pureed canned chipotle in adobo (depending on how spicy you prefer it)
- 1/4 tbs. kosher salt
- 1/4 tbs. freshly ground black pepper
- Whisk together ketchup, chipotle, salt, and pepper in small bowl. Cover and refrigerate at least 30 minutes to allow flavors to blend. Sauce will keep for one week in a tightly sealed container in the refrigerator.

349.   Wild Rice And Mushroom Burgers With Red Pepper Mayo Recipe

Serving: 4 | Prep: | Cook: 15mins |Ready in:

Ingredients

- 1/3 cup mayo
- 3 Tablespoons chopped roasted red peppers
- 2 3/4 cups water

- 1 large bouillon cube or equivalent for 2 cups water
- 1 cup uncooked wild rice
- 2 cups sliced mushrooms
- 1/4 teaspoon salt
- 3/4 cup Italian bread crumbs
- 1 egg
- 4 slices provolone cheese
- 4 buns

Direction

- Roasted Red pepper mayo
- Combine mayo and peppers, mix well. Refrigerate till ready to serve.
- Heat Grill (medium heat)
- Burgers
- In medium pan bring water and bouillon to a boil over medium heat, stir to dissolve
- Rinse and drain wild rice with cold water.
- Add rice to pan cover reduce heat to low.
- Cook about 1 hour or until kernels are opened and most or all the liquid is gone.
- Rice should be slightly overcooked. Remove from heat let cool and drain if needed.
- Put rice, mushrooms, and salt in food processor, process until finely chopped.
- Add 1/2 cup bread crumbs, pulse to combine.
- Add egg, pulse to combine
- Shape mixture into 4 patties.
- Sprinkle rest of breadcrumbs on plate, Dip patties into crumbs coat both sides.
- Cook on grill over medium heat, covered about 6 minutes on each side.
- Top each patties with slice of provolone last minute of cooking.
- Put on bun top with red pepper mayo.

350.   Wine Soaked Burgers Recipe

Serving: 6 | Prep: | Cook: 12mins |Ready in:

Ingredients

- 2 pounds ground round beef
- 6 fresh bay leaves
- 8 cloves garlic, minced
- 2-1/2 cups dry white wine
- 1-1/2 cups lemon juice
- 2 tablespoons red-wine vinegar
- 1 tablespoon extra-virgin olive oil
- Salt and freshly ground black pepper

Direction

- Form the beef into 6 patties. Place a bay leaf under each hamburger on a flat, non-reactive baking dish and sprinkle garlic over the top. Stir the wine, lemon juice, vinegar, and olive oil together and pour over the patties. Season to taste with salt and pepper. Cover and refrigerate, turning the hamburgers several times, for at least 3 hours.
- Half an hour before cooking, remove the burgers from the refrigerator and drain on paper towels. Discard the bay leaves. Grill, broil, or fry in a preheated skillet 3 to 6 minutes per side. Serve on warmed rolls and enjoy!

351. Zesty White Bean Burgers Recipe

Serving: 4 | Prep: | Cook: 15mins | Ready in:

Ingredients

- 1-16 ounce can great northern beans, undrained
- 1-4 ounce can chopped green chilies, undrained
- 2 medium green onions, chopped
- 1 cup dry bread crumbs
- 1 egg, beaten
- 1/4 cup yellow cornmeal
- 2 tablespoons vegetable oil
- 8 slices monterey jack cheese
- 4 kaiser rolls
- Shredded lettuce

- guacamole
- salsa

Direction

- Place beans in food processor or blender.
- Cover and process until slightly mashed.
- Mix beans, chilies, onions, bread crumbs and egg.
- Shape into 4 patties.
- Coat each patty with cornmeal.
- Heat oil in a large skillet over medium heat.
- Cook patties in oil for about 10 minutes, turning once, until crisp and thoroughly cooked on both sides.
- Top patties with cheese.
- Cover and cook about 1-2 minutes until cheese is melted.
- Serve patties on bottom halves of Kaiser rolls, top with lettuce, guacamole and salsa. Cover with tops of rolls.

352. Zwaanendael Bacon Wrapped Sausage Burgers Recipe

Serving: 6 | Prep: | Cook: 20mins | Ready in:

Ingredients

- 1 Tablespoon ground coriander
- ½ tsp ground cloves
- ½ tsp ground mustard
- pinch ground nutmeg
- pinch ground allspice
- 1 1/2 tsp fine salt
- 1/2 tsp freshly ground black pepper
- 2 medium eggs
- 2 oz red wine vinegar
- ½ tsp brown sugar
- 1 lb lean ground beef or venison
- 1 lb ground pork
- 12 bacon strips
- 6 hamburger buns

Direction

- Combine the first ten ingredients in a large bowl. Crumble beef into the mixture and mix well. Shape into six patties.
- Lay a strip of bacon on a flat surface and lay another strip on top the first forming an X place a burger patty in the center of the X. Wrap the bacon strips around each burger; secure with a toothpick.
- Grill for 4-5 minutes on each side until meat is no longer pink or bake burgers in a baking dish at 350° for 25 to 30 minutes or until meat is no longer pink.
- Discard toothpicks. Serve on buns with all you favorite burger toppings.

353.   Burger Bundles Recipe

Serving: 4 | Prep: | Cook: 60mins | Ready in:

Ingredients

- 1 lb ground beef
- 1/3 cup evaporated milk
- 1 cup mushroom soup
- 1 cuppepperidge farm stuffing, prepared as directed on package

Direction

- Mix milk and beef, divide into 4 patties, approx. 6 inch in diameter
- In center of each patty, place 1/4 cup of stuffing.
- Mold the meat around the stuffing to form a ball
- Place in an 8x8 inch pan, and add the soup
- Bake at 350 degree for 1 hour, baste several times

354.   Burgers With Ranch Dressing Recipe

Serving: 6 | Prep: | Cook: 15mins | Ready in:

Ingredients

- 2 lbs ground beef
- 1 1oz pack ranch dressing mix
- 1 egg
- 3/4 cup crushed saltines
- 1 diced onion
- add bacon and cheese

Direction

- Using a large bowl mix beef, egg, and other ingredients
- Make into patties
- Grill about 5 minutes each side
- Put bacon and cheese on a toasted bun with the patty
- You can substitute Lipton onion soup for the ranch if you prefer

355.   Cheesey Burger Chowder Recipe

Serving: 4 | Prep: | Cook: 10mins | Ready in:

Ingredients

- 1 LB. lean ground beef
- 2 (16 oz.) cans cheddar potato soup
- 1 cup milk
- 1/4 cup pasteurized process cheese spread with bacon (from 5 oz. jar)
- 1 oz. shredded cheese

Direction

- 1. Cook ground beef in Dutch oven or large saucepan over medium heat for 8 to 10 mins. or until thoroughly cooked, stirring frequently. Drain

- 2. Add soup and milk, mix well. Bring to a boil. Reduce heat to low. Add cheese spread, cook and stir until cheese spread is melted. Top individual servings with shredded cheese

356.   Chicken Burger With Bbq Sauce Recipe

Serving: 3 | Prep: | Cook: 15mins | Ready in:

Ingredients

- 2 boneless ,skinless, chicken breasts
- onion
- 1 -2 stalks celery
- 1/2 cup or more of honey and garlic bbq sauce
- hamburger buns
- salt and pepper
- olive oil or butter

Direction

- Cut up chicken in small pcs.
- Fry in oil or butter until cooked through
- Remove from pan, season the chicken with salt and pepper
- Add more oil if needed in the fry pan
- Sauté the chopped onion and celery until softened
- Add the cooked chicken to the onion and celery
- Put in 1/2 cup or more of bbq sauce, stir well and simmer on low heat for a few mins.
- Meanwhile toast buns in oven on cookie sheet
- Butter them and spoon bbq chicken on the buns.

357.   Crock Pot Chilli Beans With Pepperjack Cornbread Cakes Recipe

Serving: 6 | Prep: | Cook: 260mins | Ready in:

Ingredients

- Chili Beans:
- 1 large can of pinto beans
- 2 lbs of ground beef
- 2 cans of mexican stewed tomatoes
- 1 half of sliced onion
- 1cup of Gebhardt chili powder (add more for taste, if desired)
- 2 tbs salt
- 3 tbs pepper, garlic powder, onion powder
- 2 tbs of paprika
- pepper Jack cornbread cakes
- 3 cups of pepper jack cheese
- 2 boxes of "jiffy" cornbread mix

Direction

- Chili beans
- Brown and season the ground beef, then drain grease after cooking
- In crock pot put ground beef, beans (do not drain), stewed tomatoes, sliced onion and half a cup of warm water.
- Stir in all of the seasonings, cover and set on low for 6-7 hrs. or high for 3-4 hours.
- Pepper Jack Cornbread cakes
- Preheat and spray griddle with pam or whatever you choose to use
- Follow the instructions on the cornbread box
- Put in 3 cups of pepper jack cheese into the cornbread mixture.
- Just like making pan cakes, put about 1-2 serving spoon of mixture onto the greased griddle. Cook for 15 minutes of on both sides or until the cake is golden brown and the cheese is melted.
- Cool down for 3 minutes and enjoy with Chili Beans.

358.   Dried Tomato Burgers Recipe

Serving: 8 | Prep: | Cook: 14mins | Ready in:

Ingredients

- 2 pounds lean ground beef
- 2 tablespoons finely chopped, drained, oil-packed dried tomatoes
- 2 teaspoons finely shredded lemon or lime peel
- 1 teaspoon salt
- 1/2 teaspoon pepper
- 1/2 cup light mayonnaise dressing or salad dressing
- 1/4 cup snipped fresh basil
- 2 jalapeno peppers, seeded and finely chopped
- 8 onion hamburger buns
- 2 cups lightly packed arugula or spinach leaves

Direction

- 1. Combine beef, tomatoes, lemon or lime peel, salt, and pepper in a medium bowl; mix lightly but thoroughly. Shape into eight 1/2-inch-thick patties. Grill patties on the rack of an uncovered grill directly over medium heat for 14 to 18 minutes or until an instant-read thermometer inserted in side of patty registers 160 degrees F., turning once.
- 2. Meanwhile, combine the light mayonnaise or salad dressing, basil, and jalapeno peppers in a small bowl; mix well. During the last 1 to 2 minutes of grilling, place buns, cut sides down, on grill rack to toast. Place burgers on bottom halves of buns. Top with the mayonnaise dressing mixture and arugula or spinach. Add the bun tops. Makes 8 servings.

---

359. Elvis Burger With Chopped Salad And Pickled Gherkin Recipe

Serving: 4 | Prep: | Cook: 10mins | Ready in:

Ingredients

- 1 dried red chilli
- • 1/2 a red onion, peeled and finely chopped
- • a sprig of fresh tarragon, leaves picked and chopped
- • 1 large free-range or organic egg
- • a handful of breadcrumbs
- • 1 teaspoon Dijon mustard
- • 2 tablespoons freshly grated Parmesan
- • a good pinch of ground nutmeg
- • 1kg beef mince
- oil, for frying
- • salt and freshly ground black pepper
- • 1 cos lettuce
- • 4 plum tomatoes
- • 1 cucumber
- • 4 ciabatta rolls
- • 4 large pickled gherkins

Direction

- Parmesan cheese may seem a little unusual in this recipe, but it really gives the burgers a great flavour – give it a bash.
- Grind up the red chilli in a pestle and mortar, and mix it in a bowl with the onion, tarragon, egg, breadcrumbs, mustard, Parmesan, nutmeg and beef. Shape into four patties and refrigerate for half an hour or so to give them a chance to firm up slightly.
- When you're ready to cook the burgers, get a frying or griddle pan nice and hot. Brush the pan with a little oil, season the burgers generously with salt and pepper, and cook them for 10 minutes, turning them carefully every minute or so, until they're nice and pink and juicy, or longer if you like them well done. Make sure they don't break up as you turn them.
- Meanwhile, roughly chop the lettuce, tomato and cucumber, mix together and set aside. Once the burgers are cooked, split the rolls into two and toast them quickly on the griddle or in a toaster. Sandwich the cooked 'Elvis' burger between the toasted rolls and serve them on individual plates with the gherkins and some of the chopped salad (add a little

extra virgin olive oil or dressing if you like) on the side.

360. Grilled Bacon Burger Dawg Recipe

Serving: 2 | Prep: | Cook: 15mins | Ready in:

Ingredients

- 2 lbs hamburger
- 4 hot dawgs or sausage
- 8 slices bacon   half cook bacon in skillet, will cook the rest of way in burger
- Velveeta cheese or parmason cheese
- 1 egg
- 3 jalapinos chopped
- 1 tbl. worchester sauce
- 1 tbl liquid smoke
- a grill basket, very important to hold burger if you try to flip burger without basket it will fall apart

Direction

- The bacon burger dawg monster burger
- Slice hot dogs long ways in half
- Wrap hot dawgs with cheese then wrap with bacon set aside
- Place hamburger in a big bowl
- Add egg, jalapenos, Worcestershire and liquid smoke
- Mash all together and make 4 patties
- Place two dawgs [4 halves] on 1 patty, place another patty on top
- Pinch sides to seal place in the grill basket
- Repeat with the other burger
- Place on the grill make sure the meat temp reaches 160 degrees

361. Pork And Appel Burgers Recipe

Serving: 4 | Prep: | Cook: 12mins | Ready in:

Ingredients

- 1 apple, peeled and cored
- 1 stick celery, wiped clean
- 1 onion
- 400g pork mince
- 1 egg, beaten
- 2 tbsp oil- if frying

Direction

- Grate the apple, celery and onion
- Mix with the minced meat and egg.
- Shape them into 4 burgers.

362. Rotell And Cheese Burger Recipe

Serving: 6 | Prep: | Cook: 8mins | Ready in:

Ingredients

- 2 lbs hamburger
- 6 oz Velveeta cheese spread
- 1 10 0z can rotel diced tomatoes with chilies
- 1 package lipton onion soup
- 2 clove garlic minced
- 1 or 2 diced jalapinos

Direction

- Diced jalapenos, minced garlic, package Lipton onion soup
- Mixed in with 2 lbs. hamburger mix well
- Make 6 burgers
- Place on the grill for 7-9 minutes or /and 160 degrees
- Place cheese on top and heat till it melts
- Put on the bun, and cover with the rotel /chilies

- Cover with the other bun
- Munch out
- These burgers are awesome

363. Stuffed Turkey Burgers Recipe

Serving: 8 | Prep: | Cook: 10mins | Ready in:

Ingredients

- 2 lbs ground turkey,all white meast or mixed
- teaspoon garlic powder
- mrs dash no salt ,1 tablespoon
- 1tablespoon worchestershire sauce
- 1tablespoon chopped basil or tarragon
- 1 egg white,beaten
- fresh ground pepper,2 teaspoons or to taste
- 1 chopped red onion
- canola oil,4 tablespoons
- barbeque sauce

Direction

- Mix first 7 ingredients together in bowl
- Meanwhile, sauté onions in 2 tablespoons oil till caramelized, slowly
- Shape turkey into 7 or 8 plump patties
- Make an indentation in center and fill with some of the onions and a tablespoon of barbeque sauce
- Enclose the patties so stuffing is inside
- Sauté in 2 tablespoons oil about 5 minutes per side
- Serve on wheat buns with lettuce, pickles and tomatoes, if desired
- Sometimes I will melt a slice of Muenster or provolone cheese on top of patty after turning over
- These can be grilled outside also

364. Veggie Burger Recipe

Serving: 56 | Prep: | Cook: 7mins | Ready in:

Ingredients

- 1/2 cup flour
- 1 small onion, diced
- 2 cloves garlic, minced
- 1/2 tsp dried oregano
- 1 small hot pepper, minced
- 1 tbsp olive oil
- 1/2 medium red pepper, diced
- 2 cups cooked/canned black beans, mashed
- 1/2 cup corn kernels
- 1/2 cup bread crumbs (or 1/2 cup flour)
- 1/4 tsp cumin
- 1/2 tsp salt
- 2 tsp chili powder
- 2 tbsp fresh cilantro, minced

Direction

- On a small plate, set aside flour for coating. In a medium saucepan, sauté the onion, garlic, oregano, and hot pepper in oil on medium-high heat until the onions are translucent. Add the peppers and sauté another 2 minutes, until pepper is tender. Set aside. In a large bowl, mash the black beans with a potato masher or fork. Stir in the vegetables (including corn), bread crumbs, cumin, salt, chili pepper and cilantro. Mix well. Divide and shape 5-6 patties. Lay down each patty in flour, coating each side. Cook on a lightly oiled frying pan on medium-high heat for 5-10 minutes or until browned on both sides.

365. ~ Wild West ~ Recipe

Serving: 0 | Prep: | Cook: | Ready in:

Ingredients

- 1lb. Ground lean beef

- 2 cloves, minced garlic
- 2 Little green onions, finely chopped
- parsley
- 1 teaspoon India relish,heaping
- 2 Tablespoons,Capers
- 1 heaping teaspoon, spice Islands sage
- 1/2 teaspoon spice Islands beau monde seasoning
- 1/2 teaspoon spice Islands Mei Yen pepper...can't get...no problem
- salt and pepper
- 1 egg, beaten in a cup with a fork
- About 1/3 Cup Dry Red or white wine
- 1 Tablespoon cooking oil

Direction

- What to do
- Break up the meat with a fork and scatter the garlic, onion and dry seasonings over it, then mix them into the meat with a fork or your fingers. Let the bowl of meat sit out of the icebox for ten or fifteen minutes while you set the table and make the salad. Add the relish, capers, everything else including wine and let the meat sit, quietly marinating, for another ten minutes if possible.
- Now make four fat, juicy patties with your hands. The patties should be an inch thick, and soft in texture but not runny. Have the oil in your frying pan hot but not smoking when you drop the patties and then turn the heat down and fry the burgers about four minutes. Take the pan off the burner and turn the heat high again. Flip the burgers over , put the pan back on the hot fire, then after one minute, turn the heat down again and cook another three minutes. Both sides of the burgers should be crispy brown and the middle pink and juicy.
- Sub for Spice Islands Mei Yen Pepper:
- Mix nine parts salt, nine parts sugar, two parts MSG, then when the recipe calls for one teaspoon Mei Yen Powder, use two thirds teaspoon of the dry mixed with one eight teaspoon soy sauce.

Index

Conclusion

Thank you again for downloading this book!

I hope you enjoyed reading about my book!

If you enjoyed this book, please take the time to share your thoughts and post a review on Amazon. It'd be greatly appreciated!

Write me an honest review about the book – I truly value your opinion and thoughts and I will incorporate them into my next book, which is already underway.

Thank you!

If you have any questions, **feel free to contact at:** *author@cuminrecipes.com*

Rita Morrow

cuminrecipes.com

Printed in Great Britain
by Amazon